I0462201

Varyscript

Music Manuscript Paper

Eros Mungal

ISBN 978-0-244-44389-4

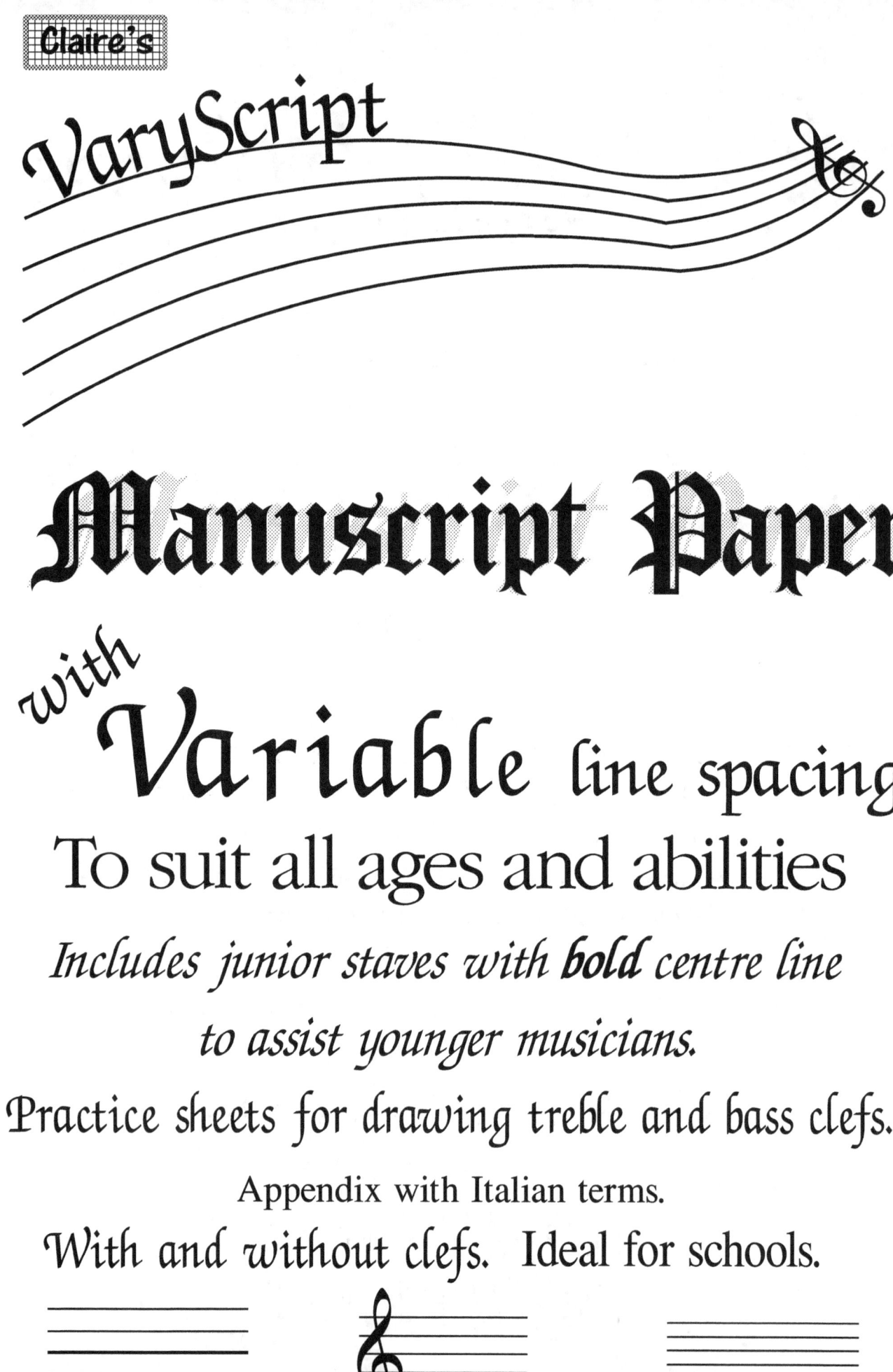

Claire's

VaryScript

Manuscript Paper

with *Variable* line spacing

To suit all ages and abilities

*Includes junior staves with **bold** centre line*

to assist younger musicians.

Practice sheets for drawing treble and bass clefs.

Appendix with Italian terms.

With and without clefs. Ideal for schools.

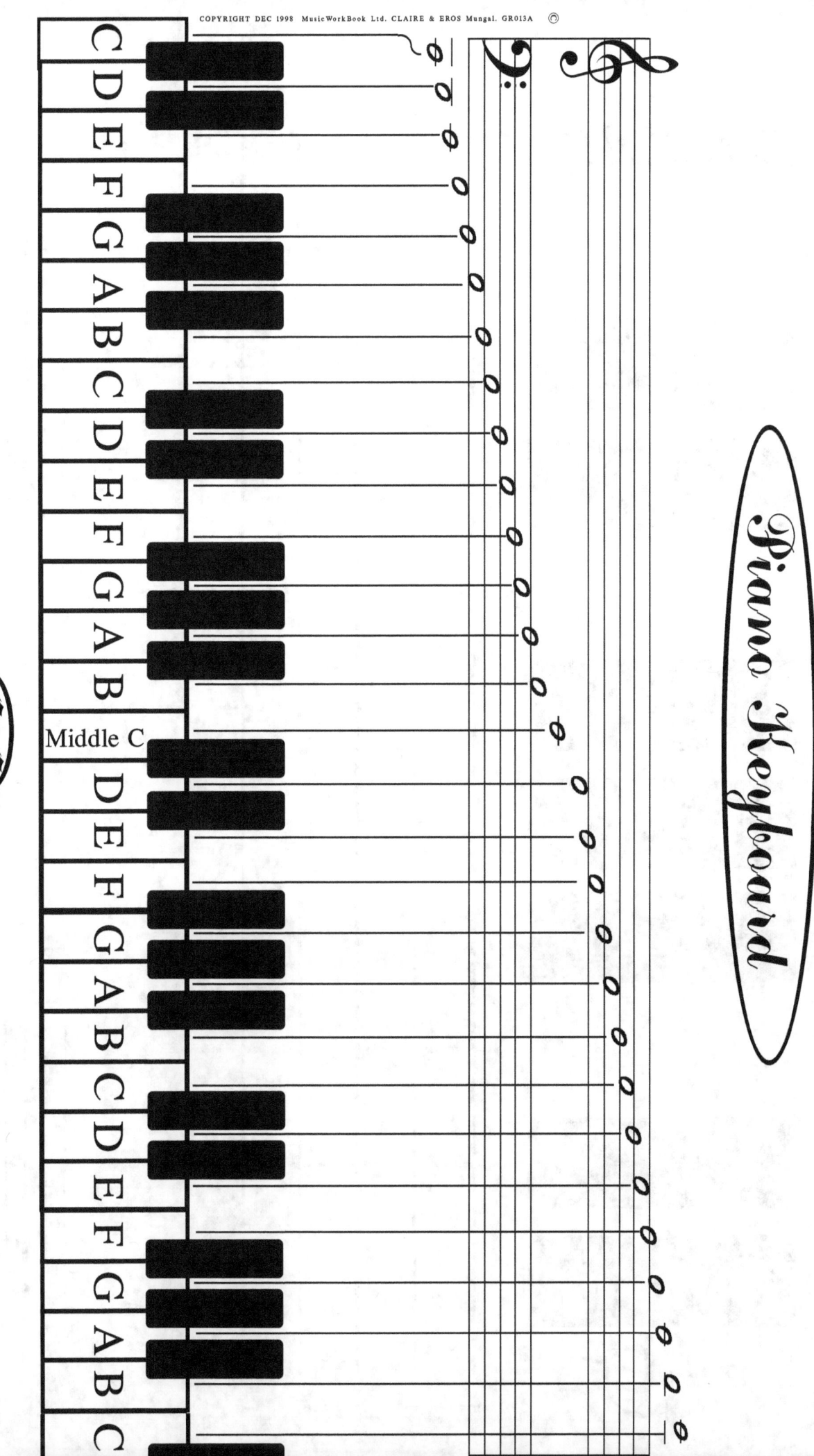

Piano Keyboard

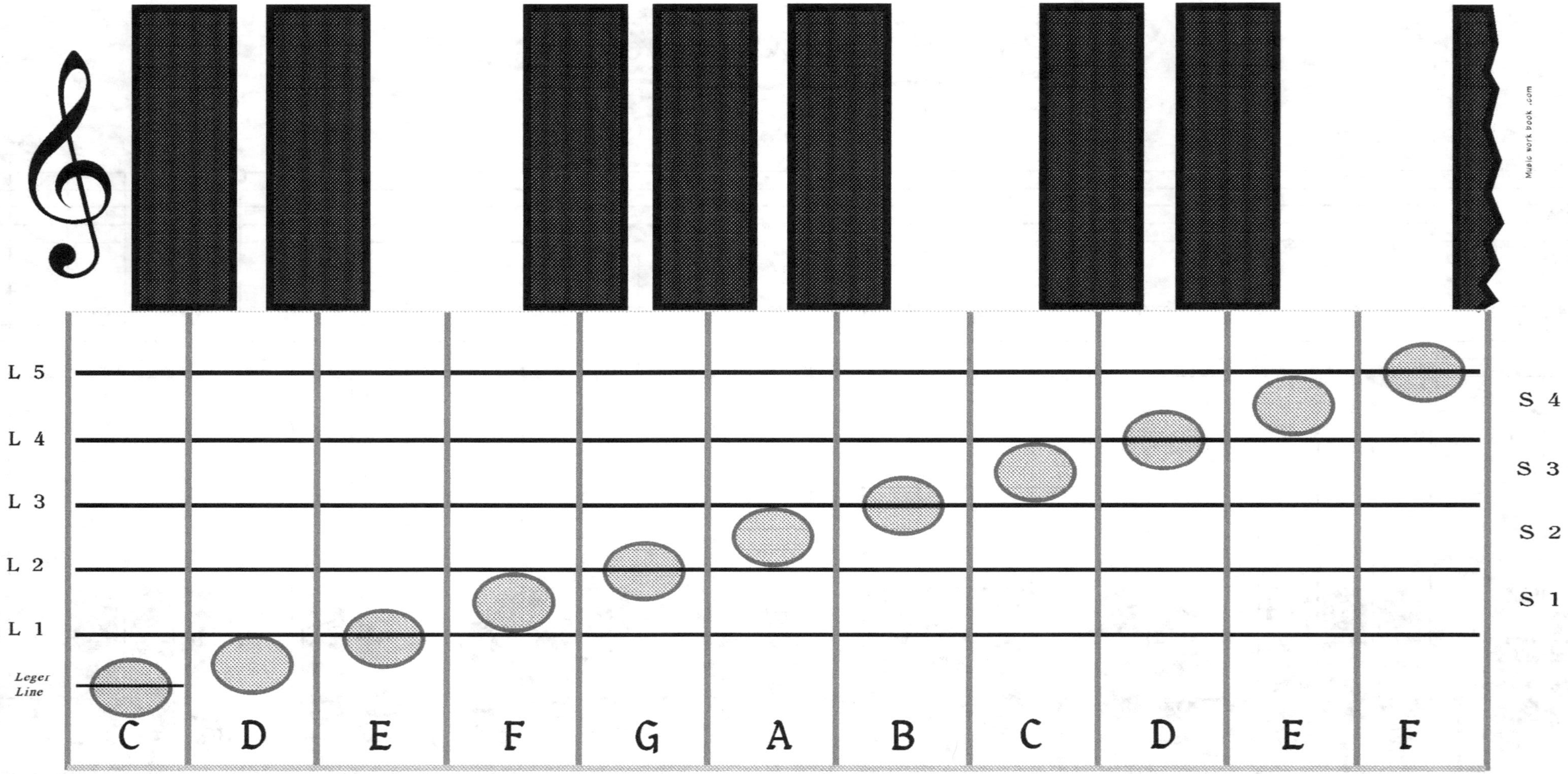
Music work book .com
L 5
L 4
L 3
L 2
L 1
Leger Line
S 4
S 3
S 2
S 1
C D E F G A B C D E F

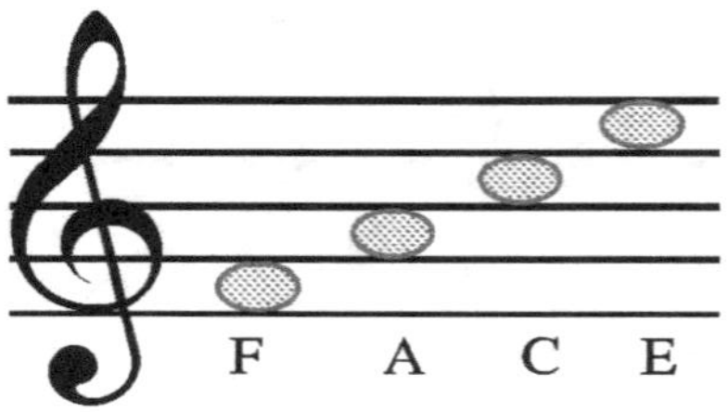
F A C E

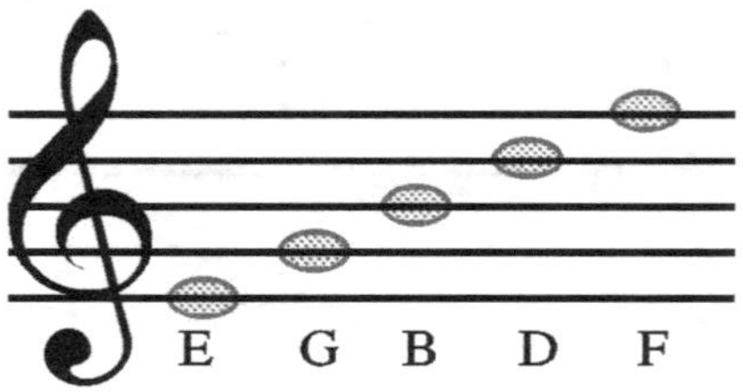
E G B D F

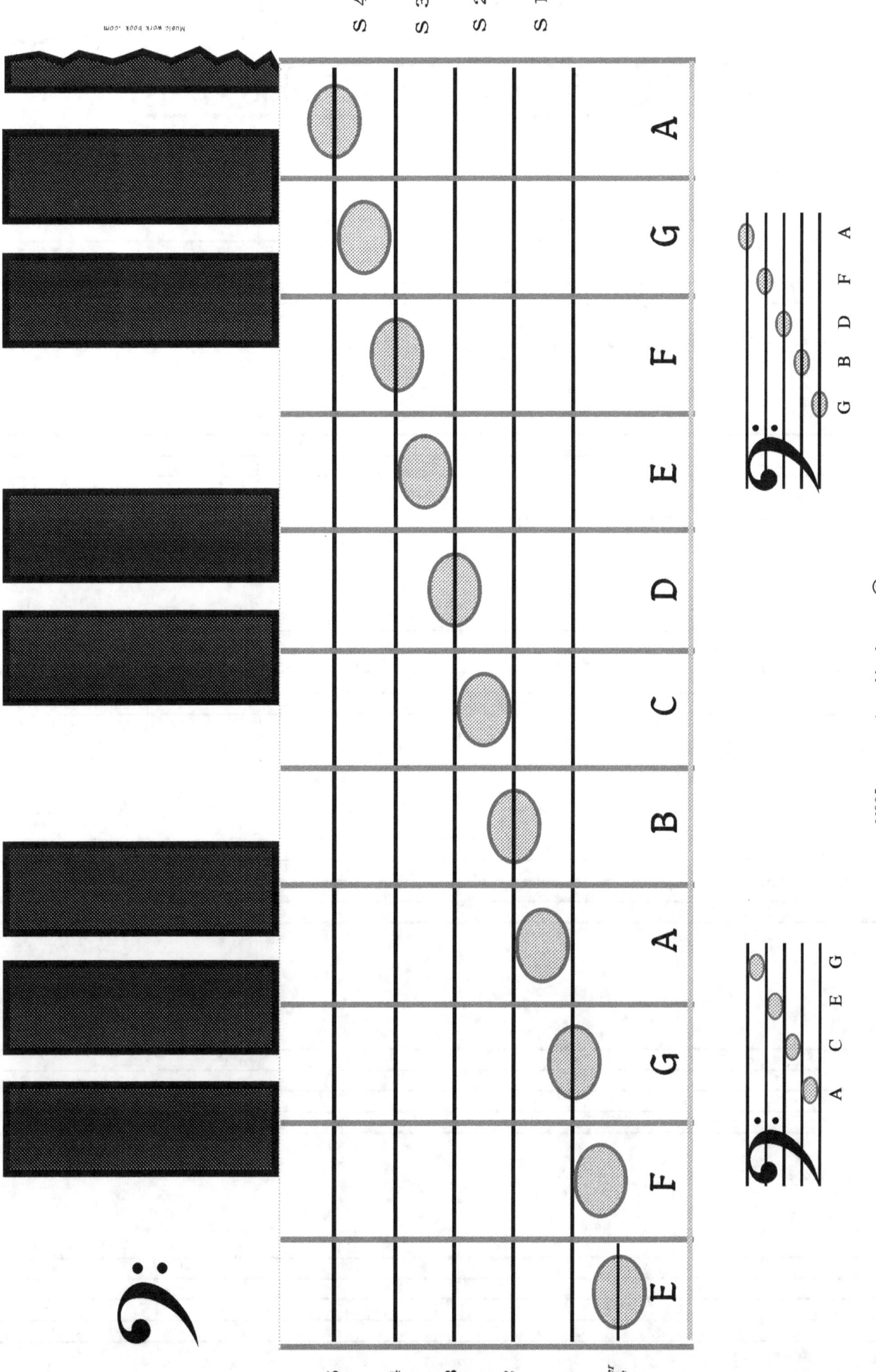

M005 www.musicworkbook.com ©

DATE:_____
Sign:_____

TRACE SYMBOLS - Treble Clefs

Treble Clefs

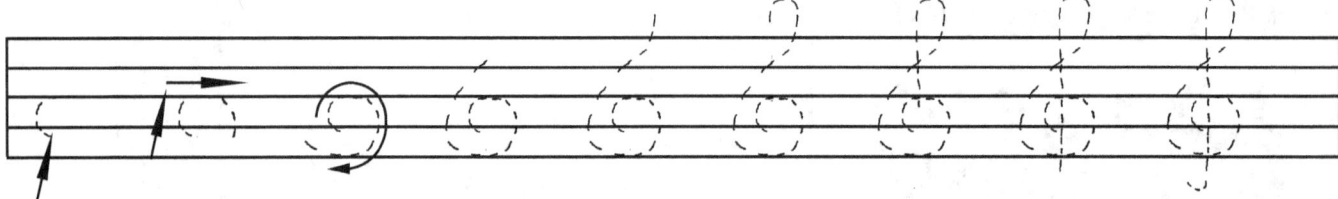

Start here and follow the trace around in a clockwise direction.

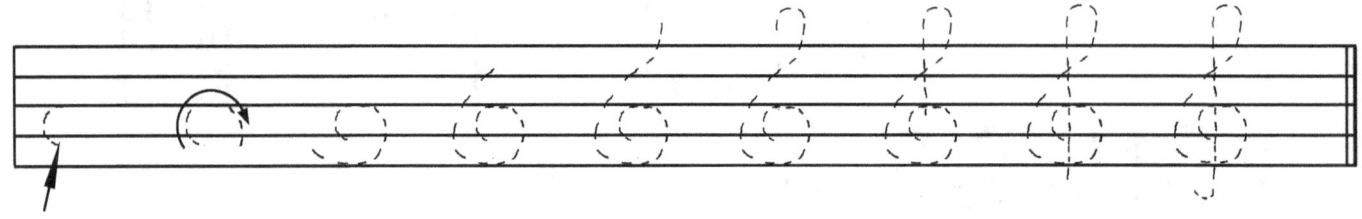

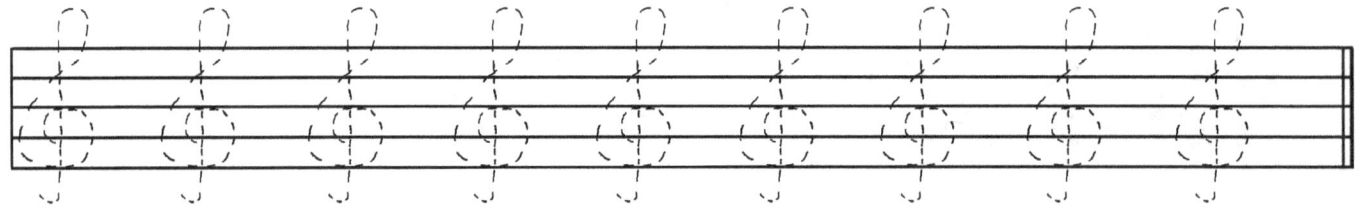

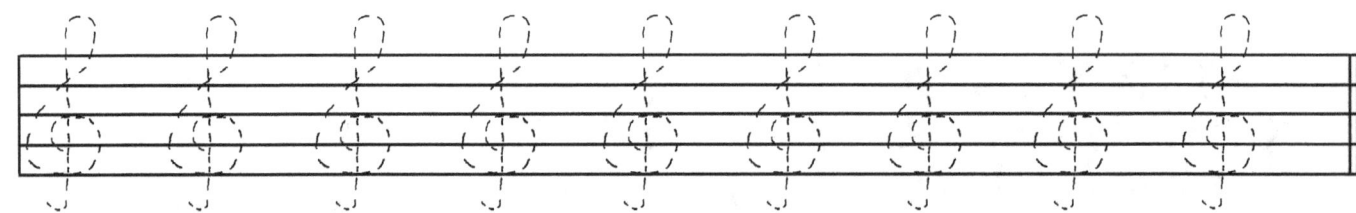

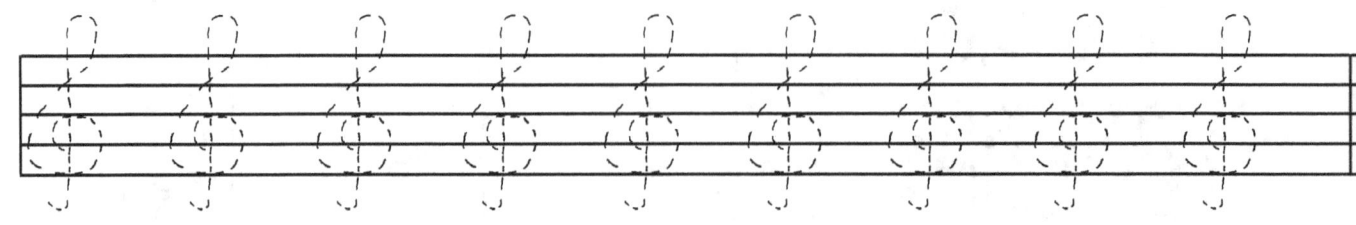

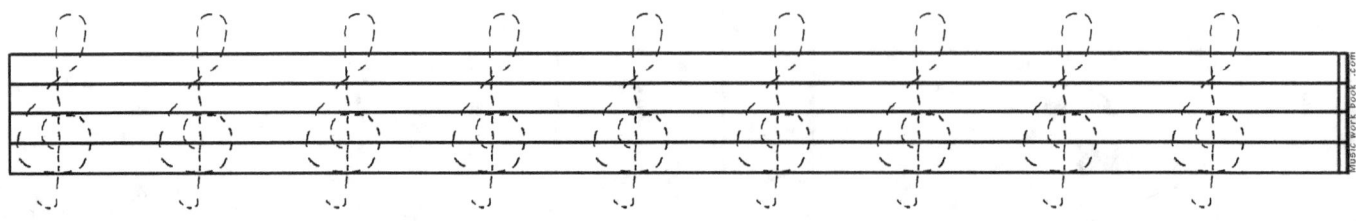

DATE:____
Sign:____

TRACE SYMBOLS - Bass Clefs

Bass Clefs (hand-drawn version)

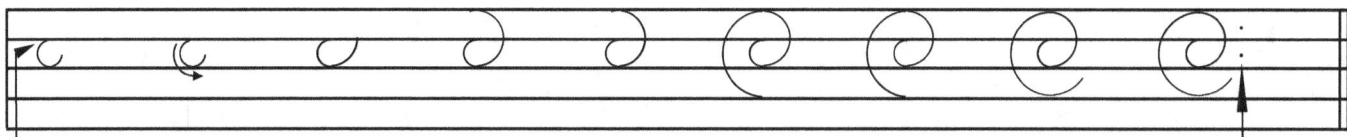

*Start here and follow the trace around in an **anti**-clockwise direction.*　　*Now add the dots.*

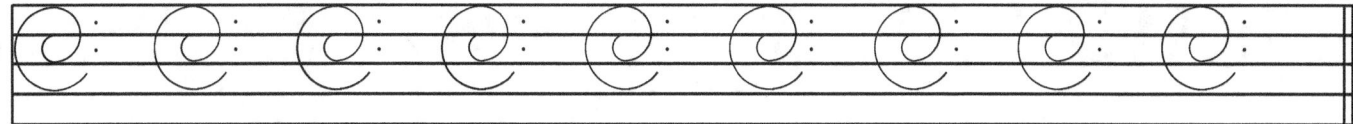

The dots are in the third and fourth spaces.

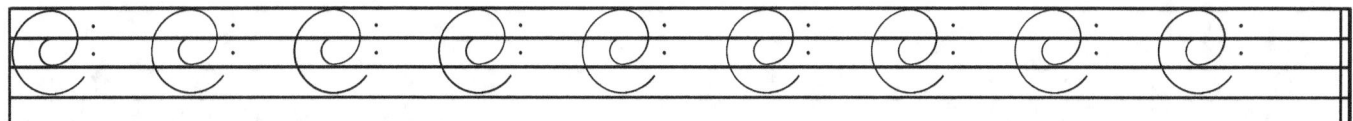

Bass Clefs (printed version)

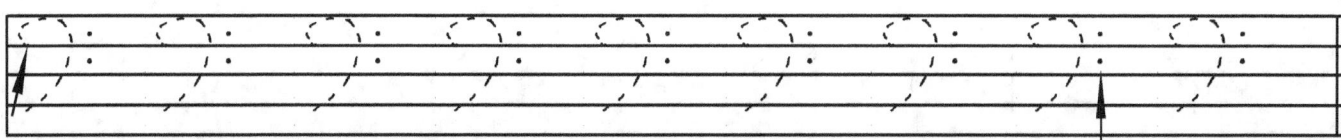

Start here and follow the trace around in a clockwise direction.　*Then add the dots.*

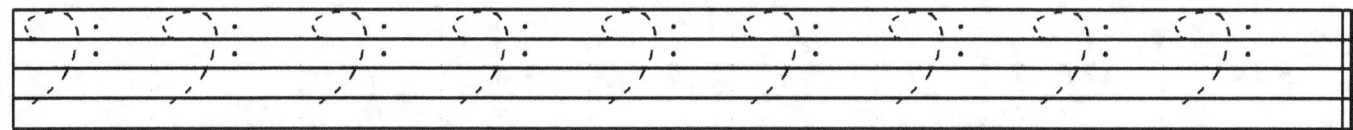

The dots are in the third and fourth spaces.

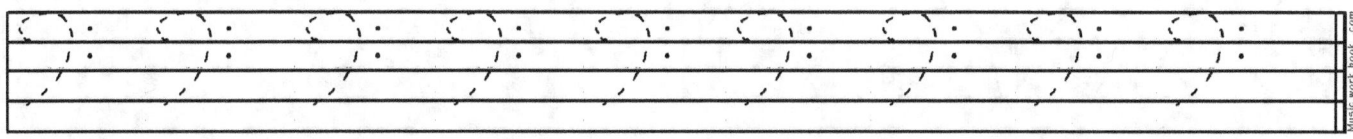

DATE:
Sign:

TRACE THESE SYMBOLS

Treble Clefs

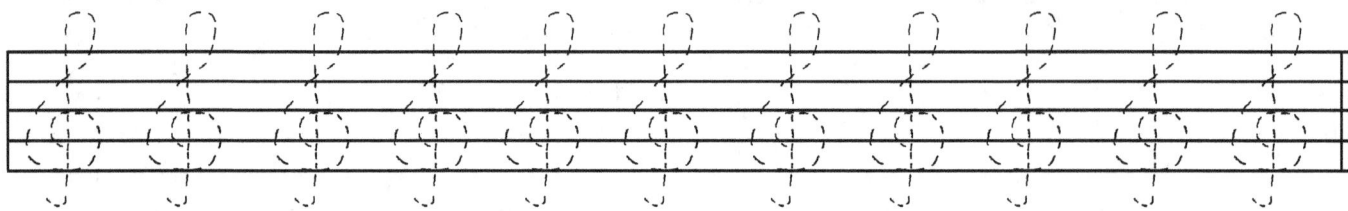

Bass Clefs

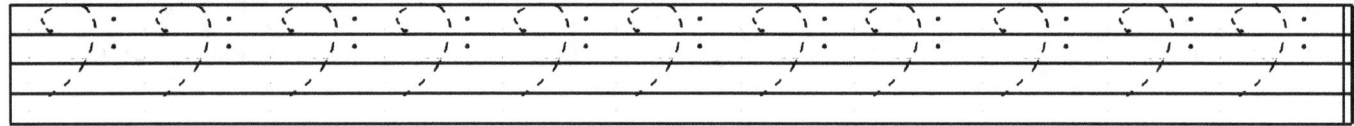

Semibreves

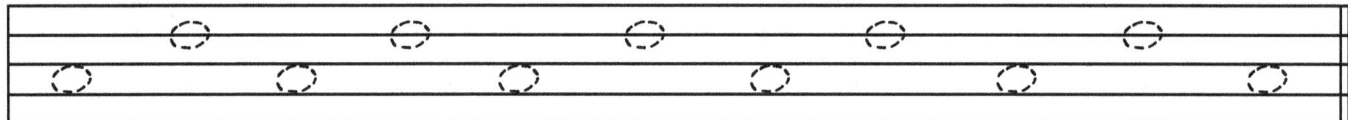

Minims

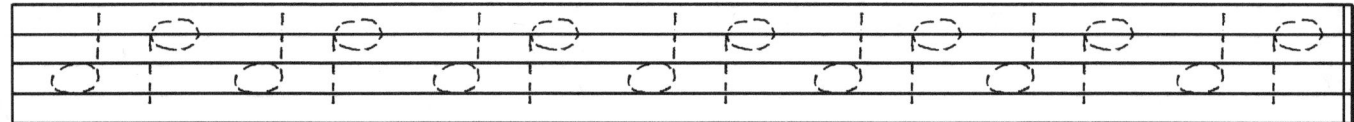

Crotchets

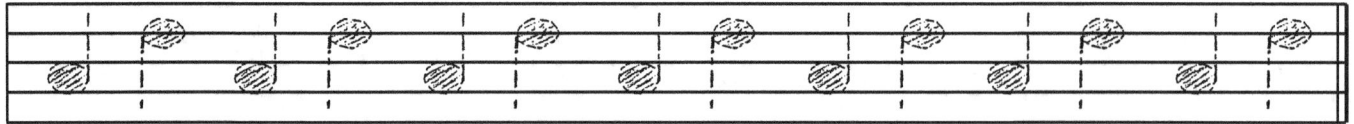

Quavers

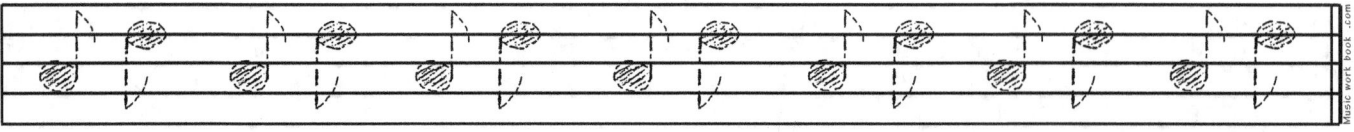

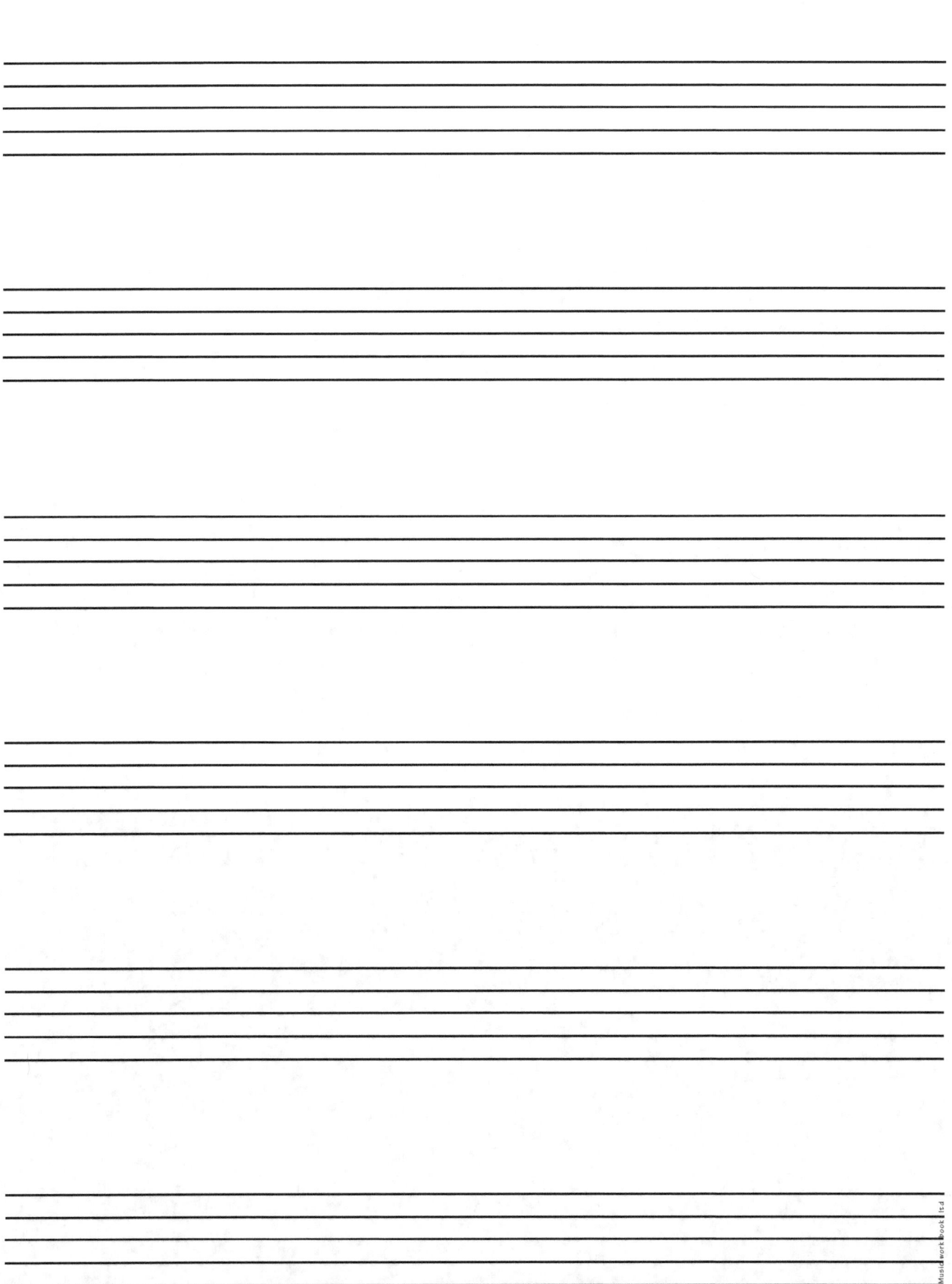

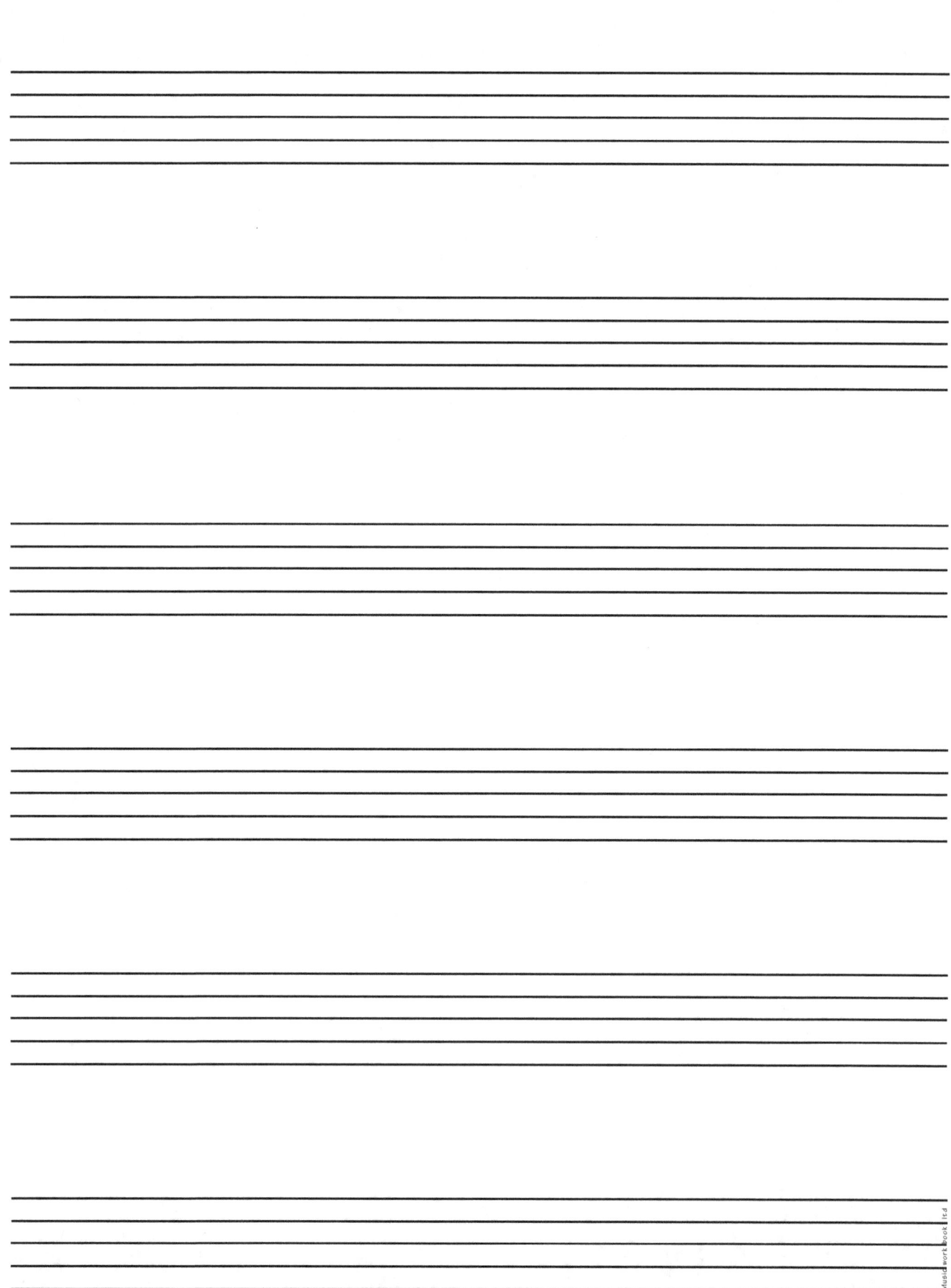

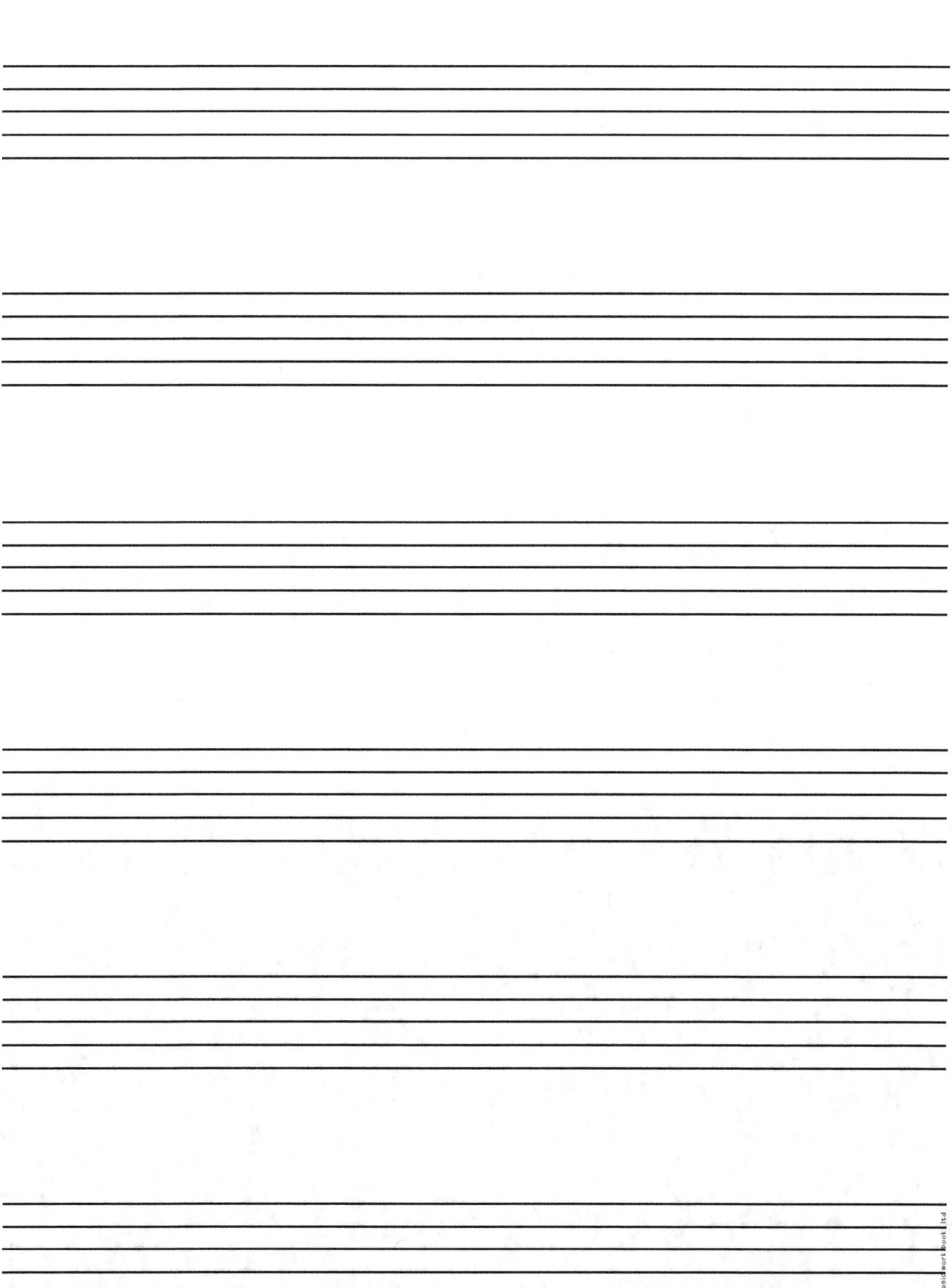

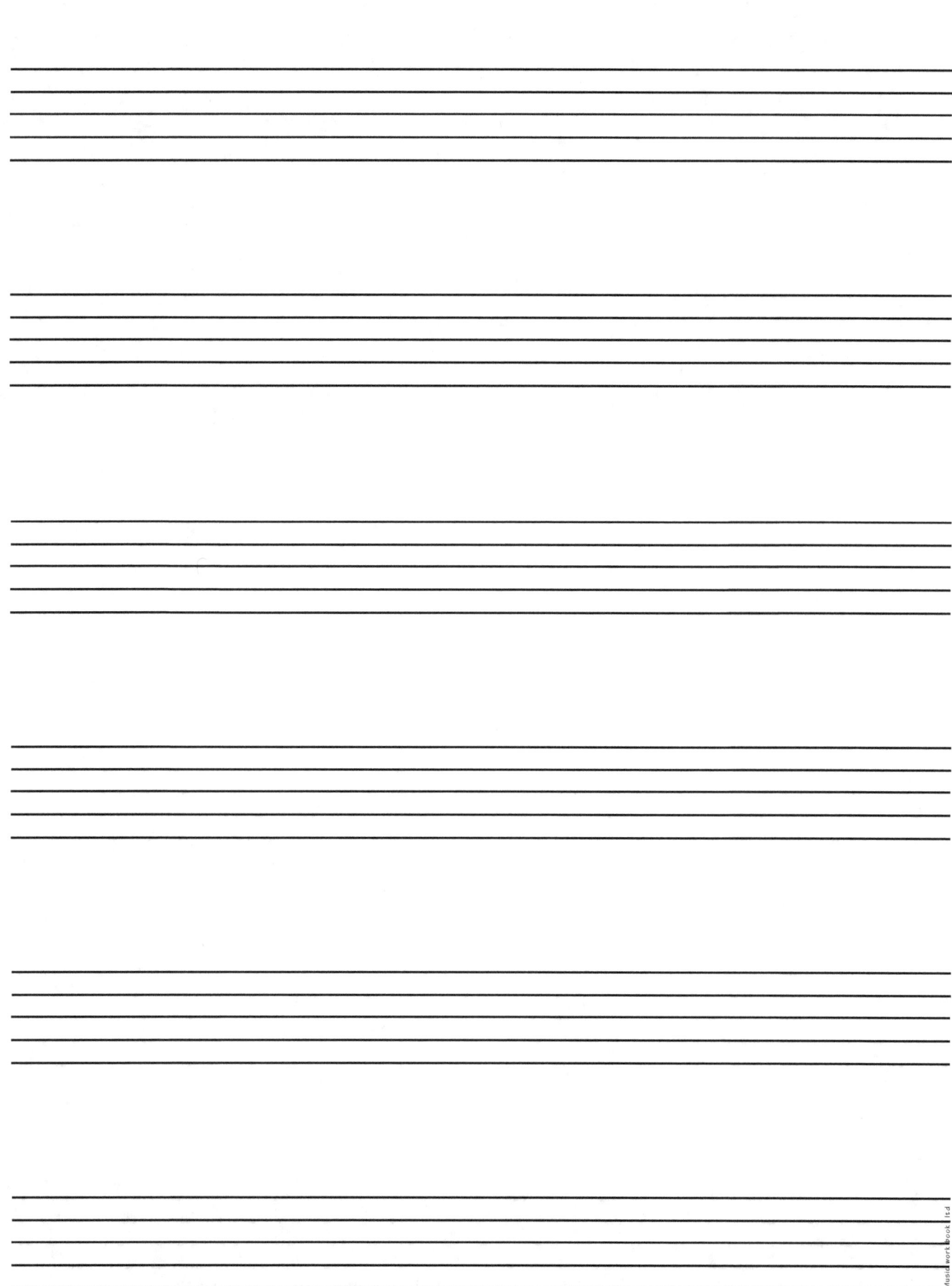

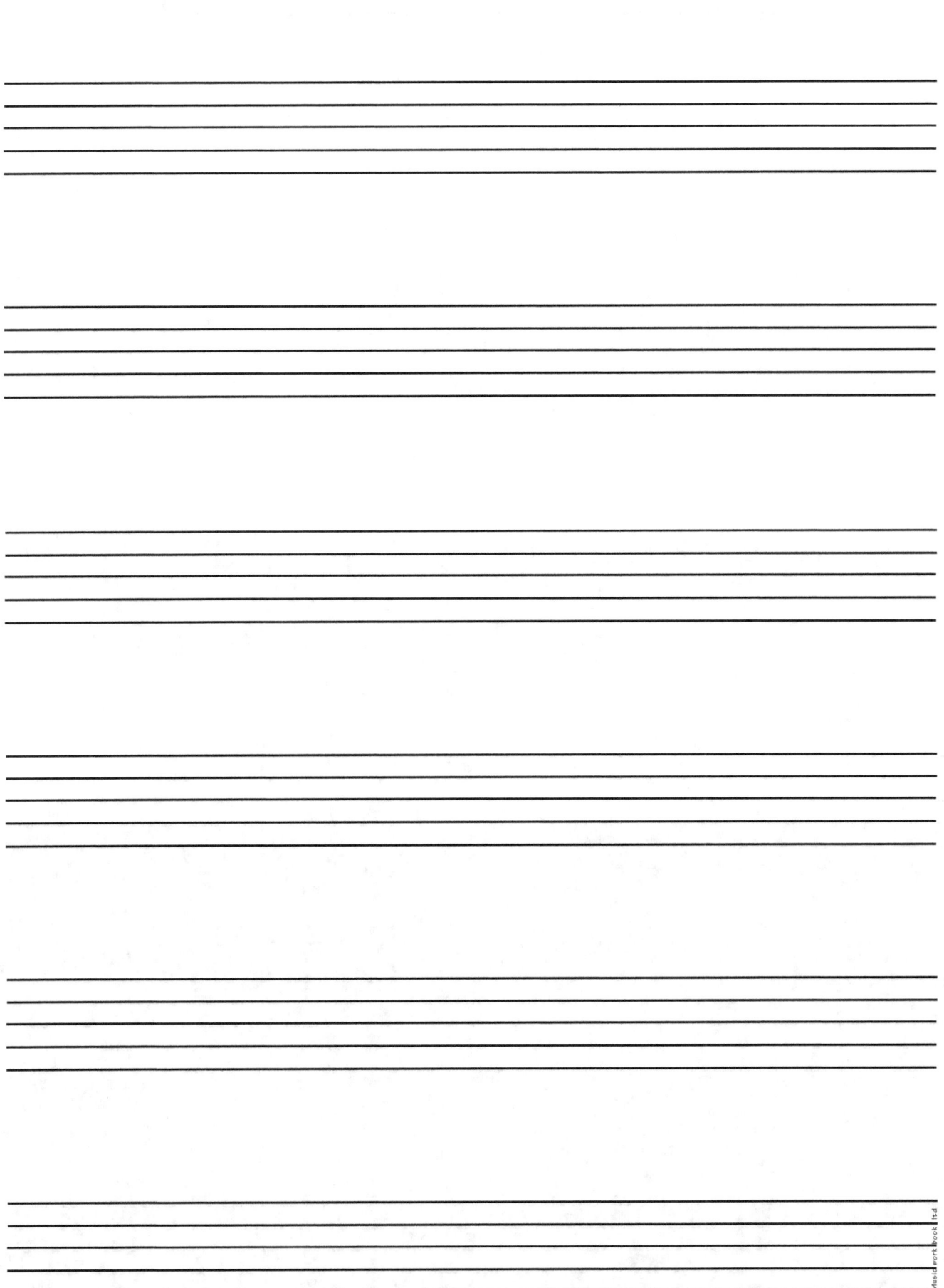

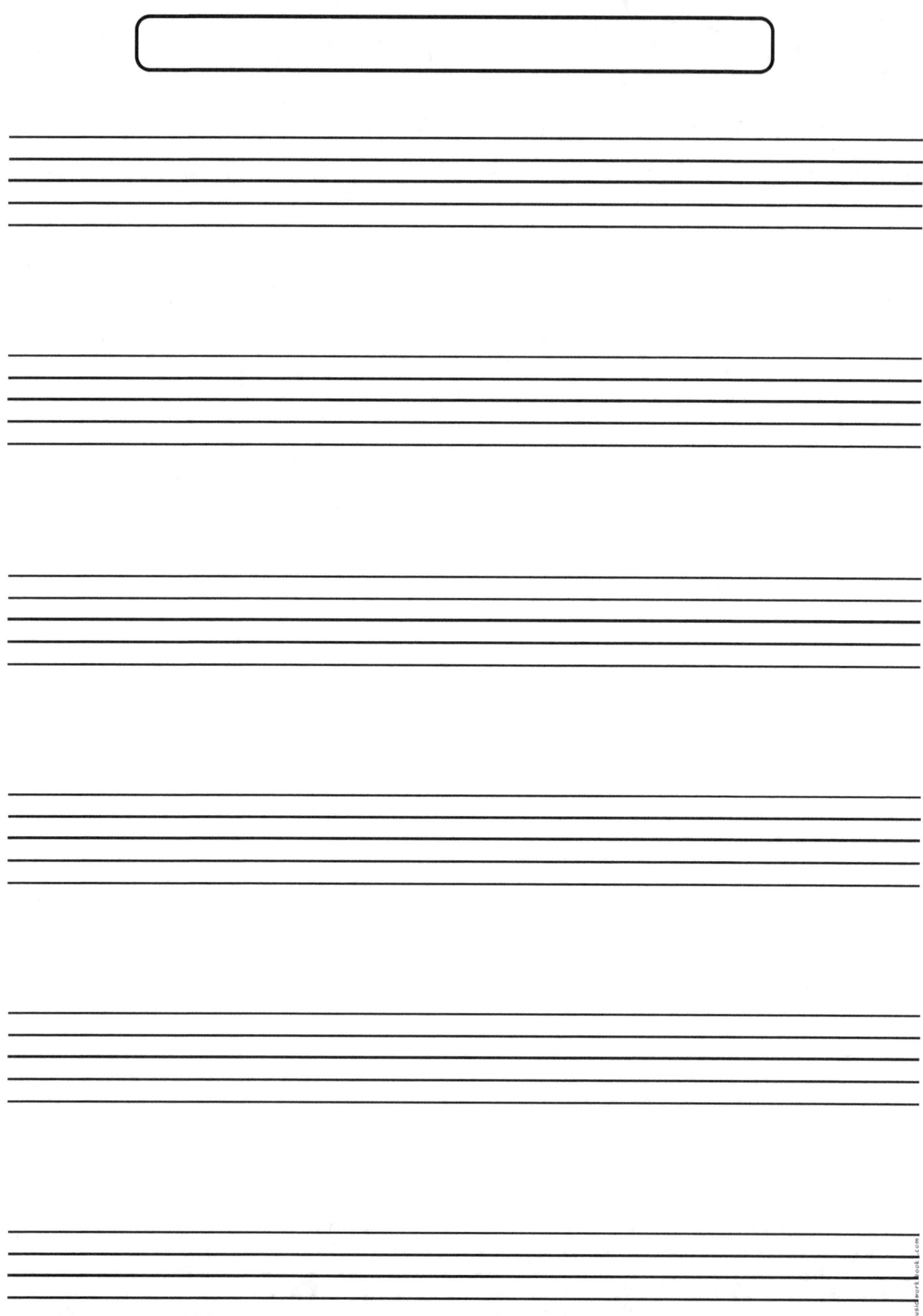

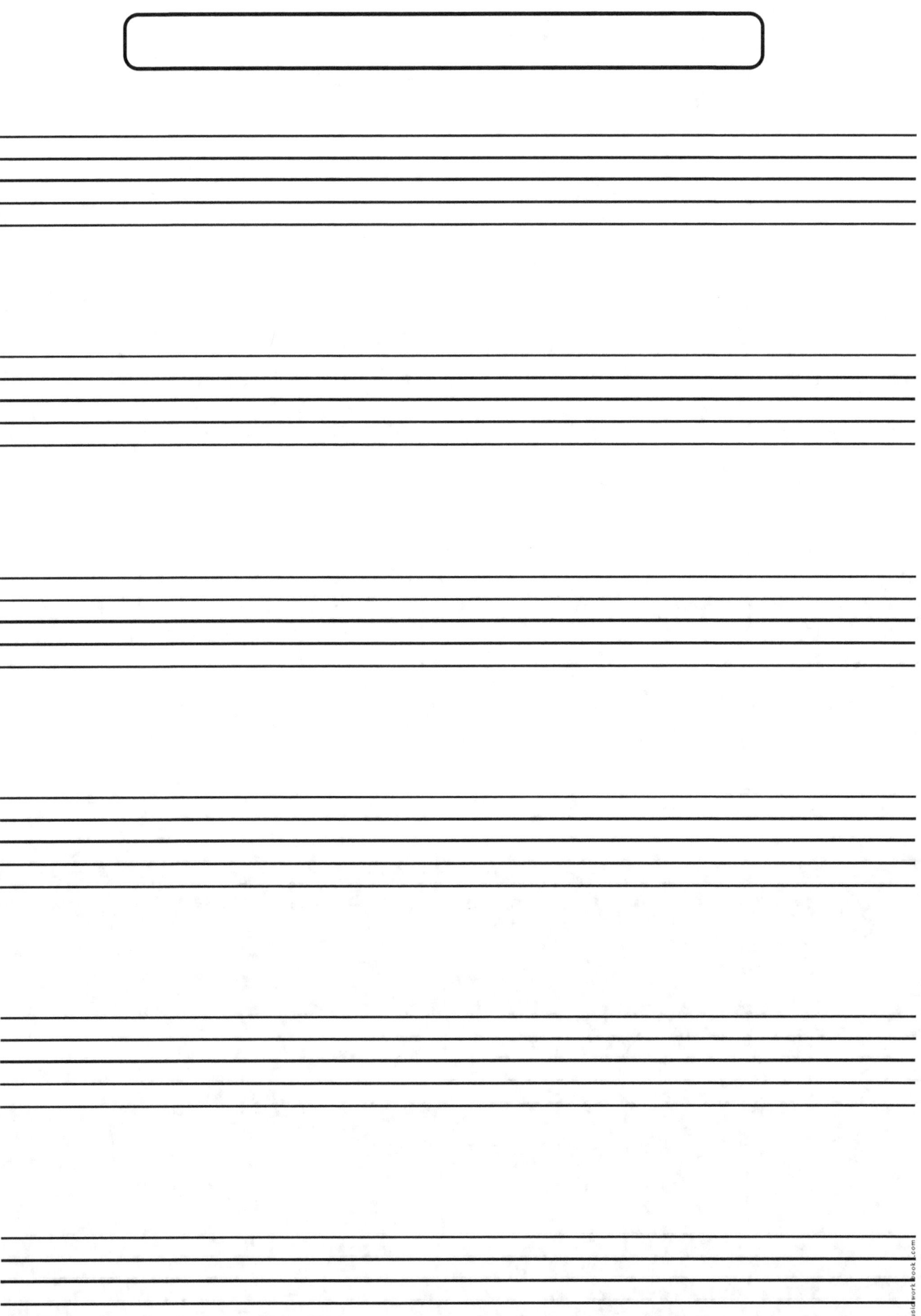

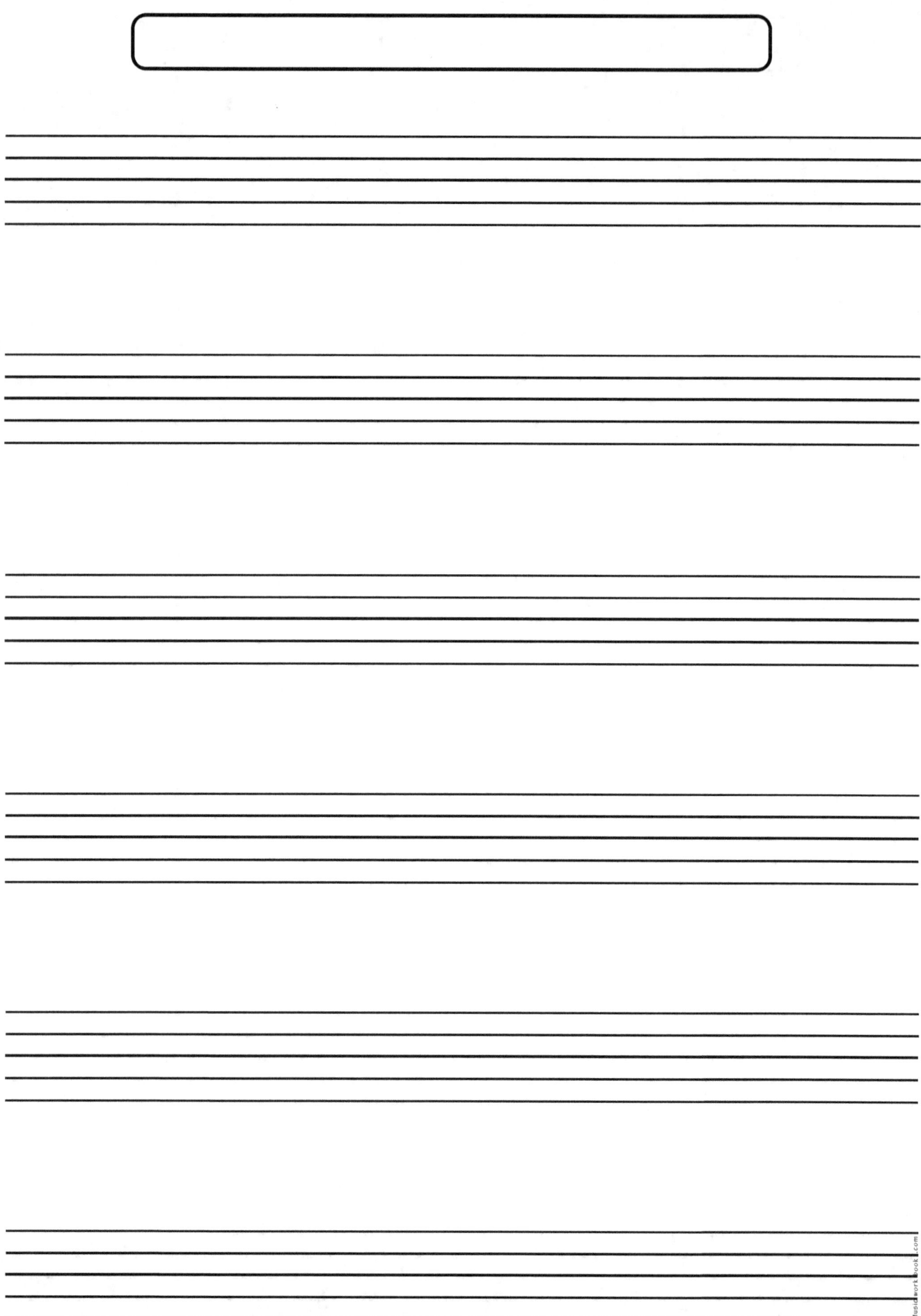

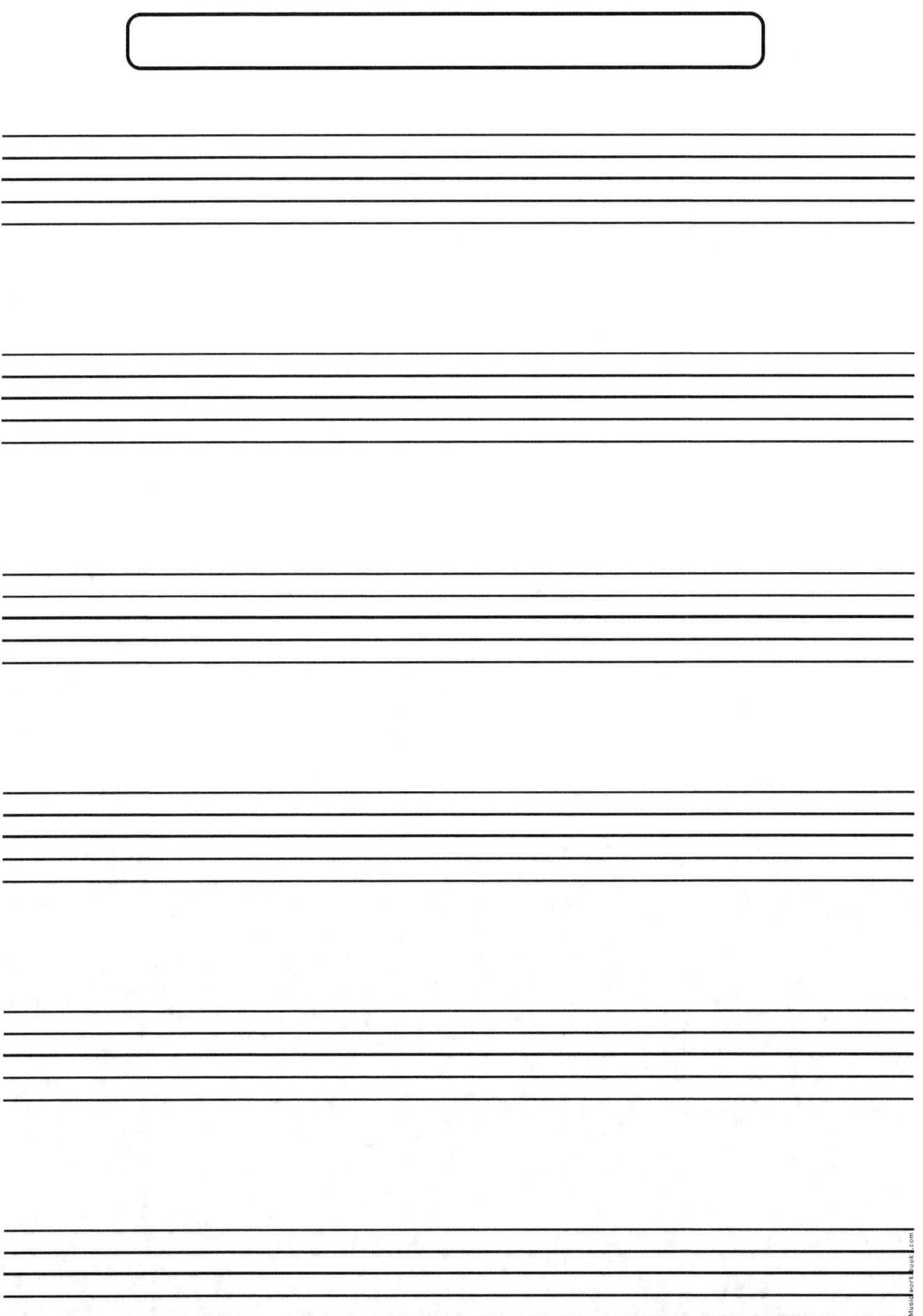

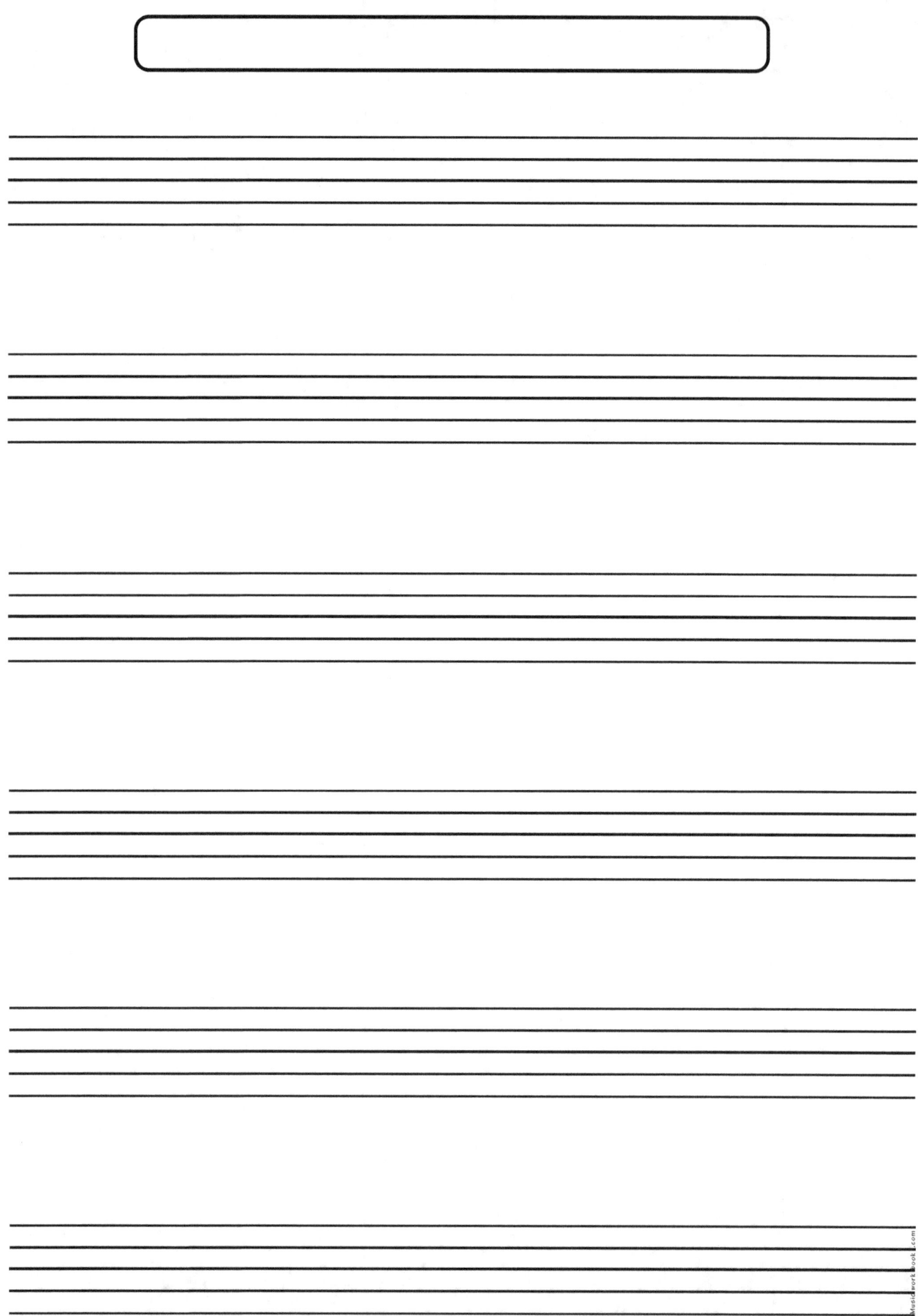

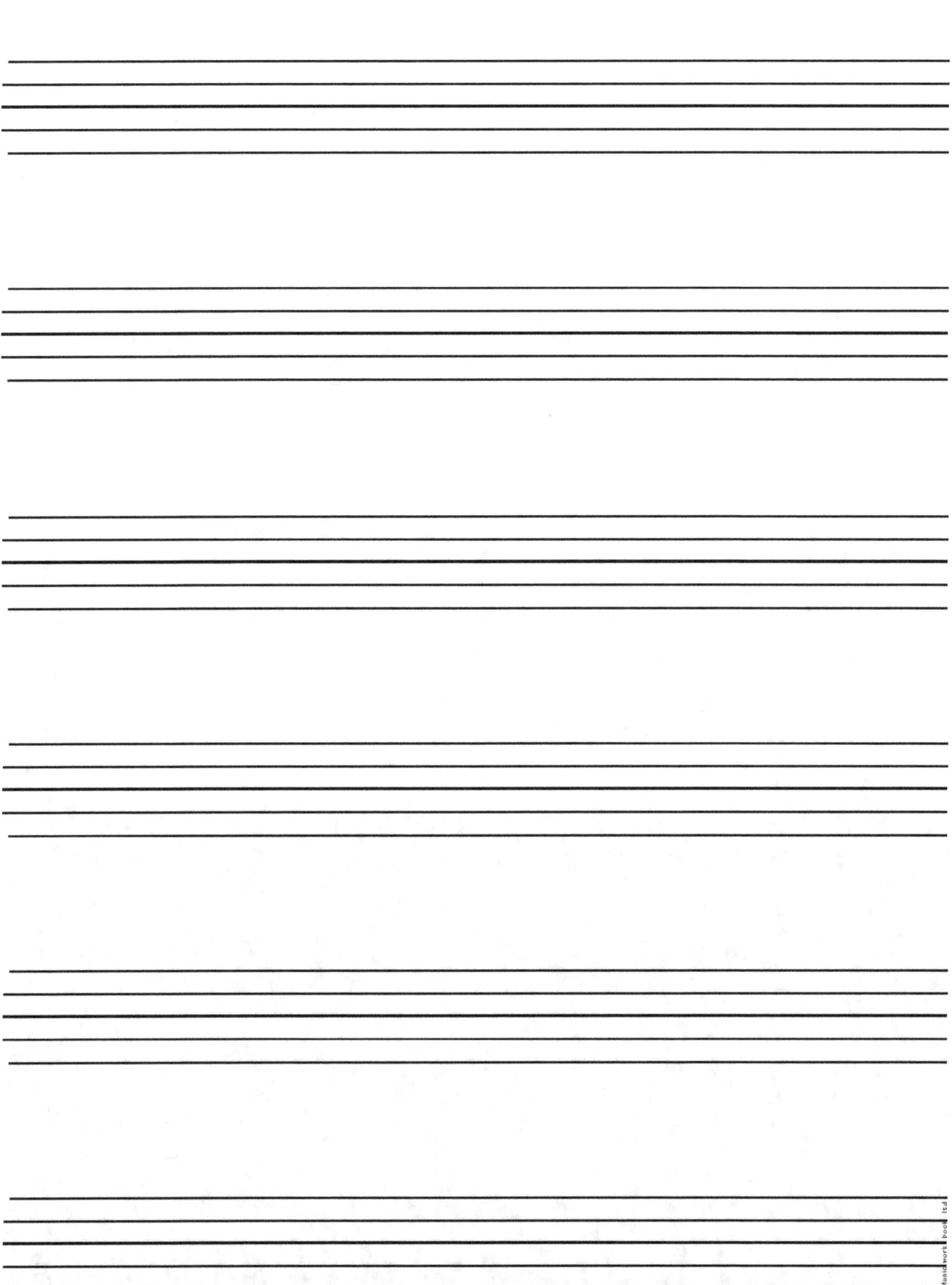

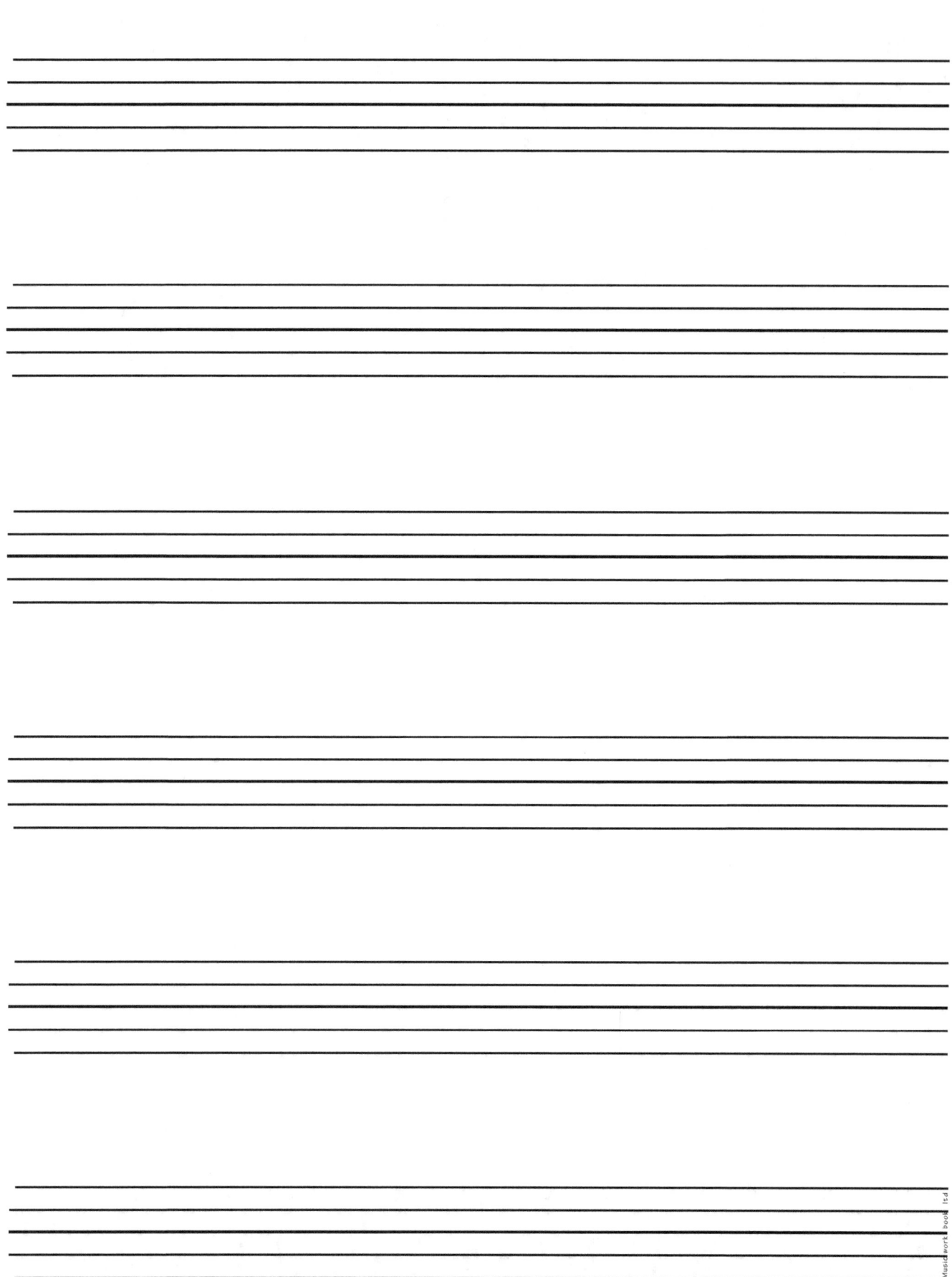

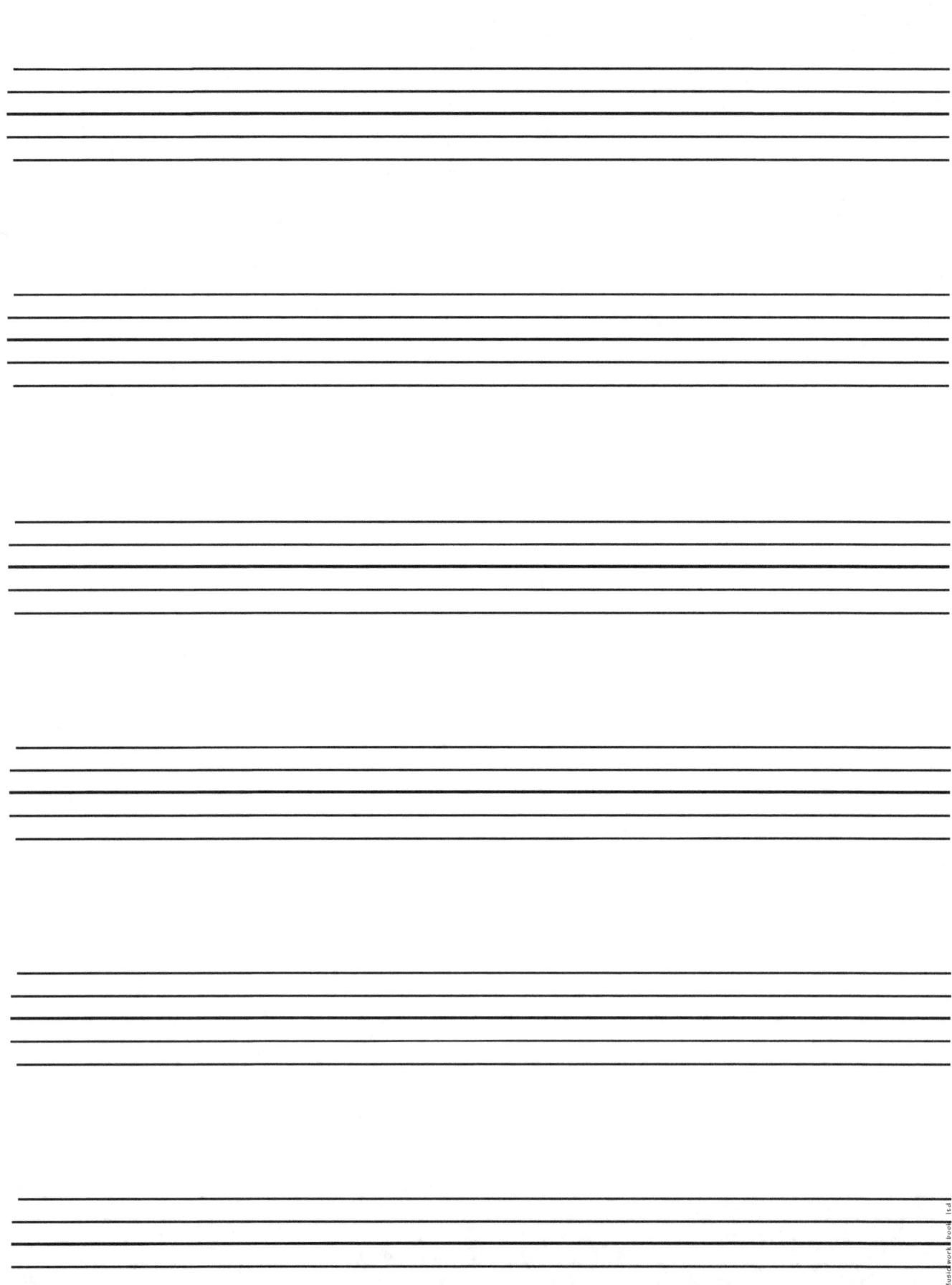

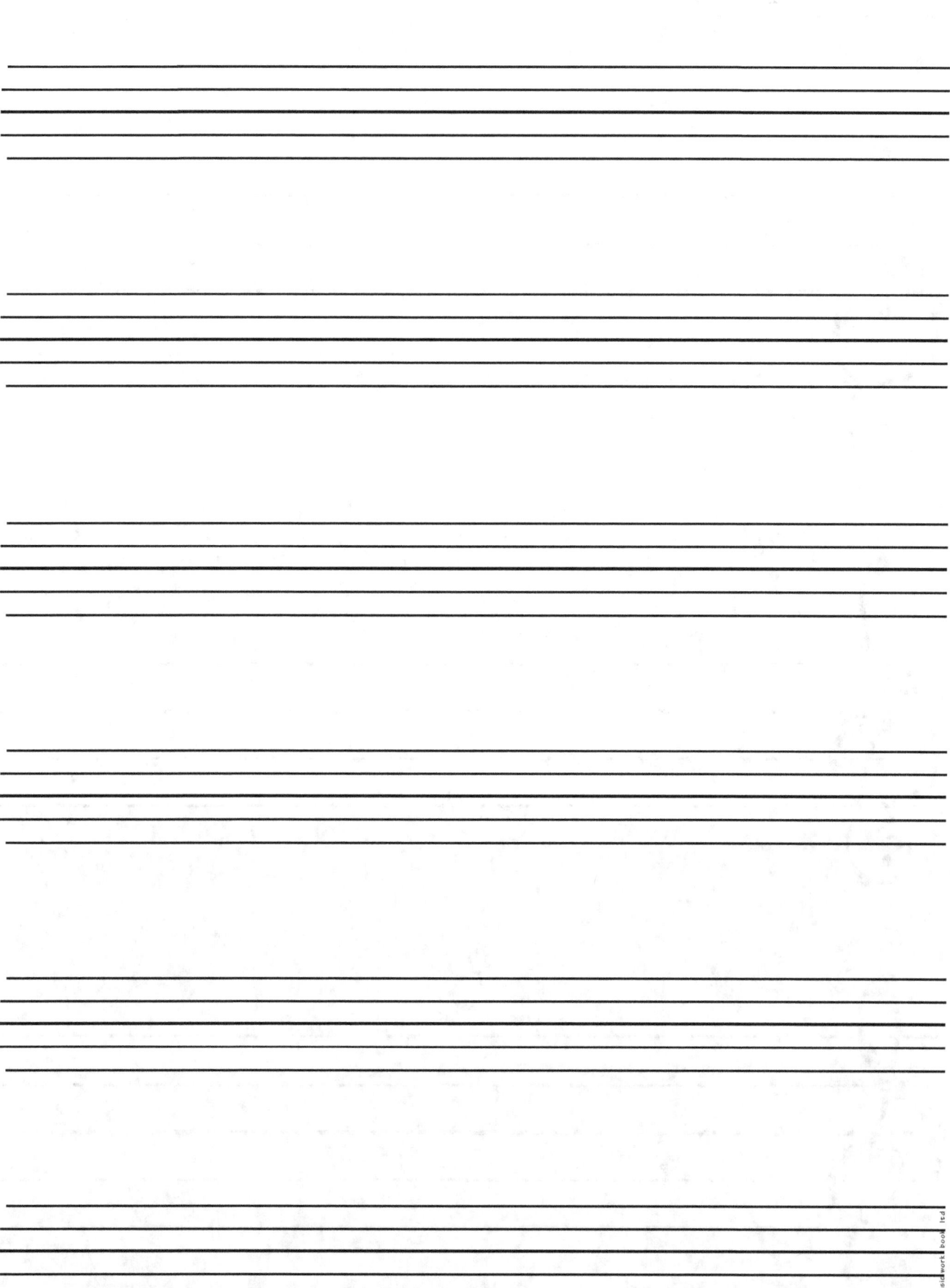

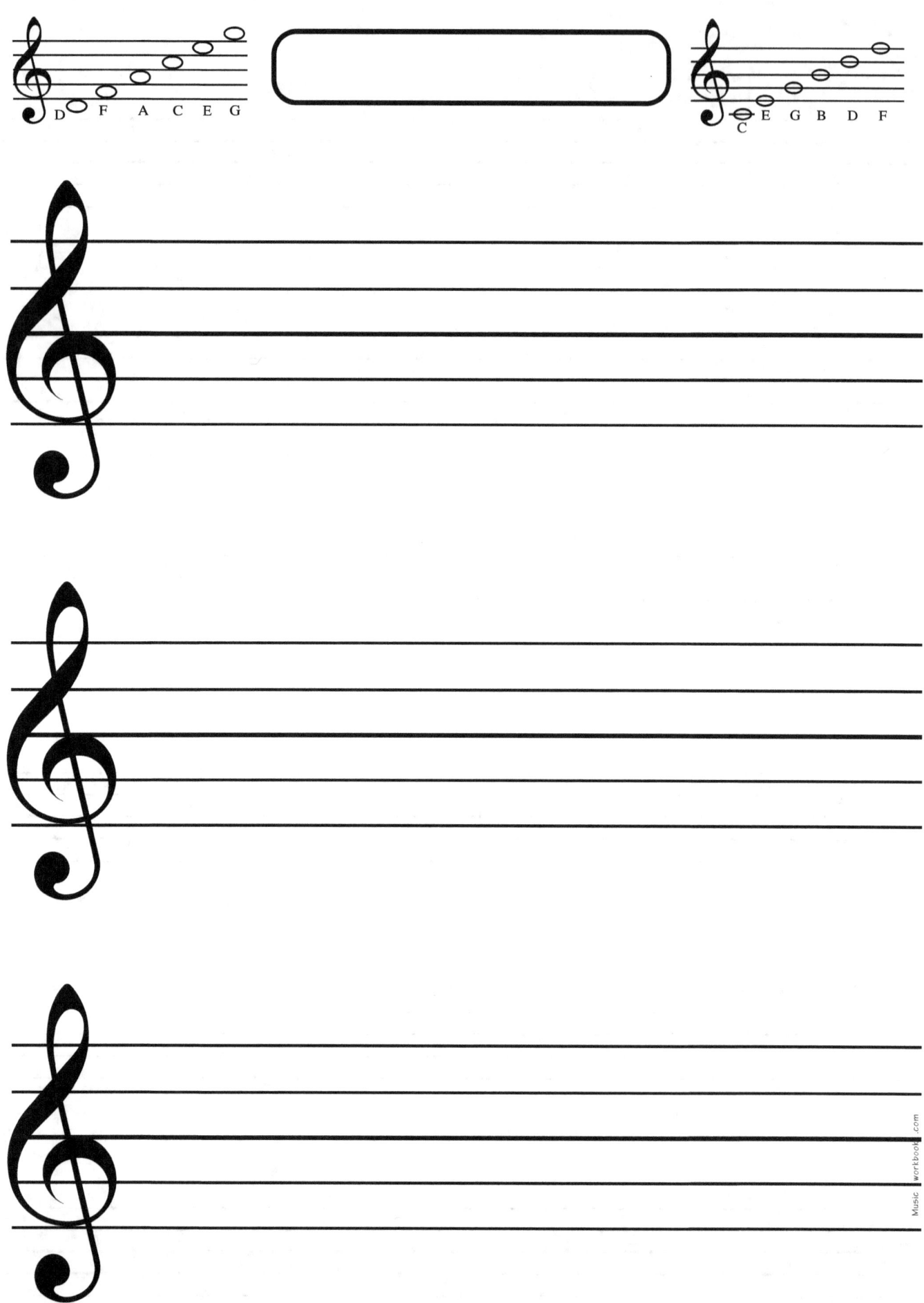

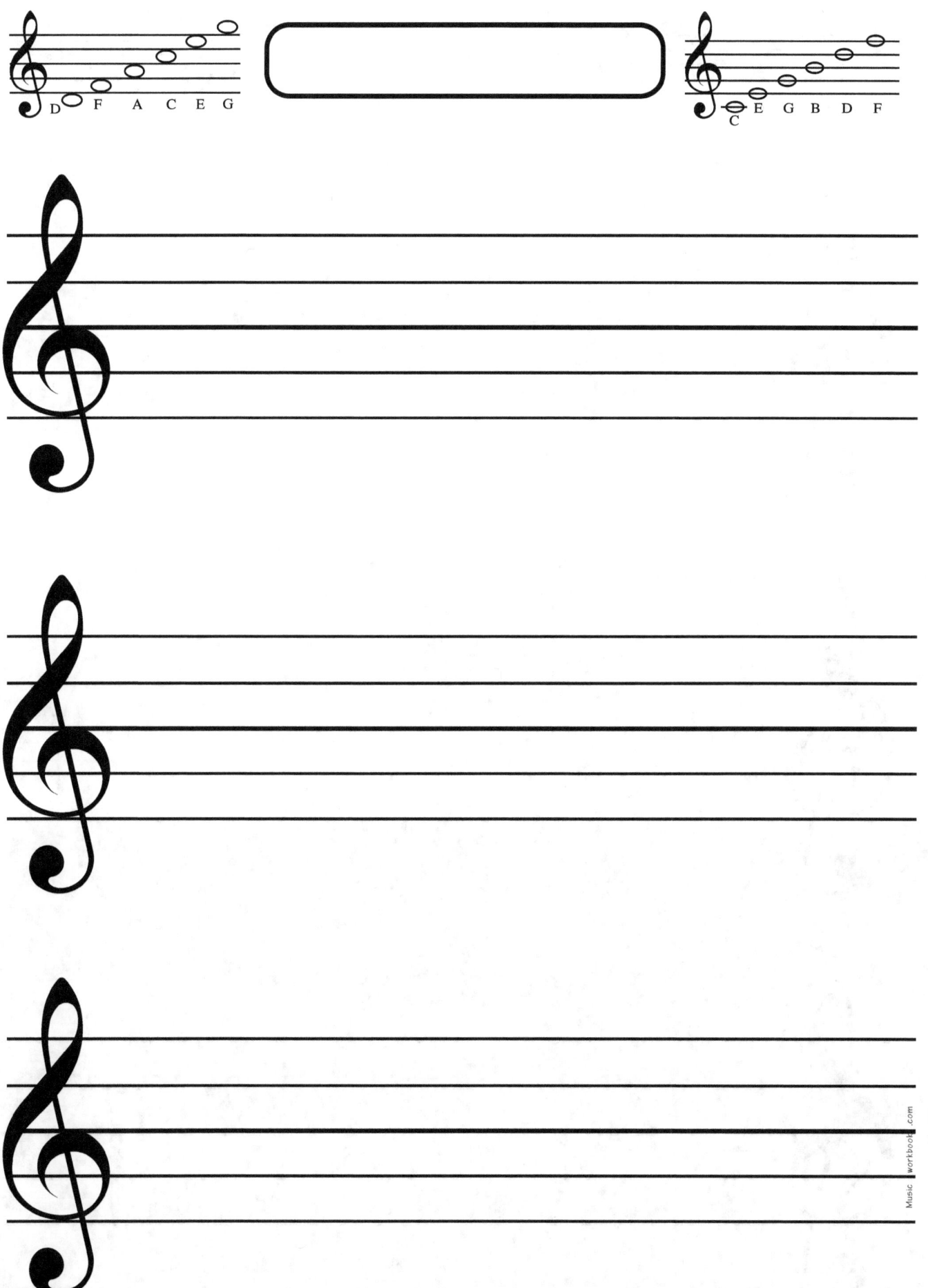

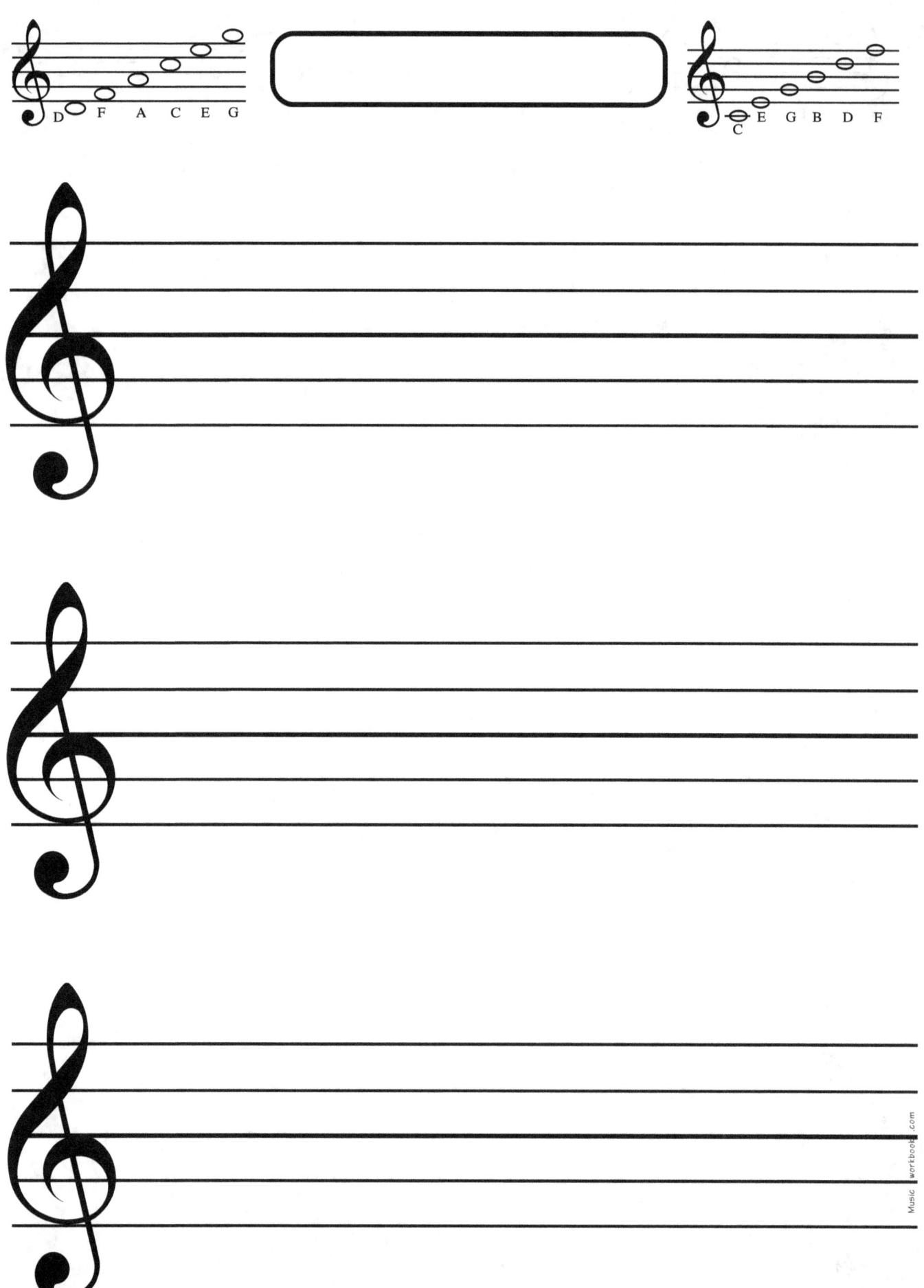

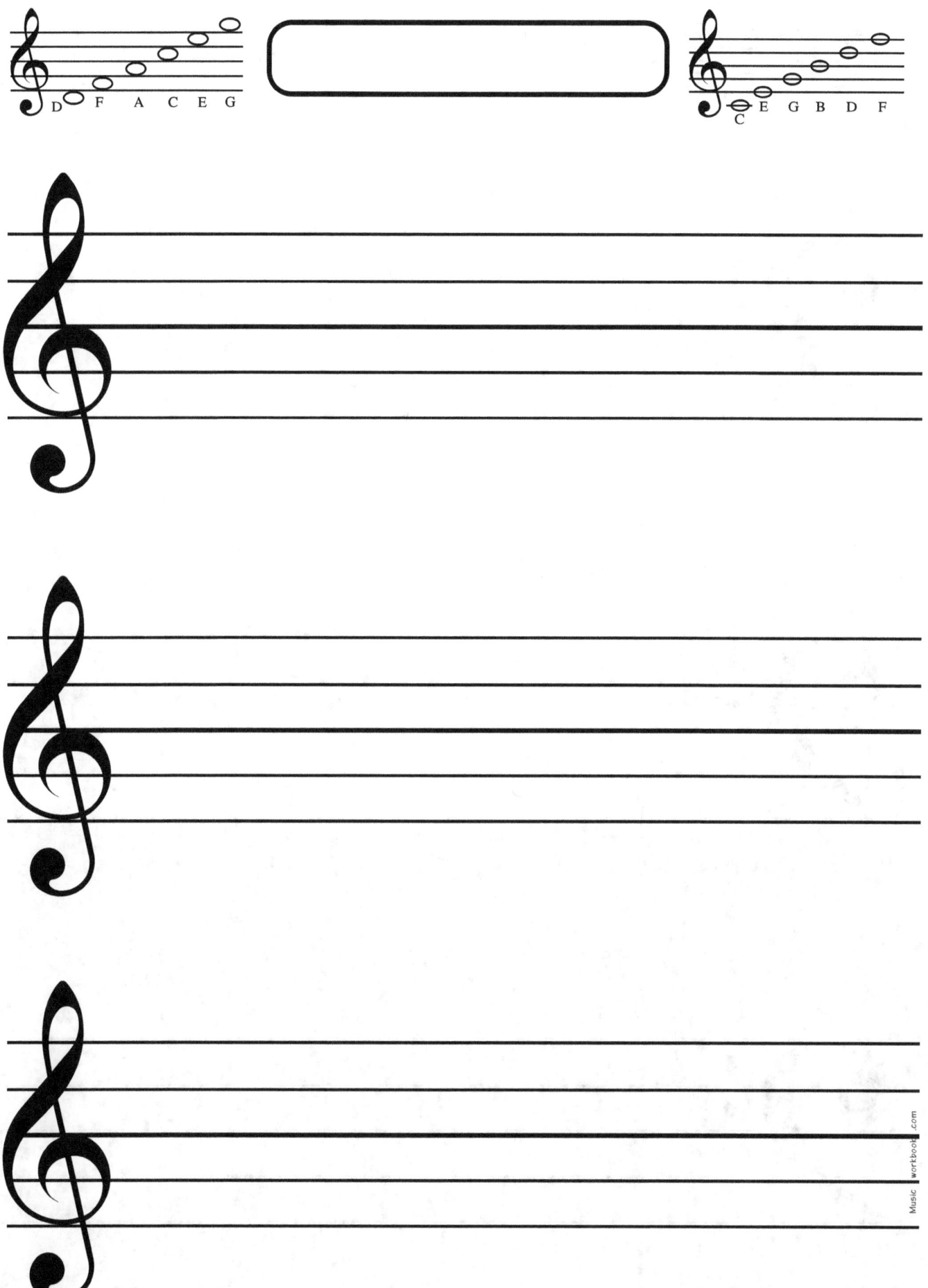

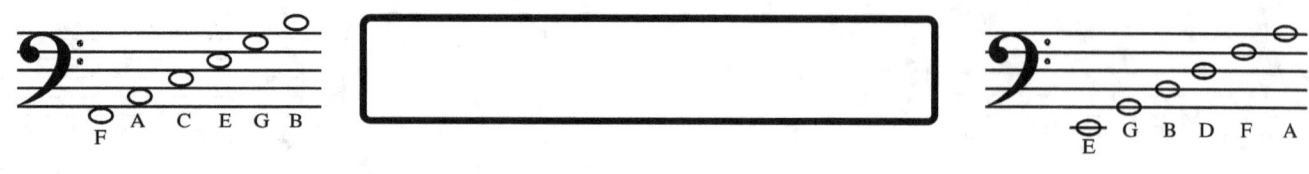

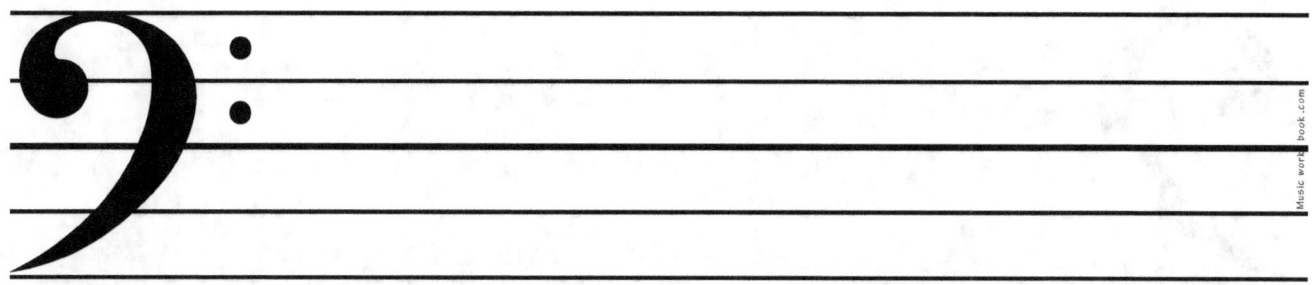

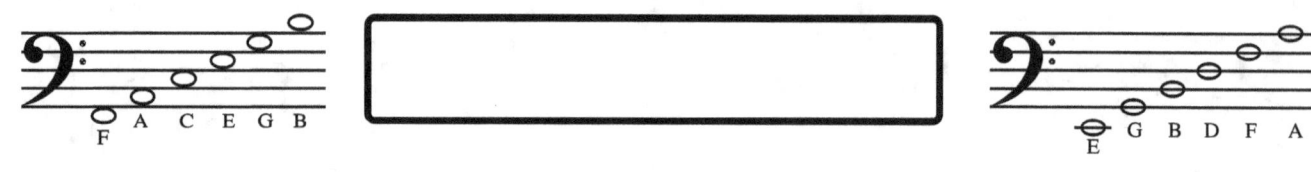

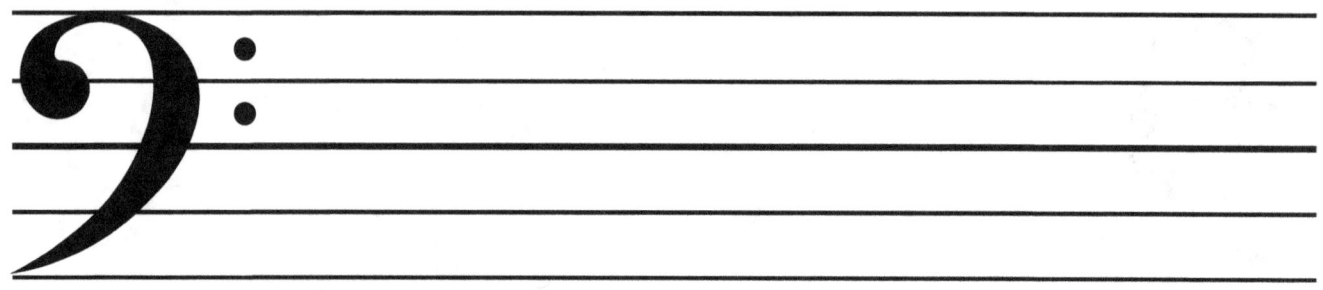

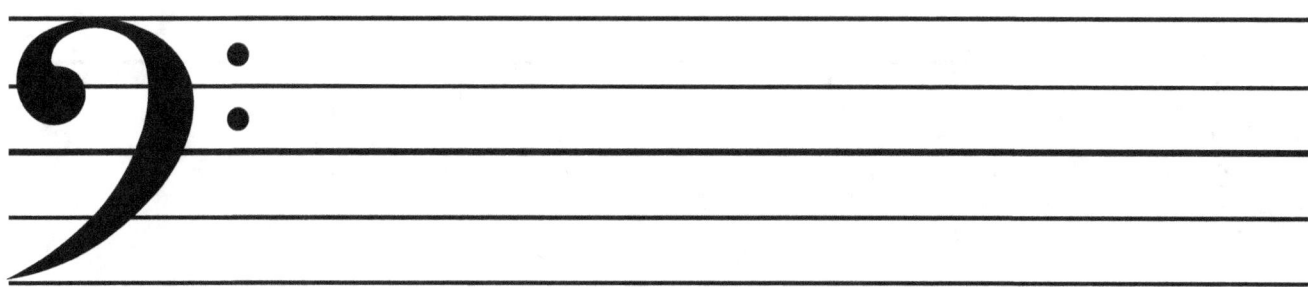

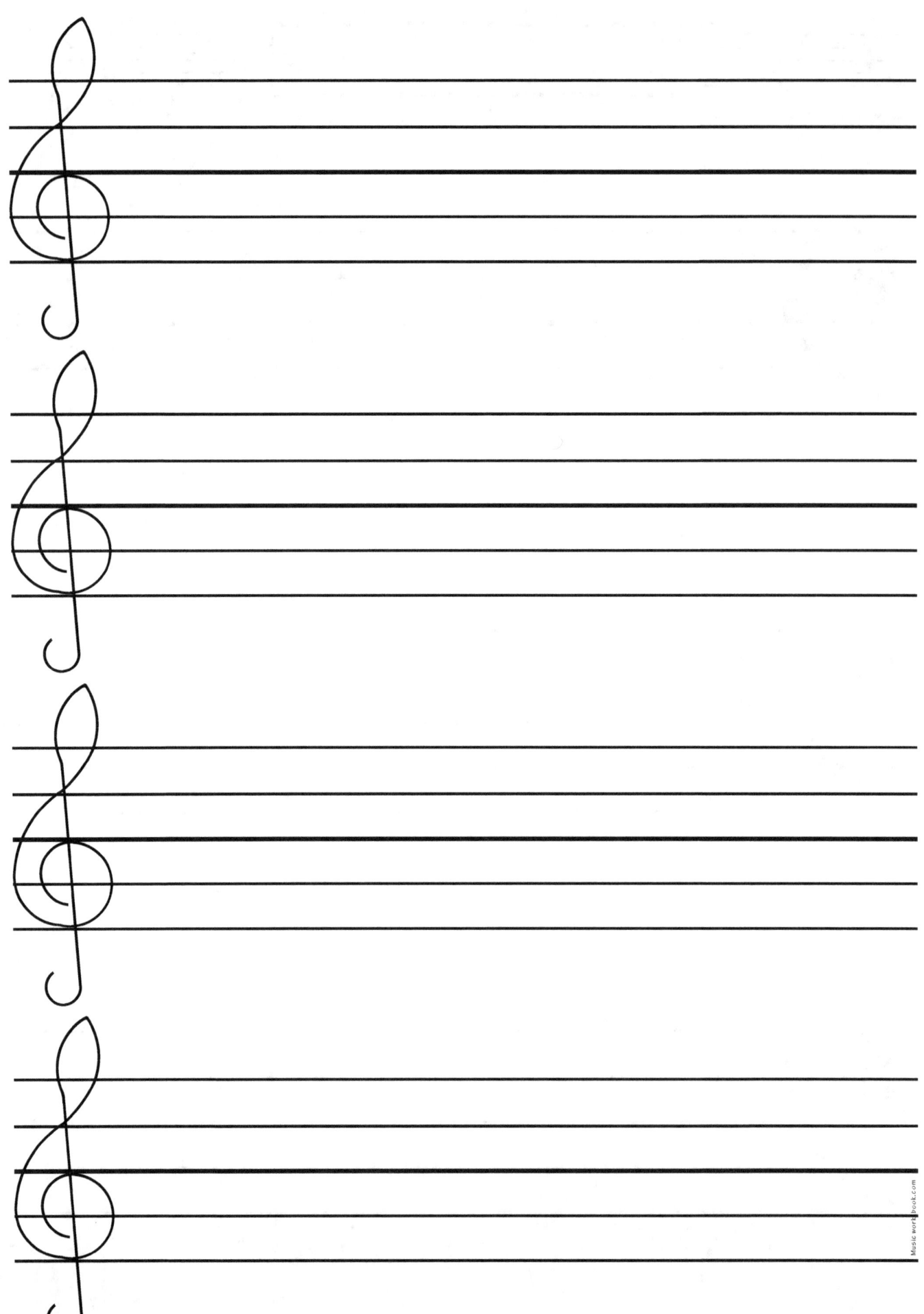

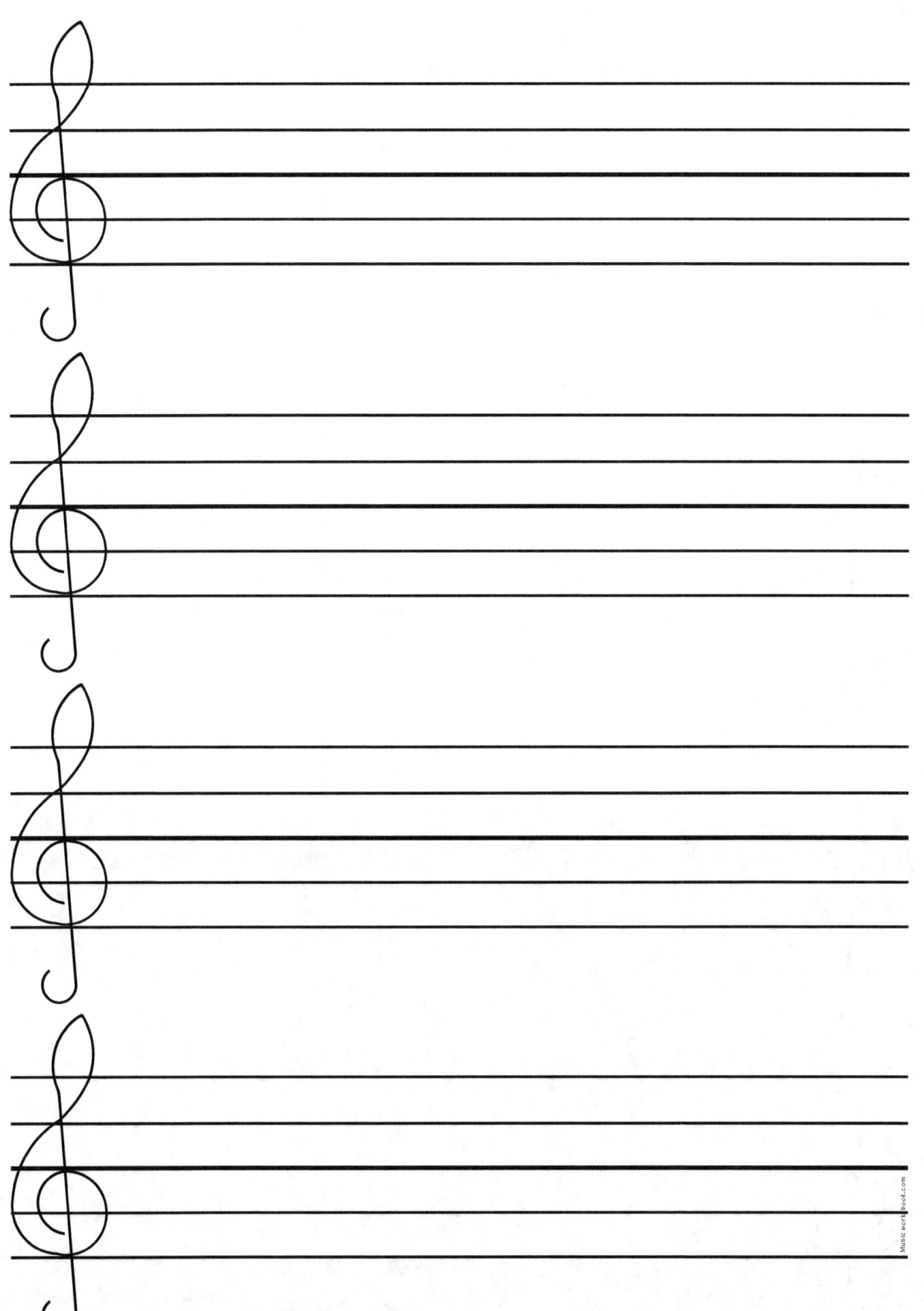

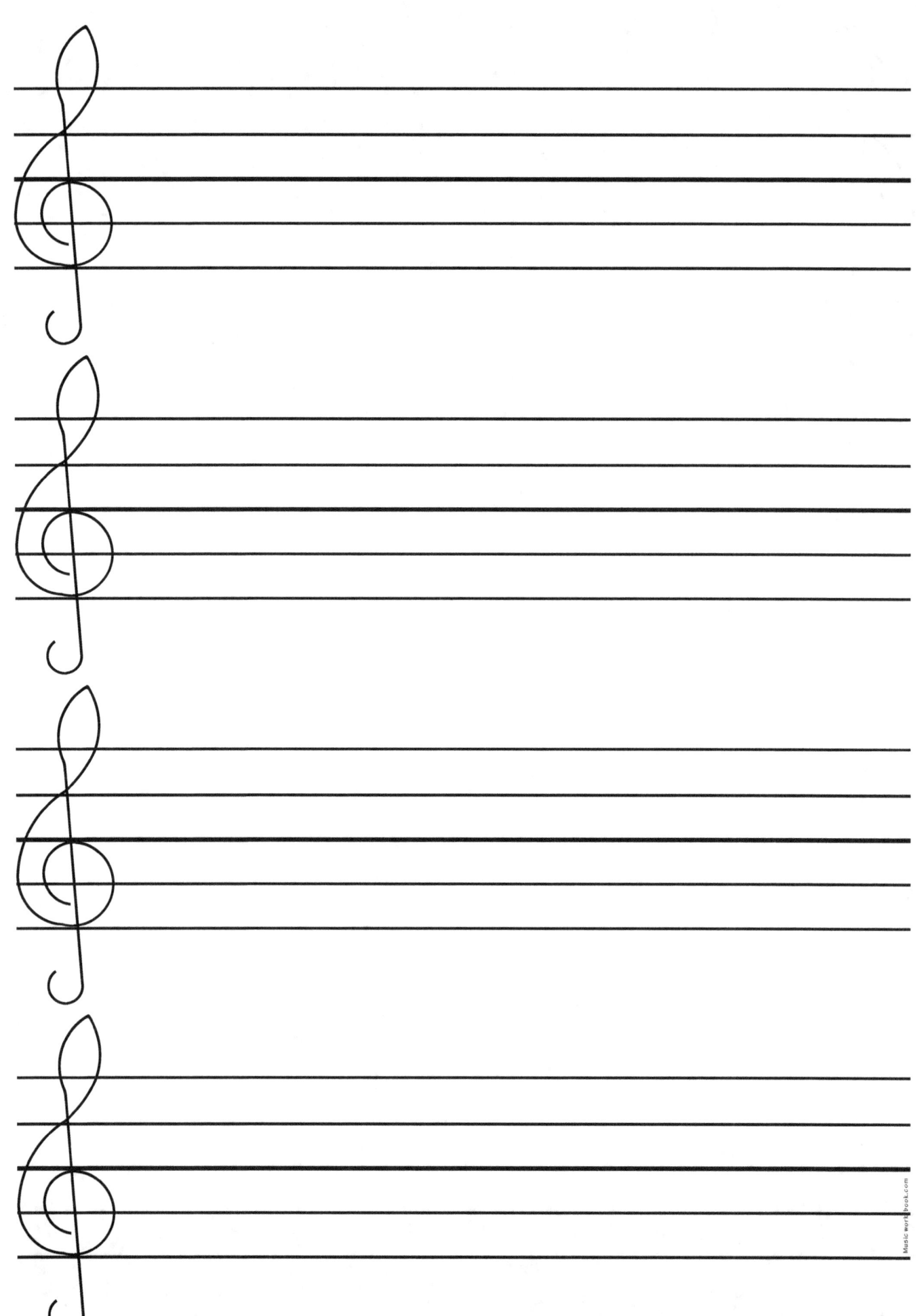

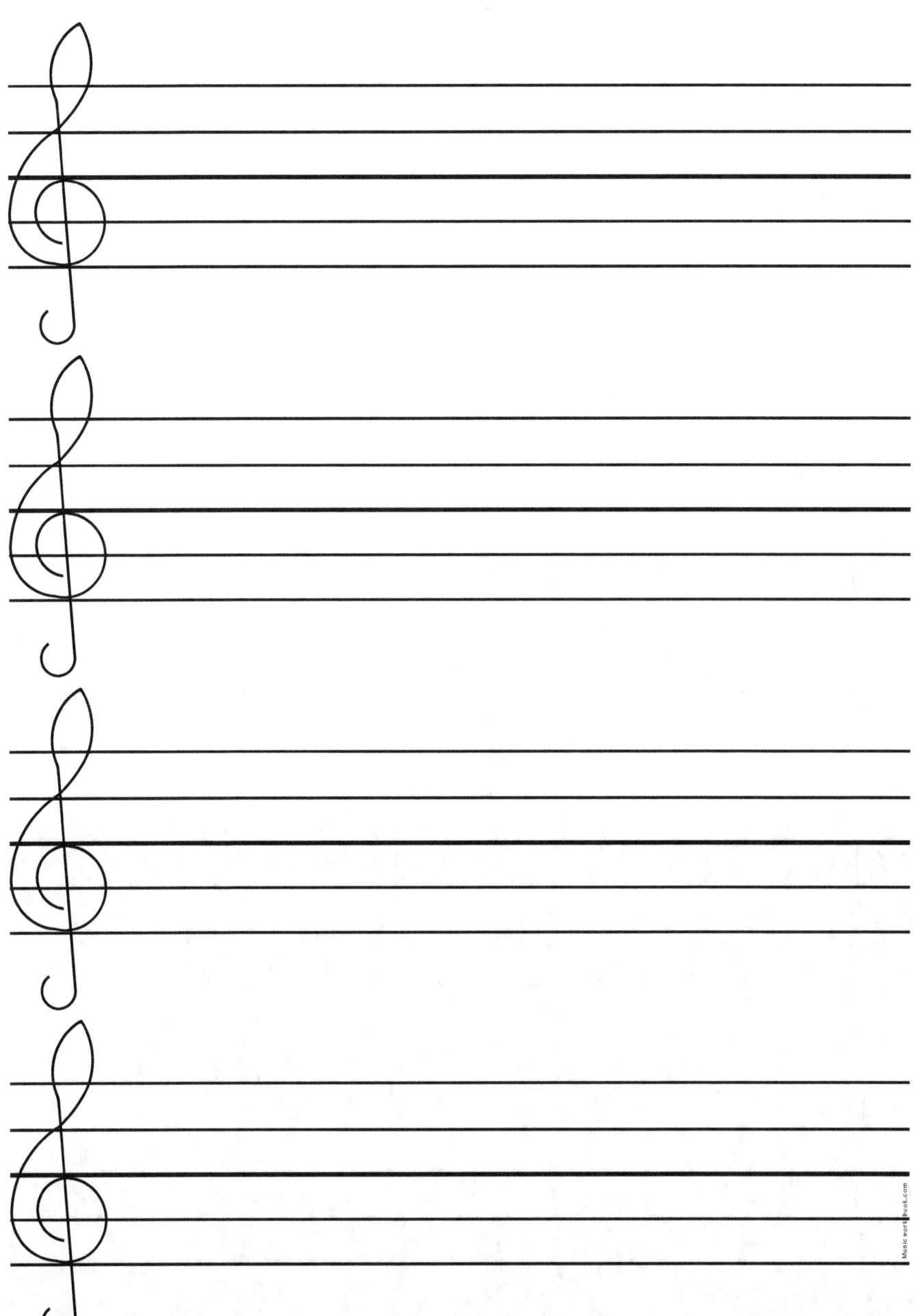

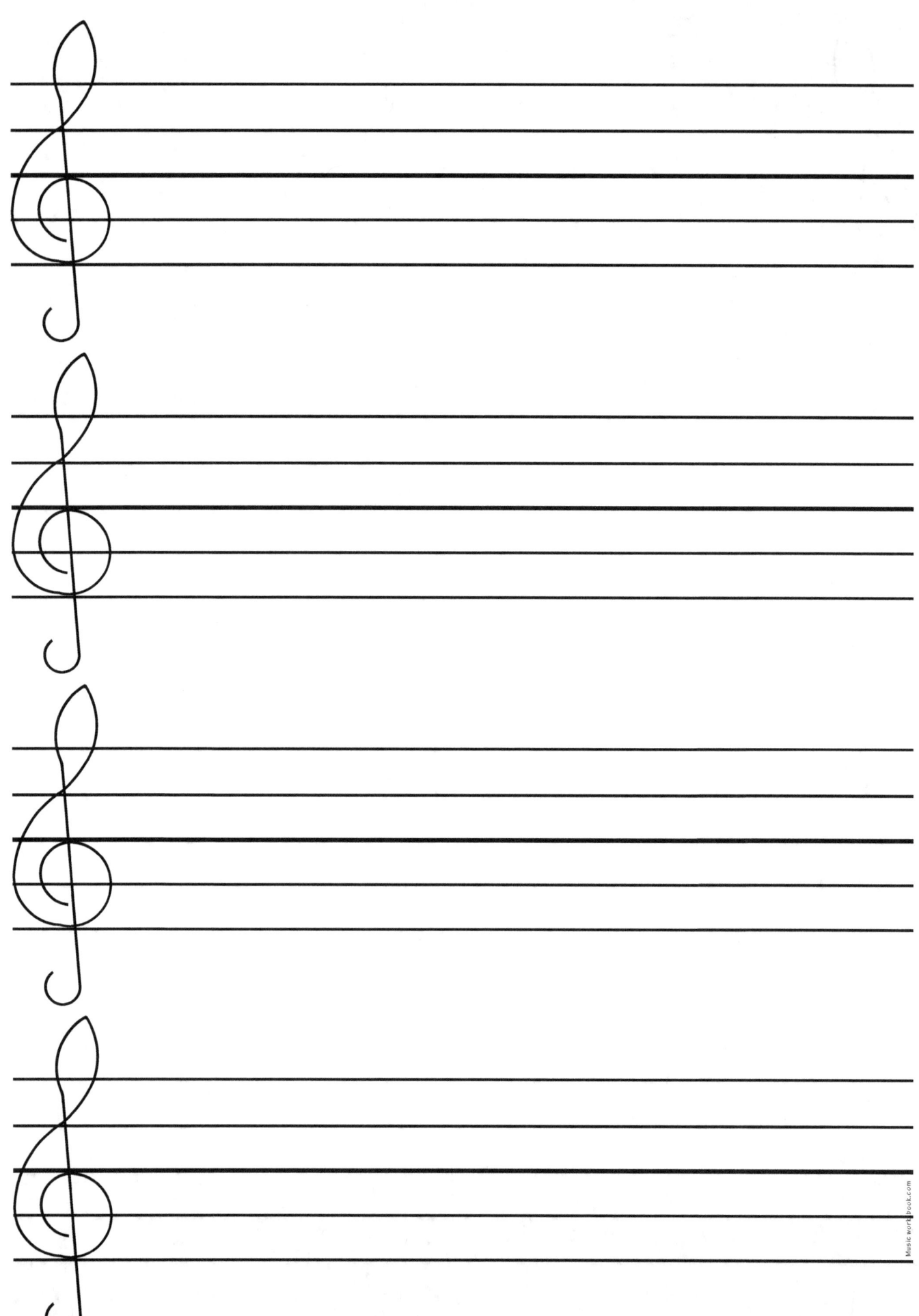

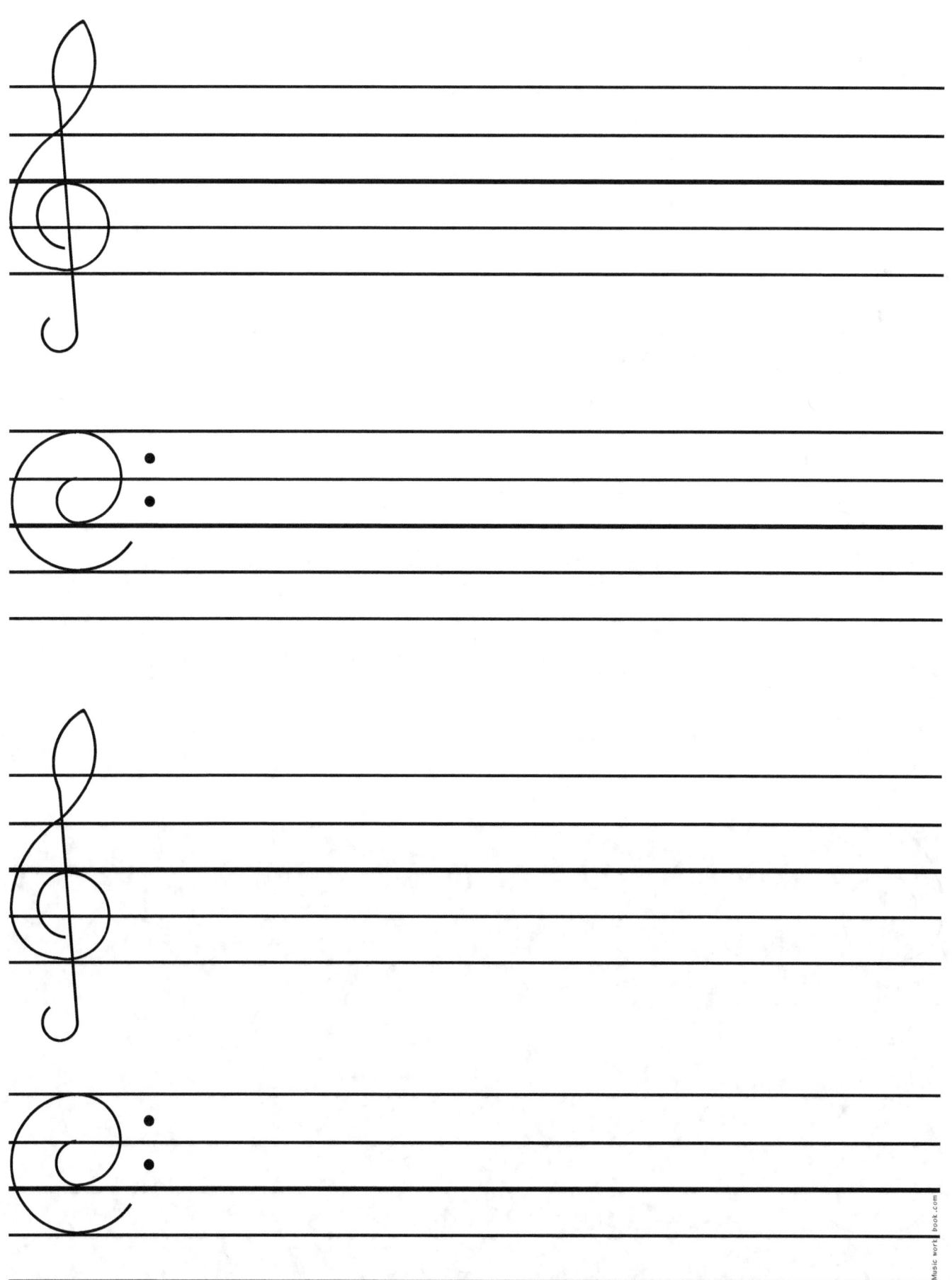

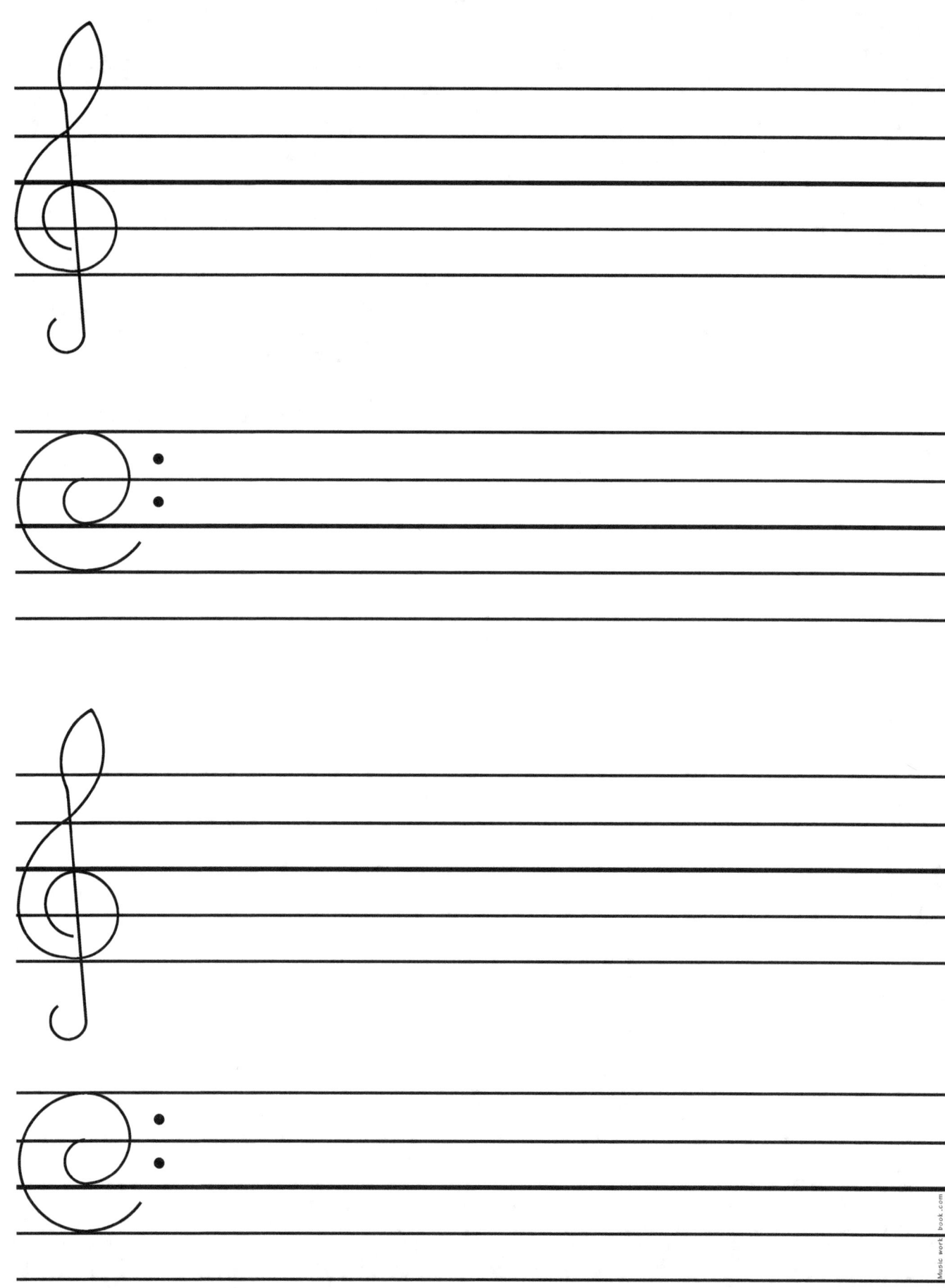

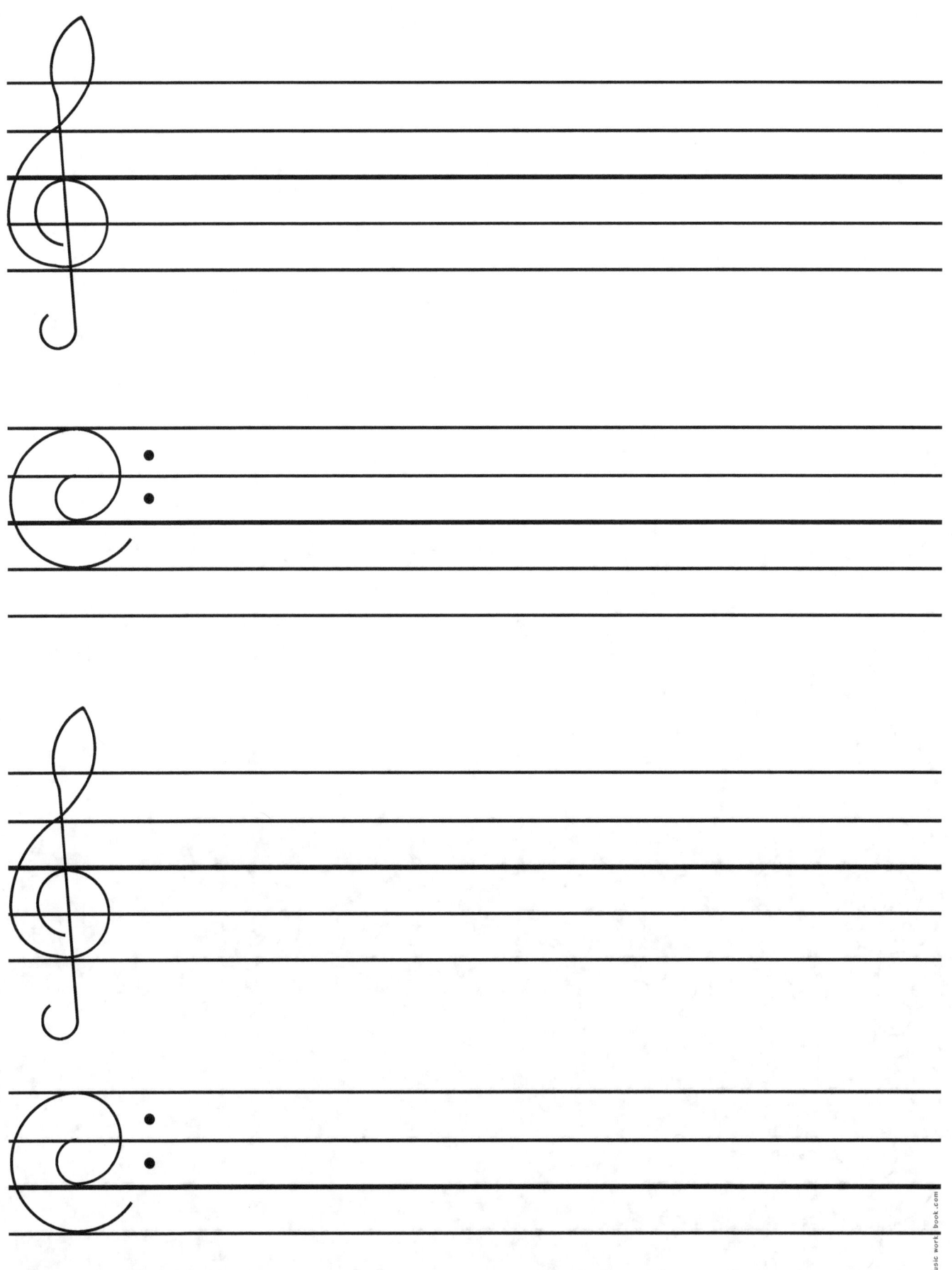

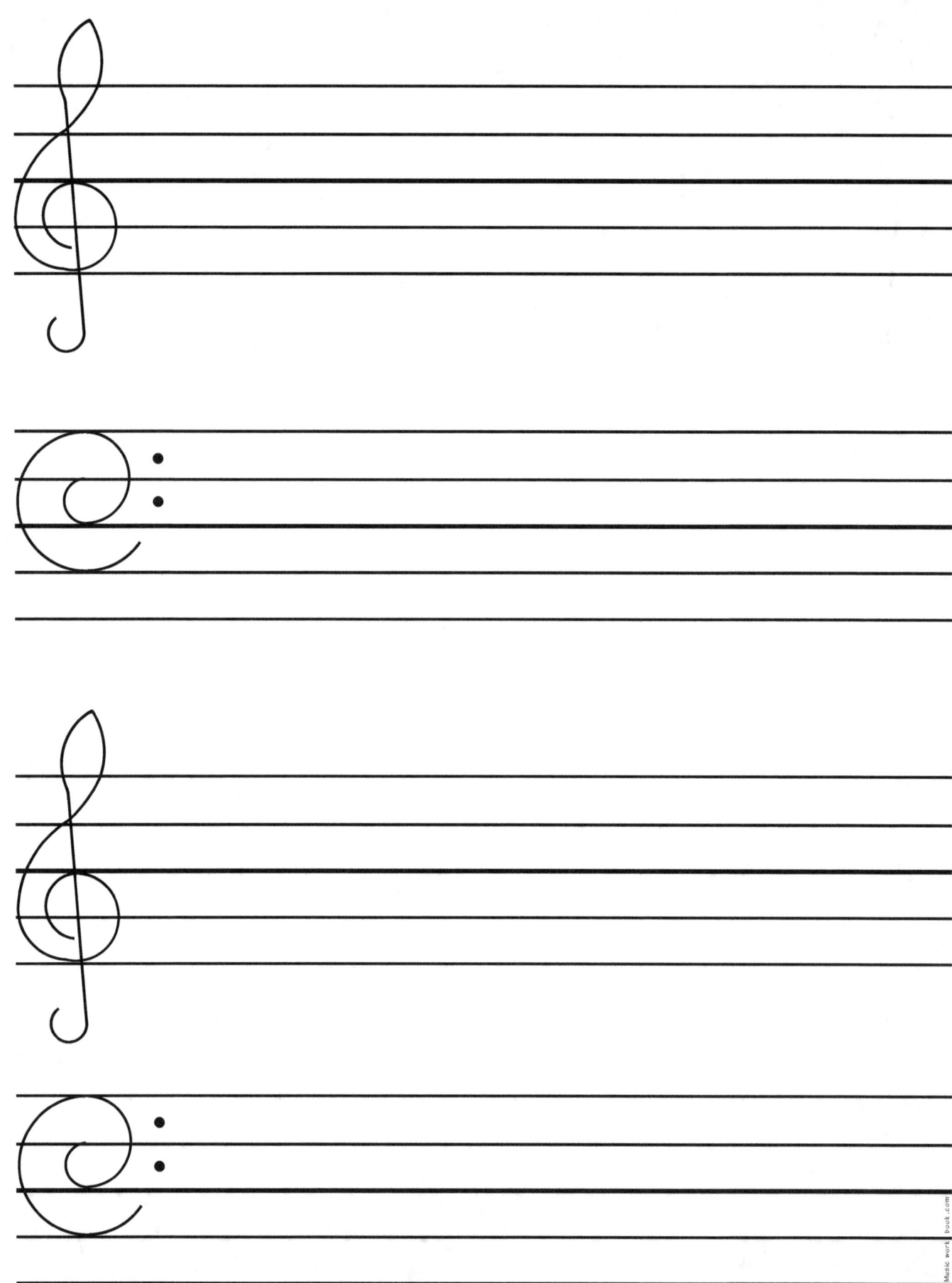

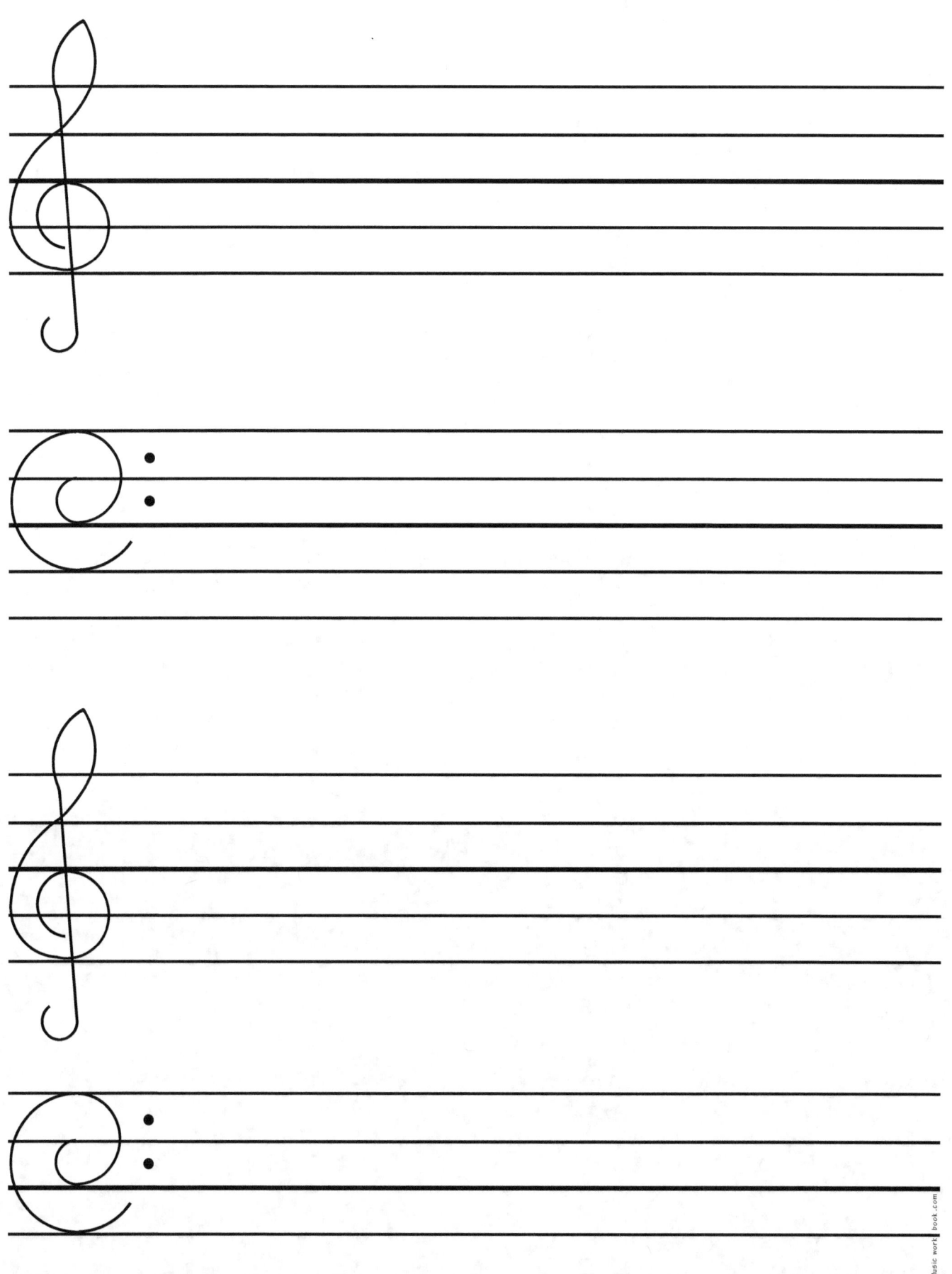

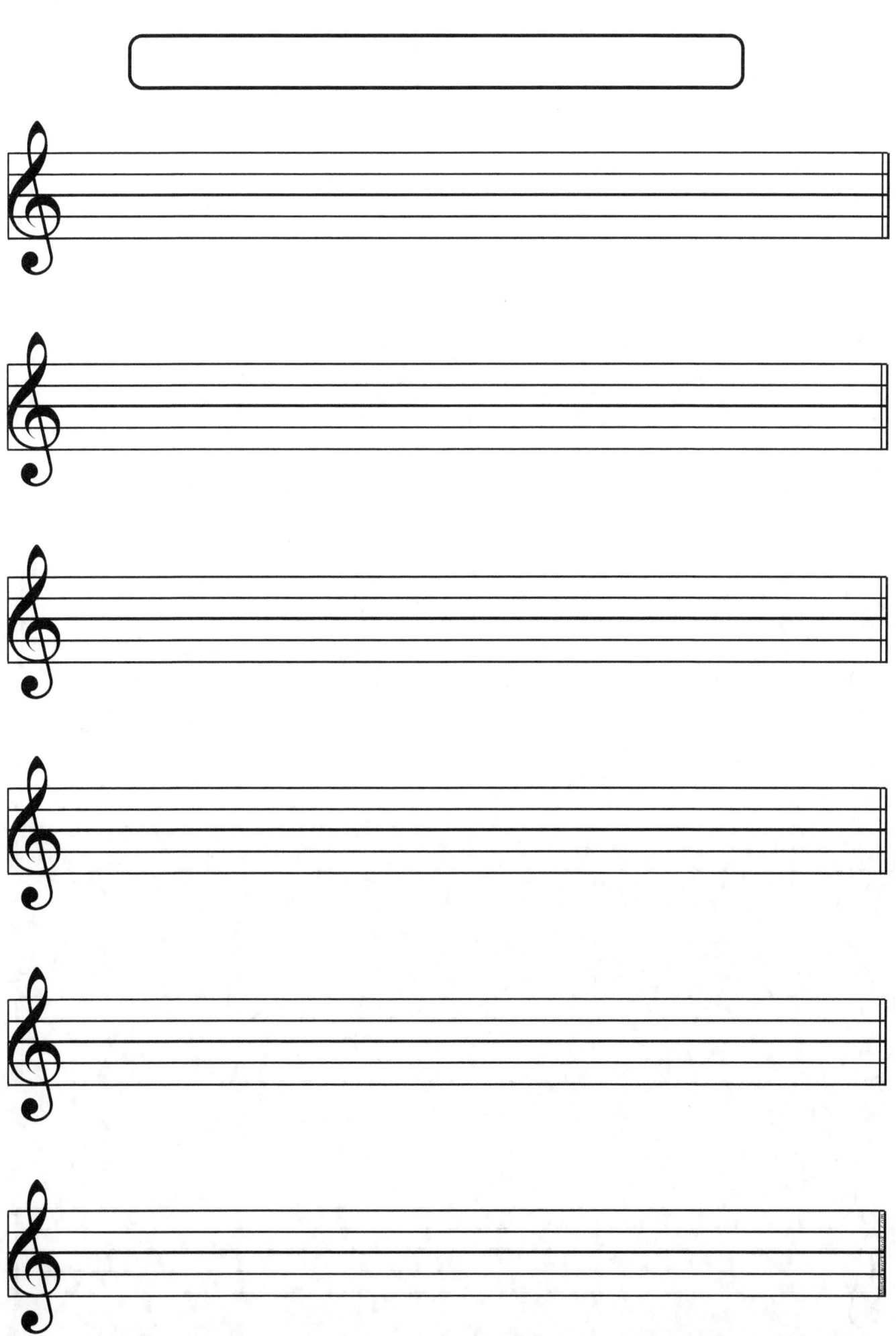

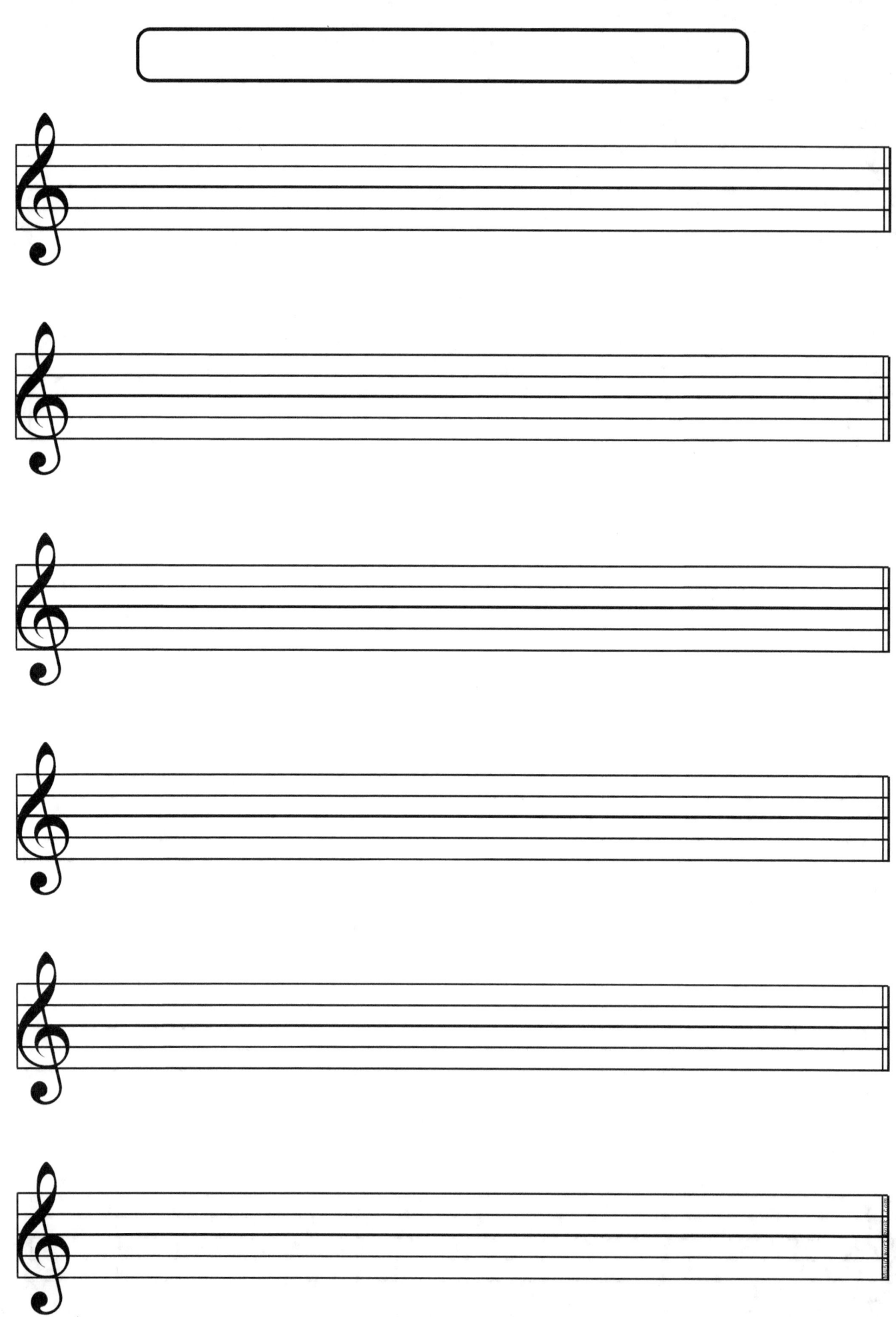

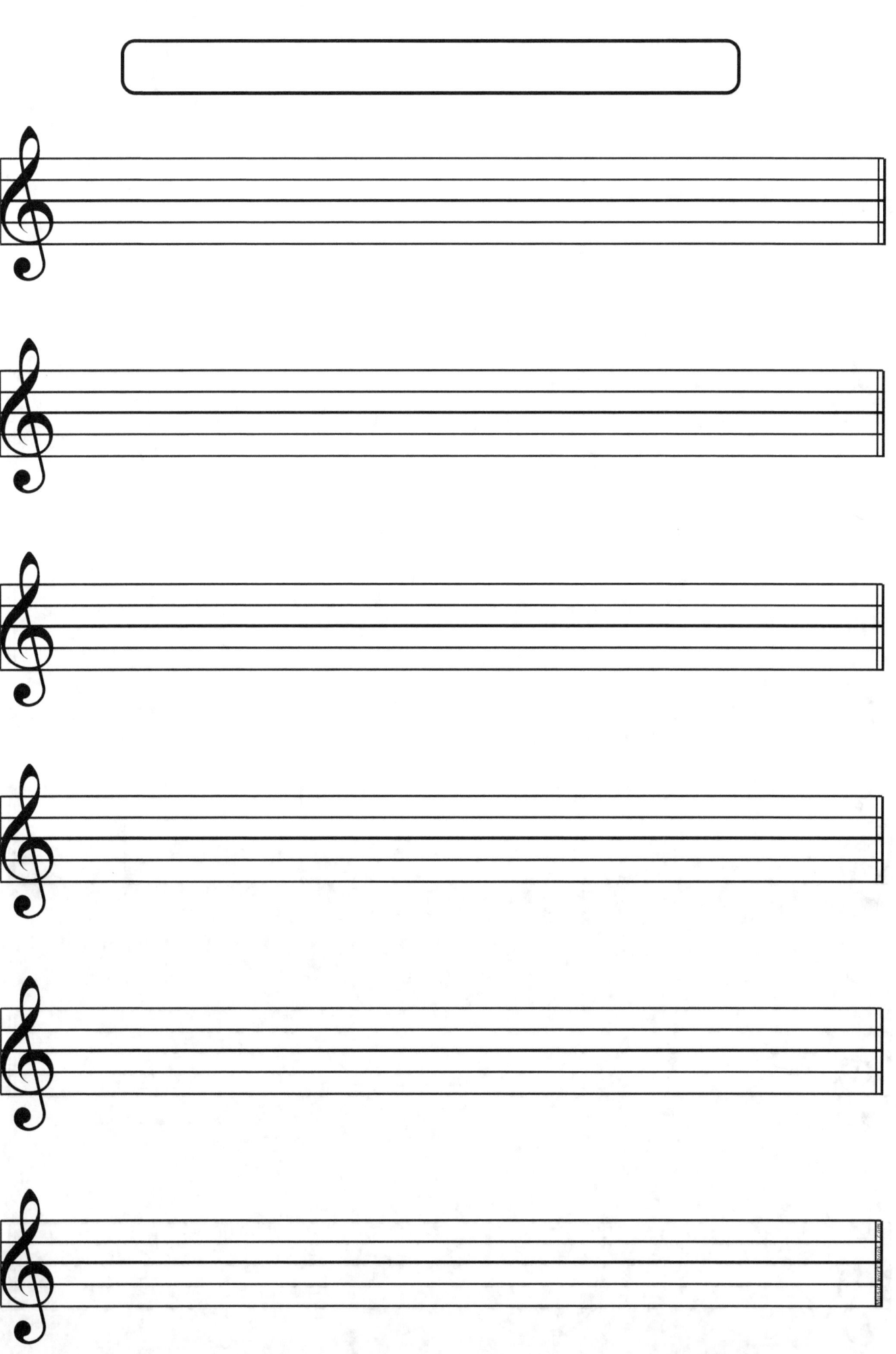

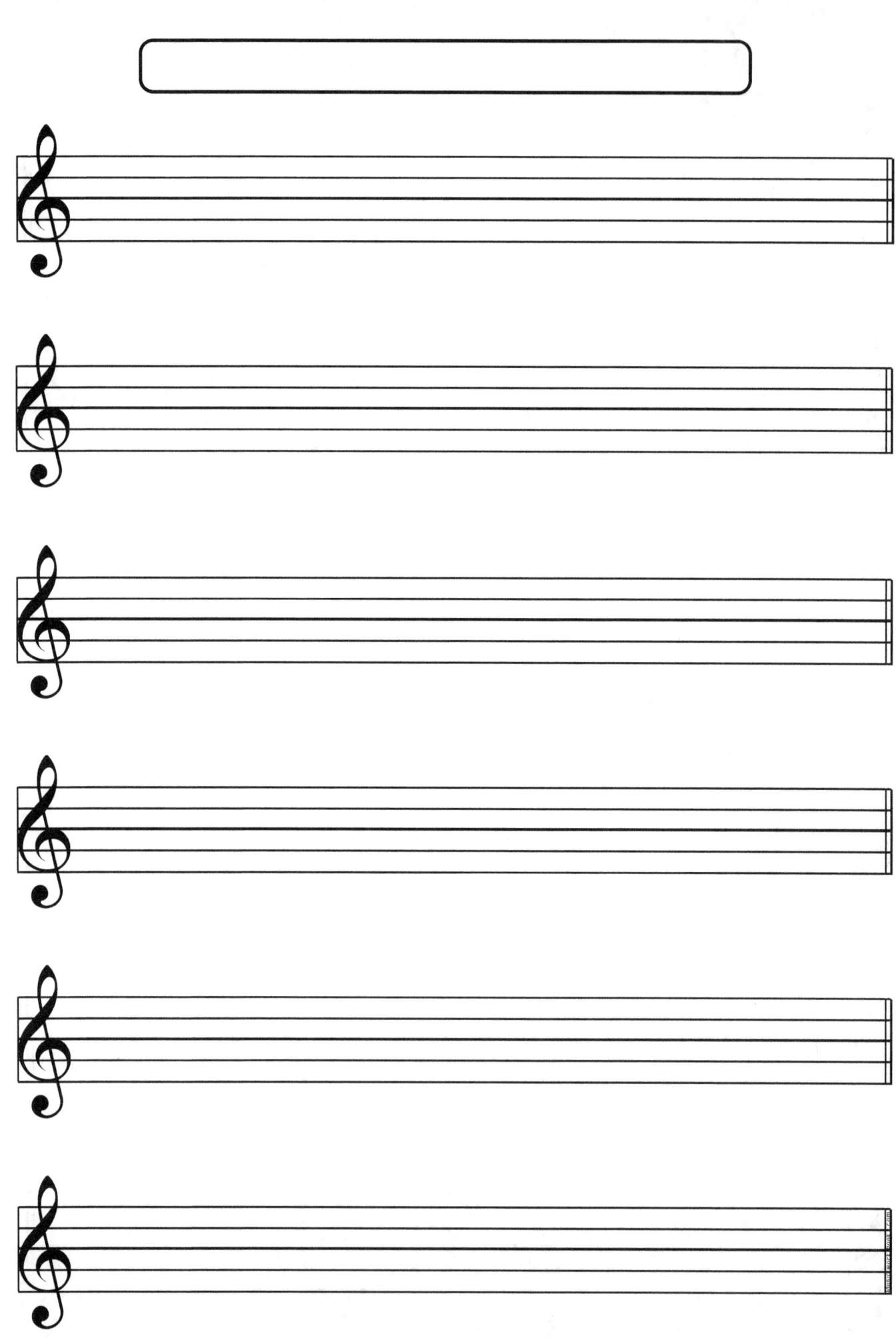

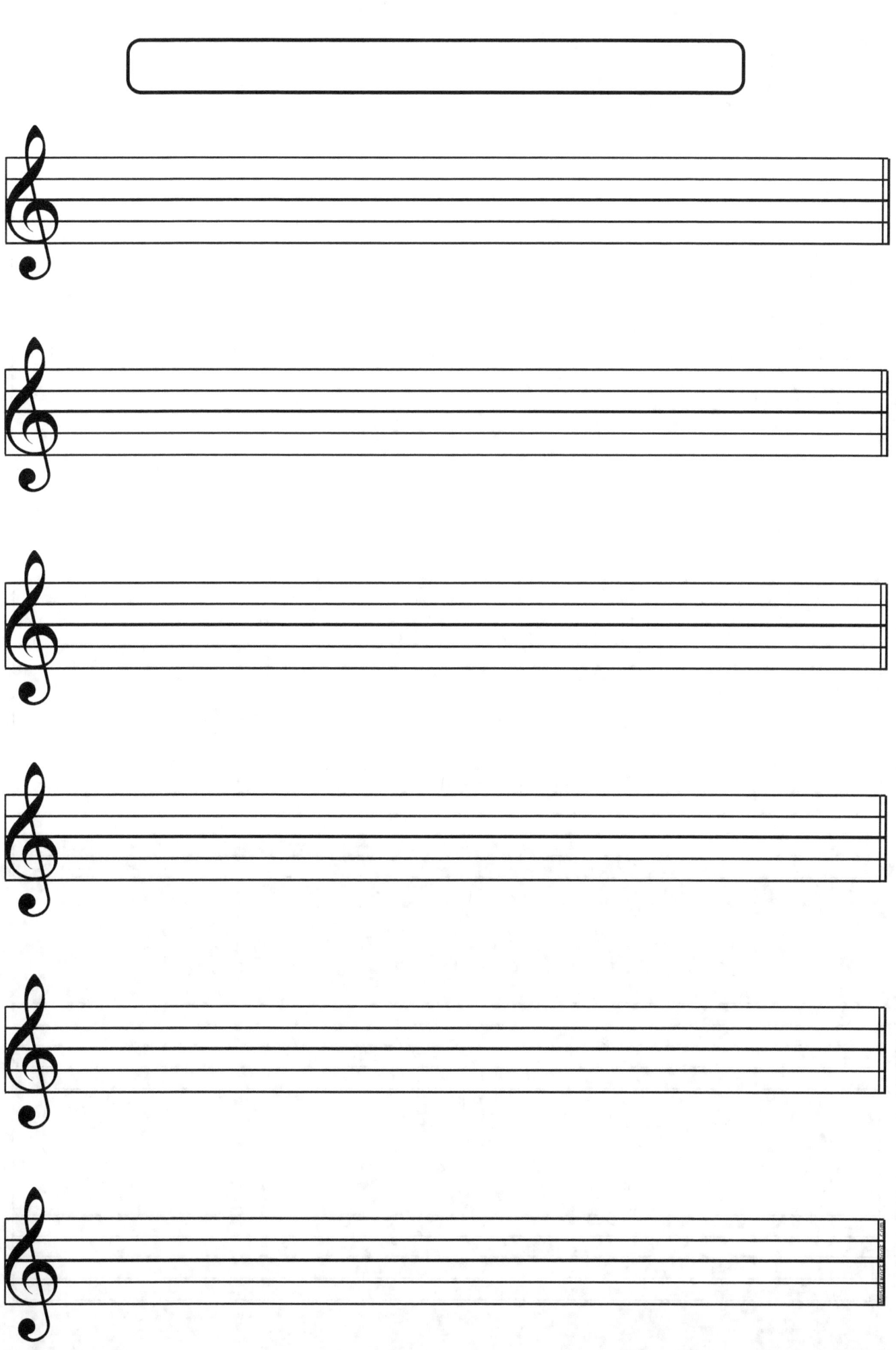

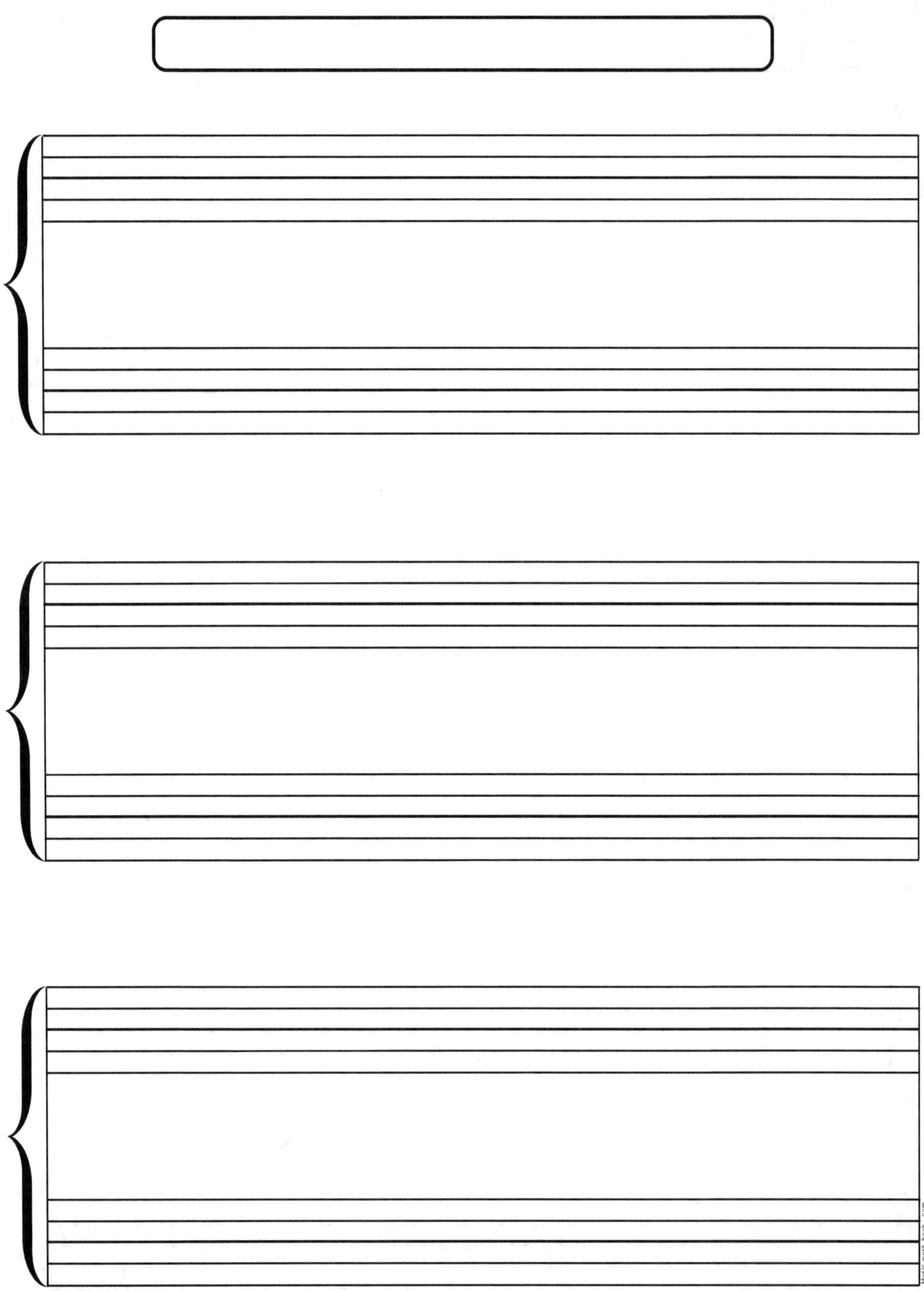

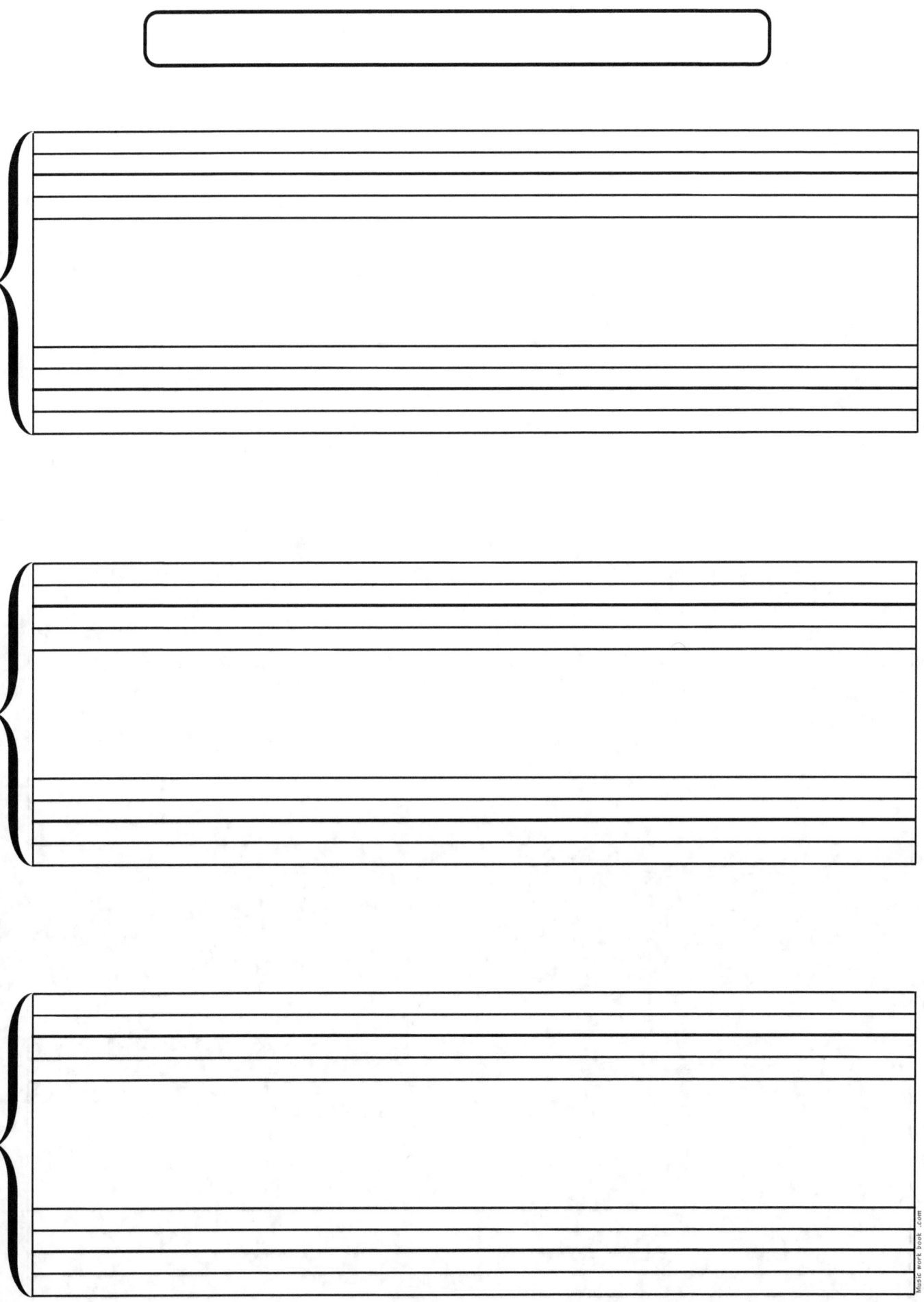

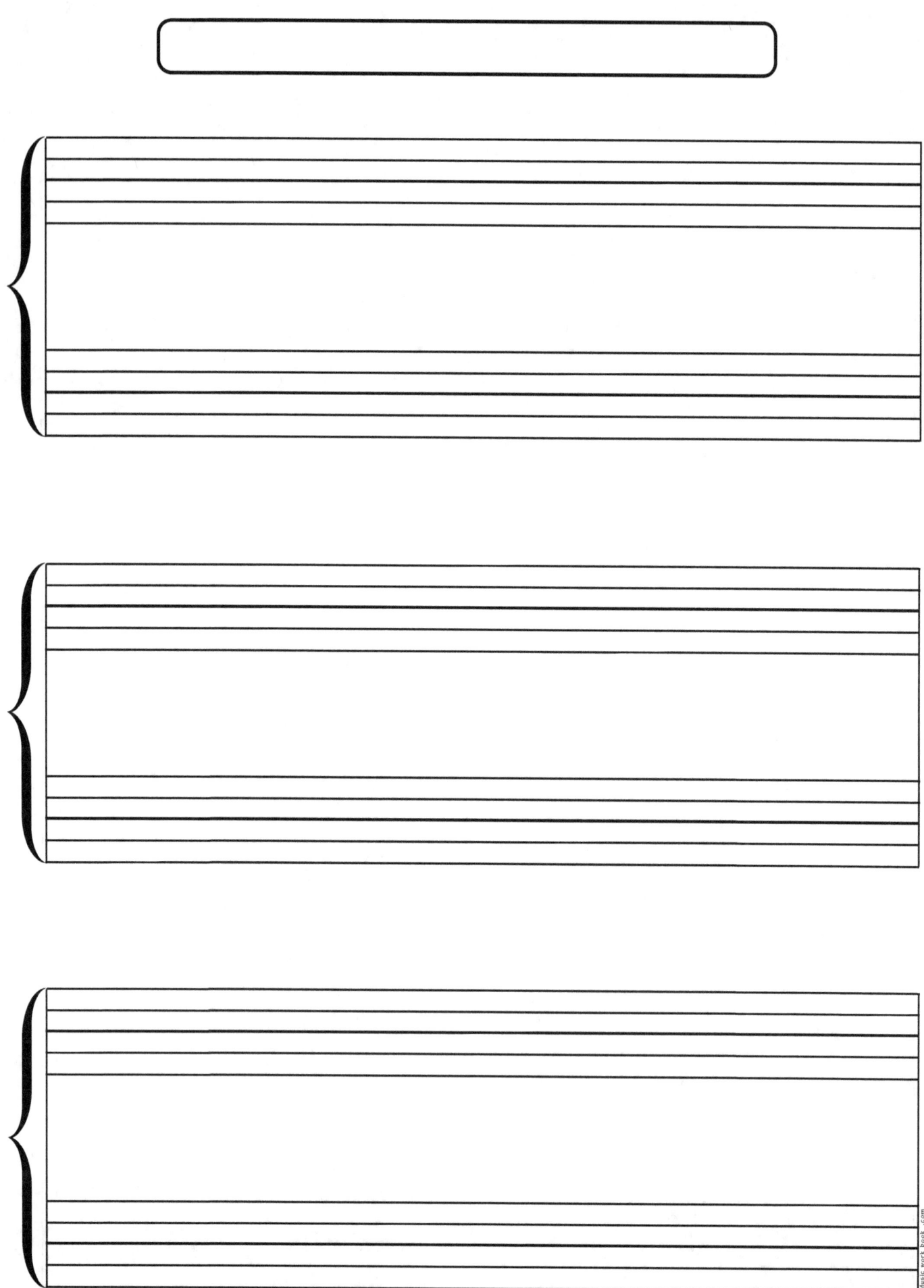

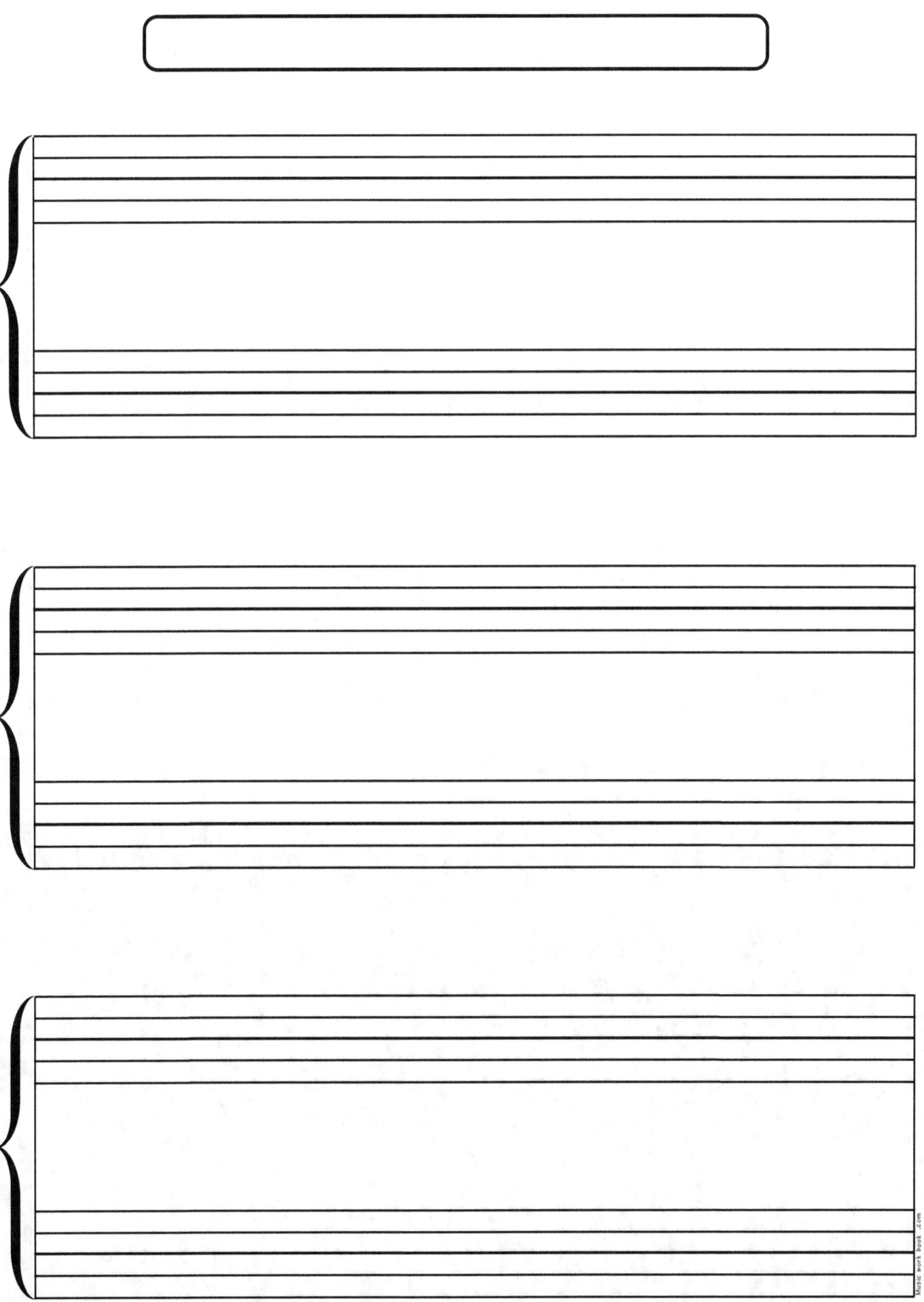

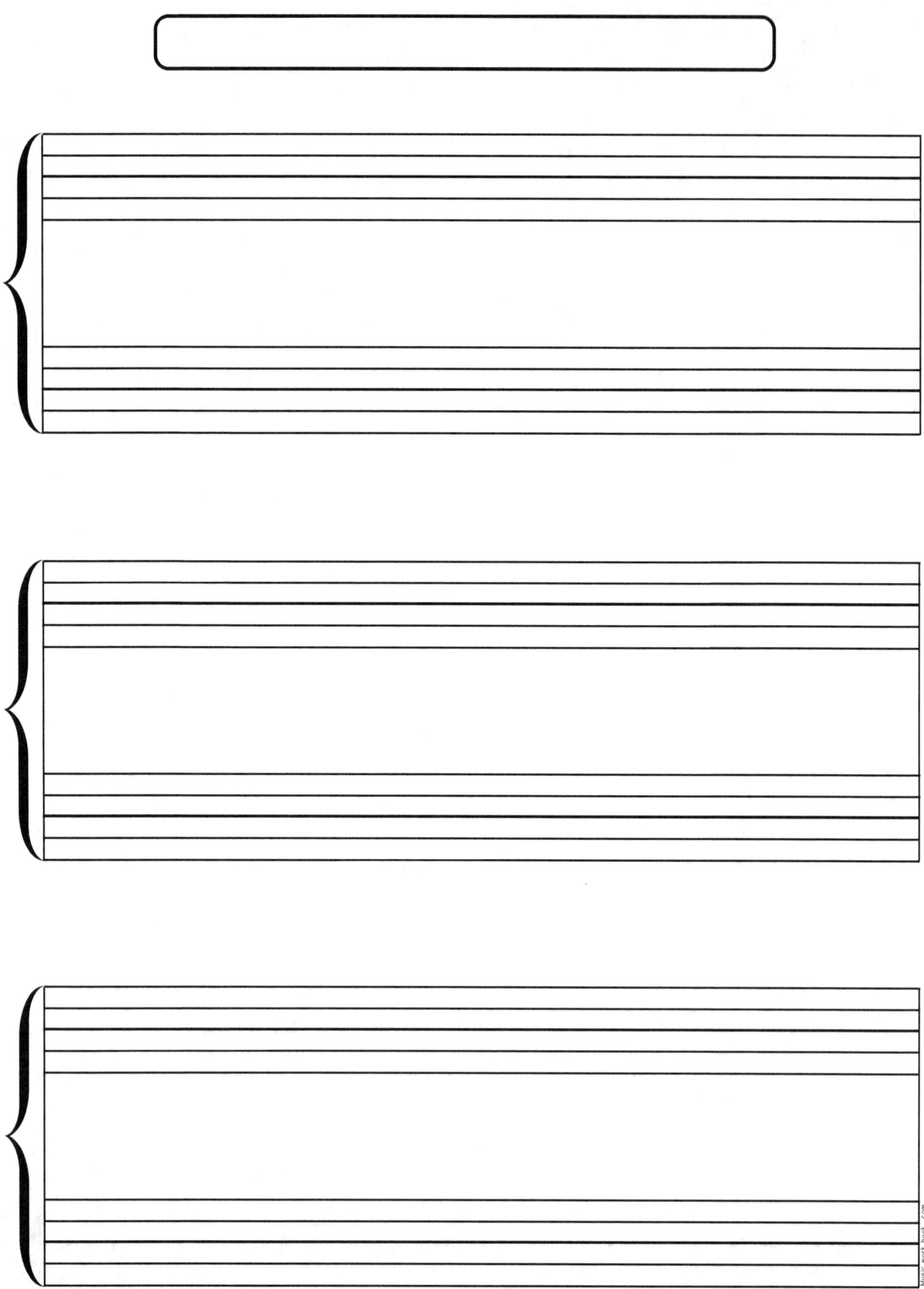

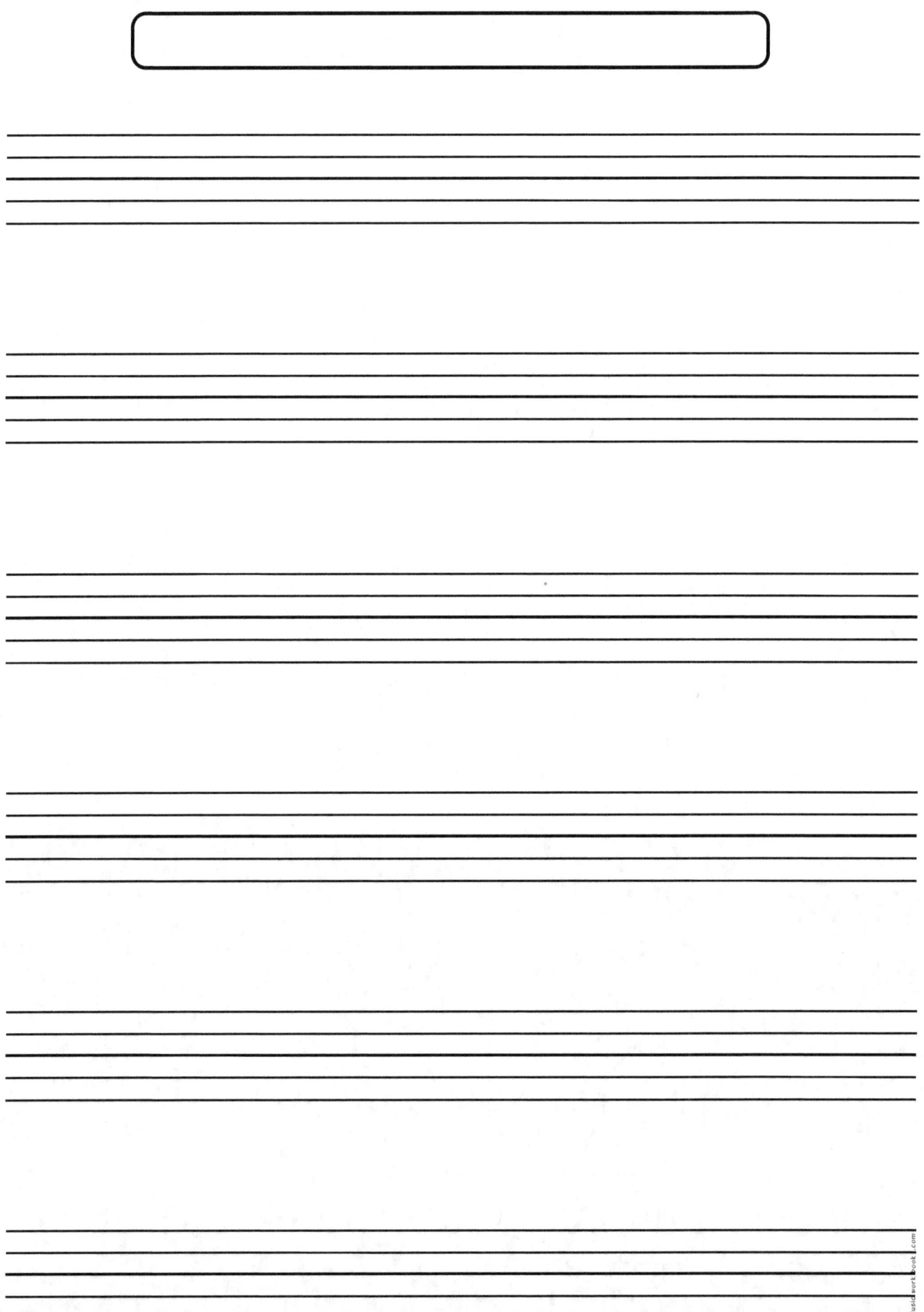

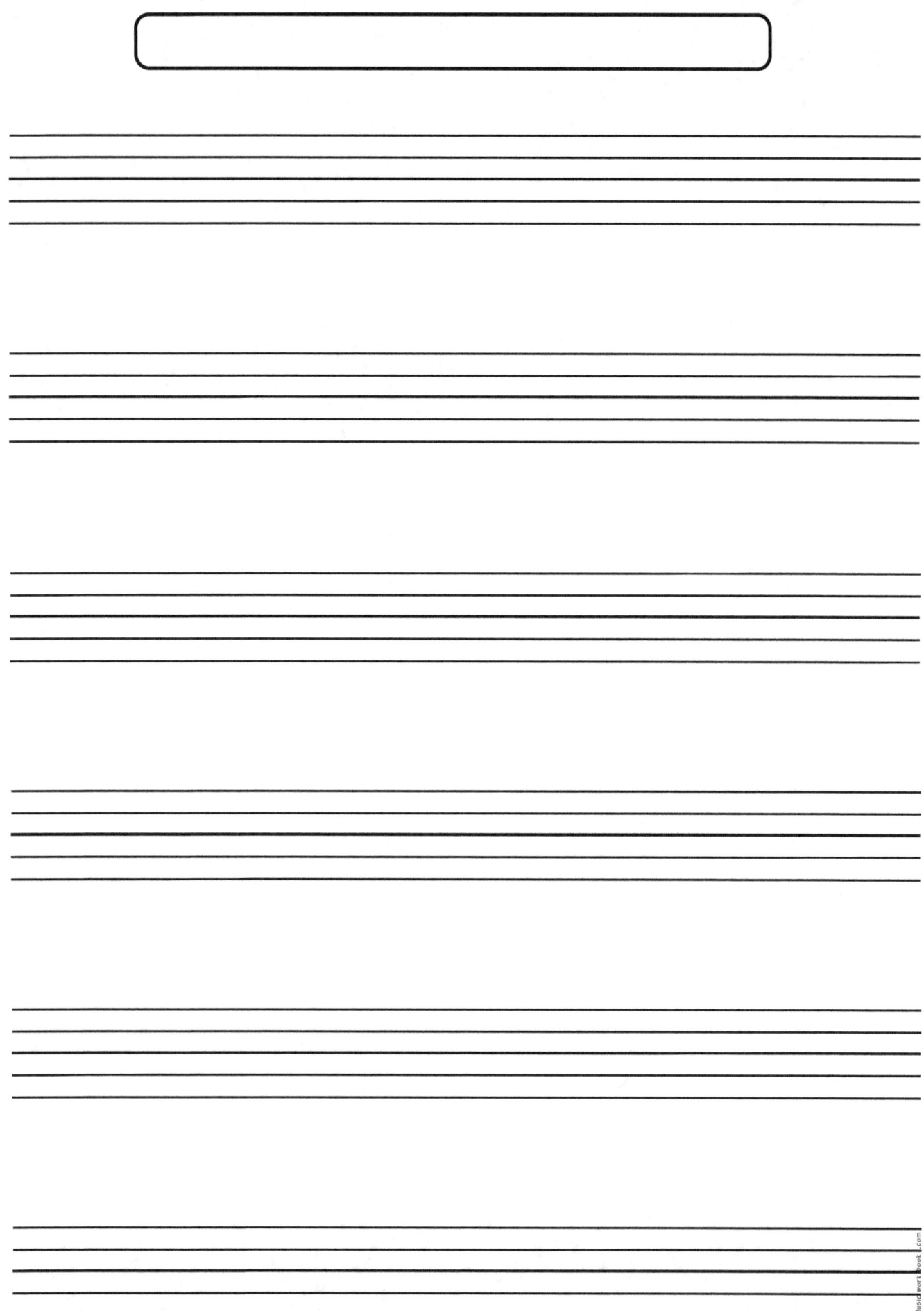

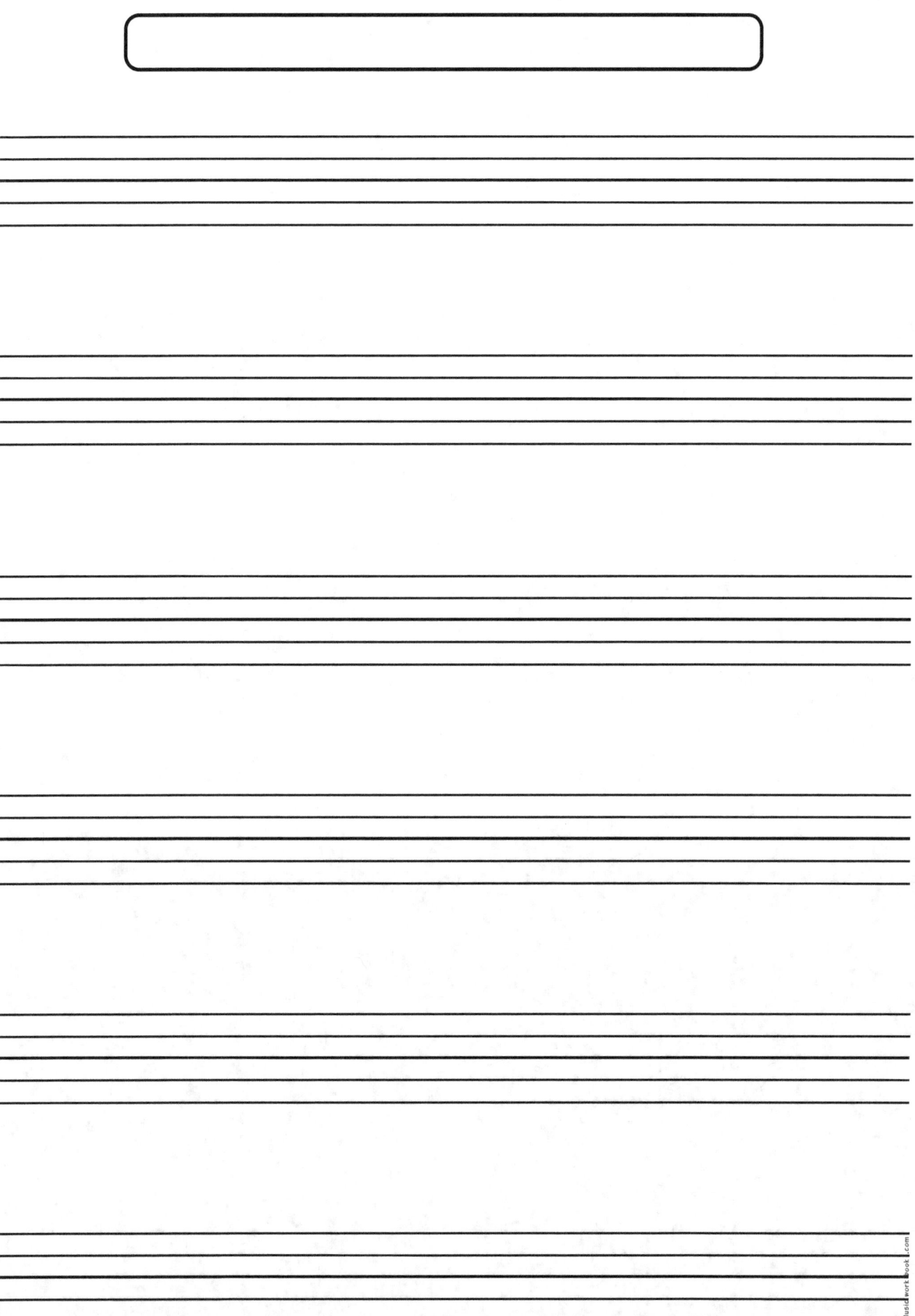

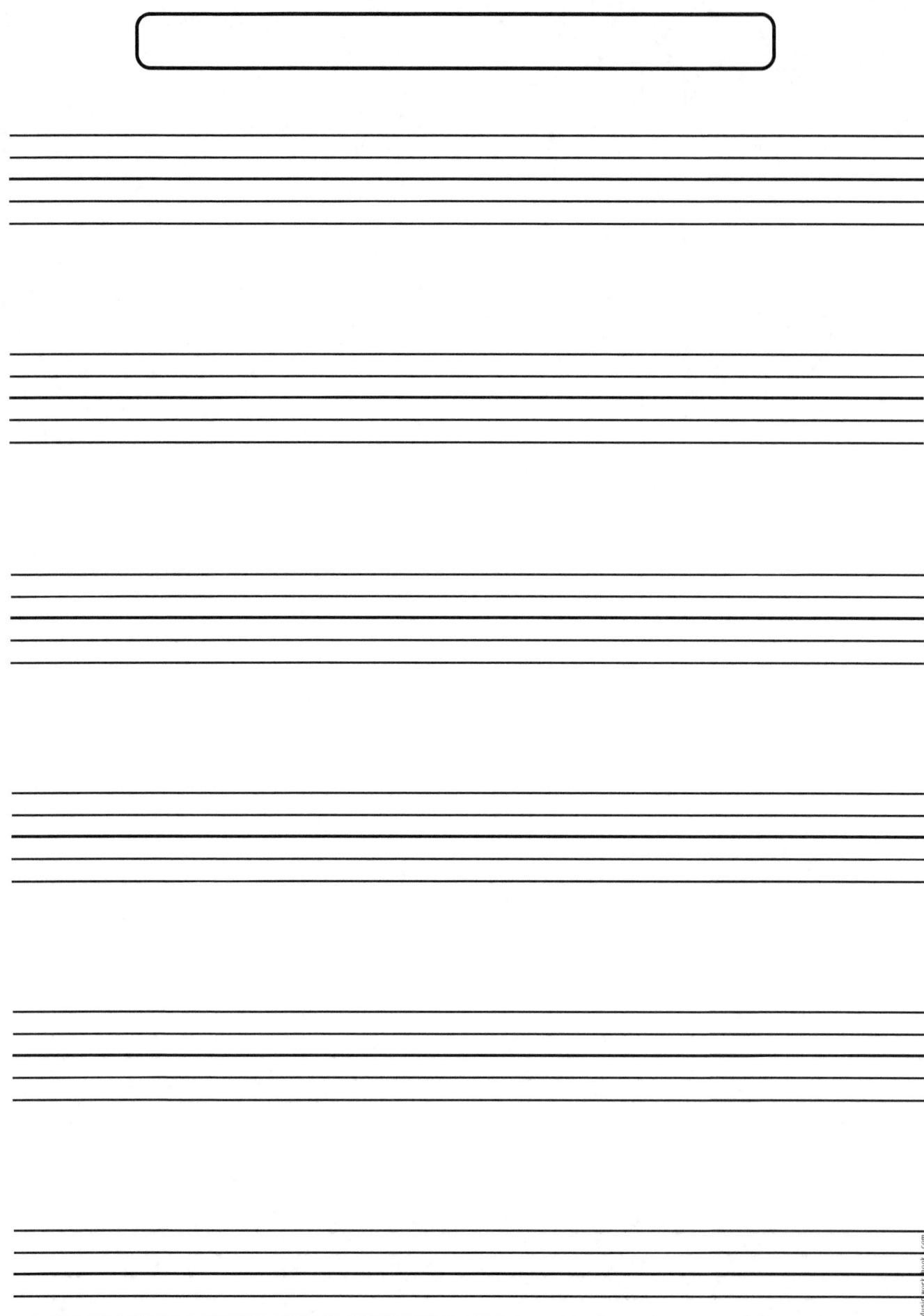

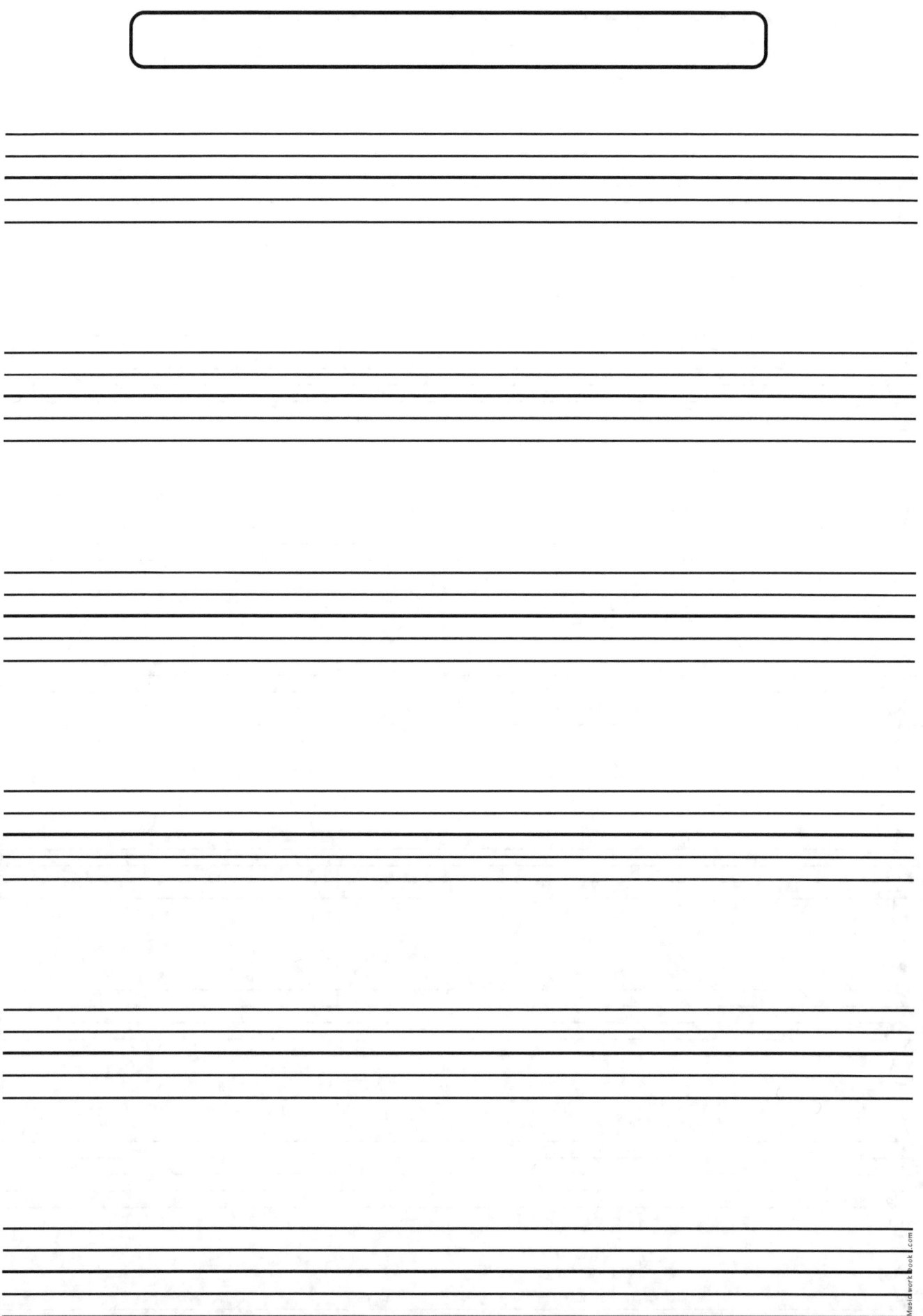

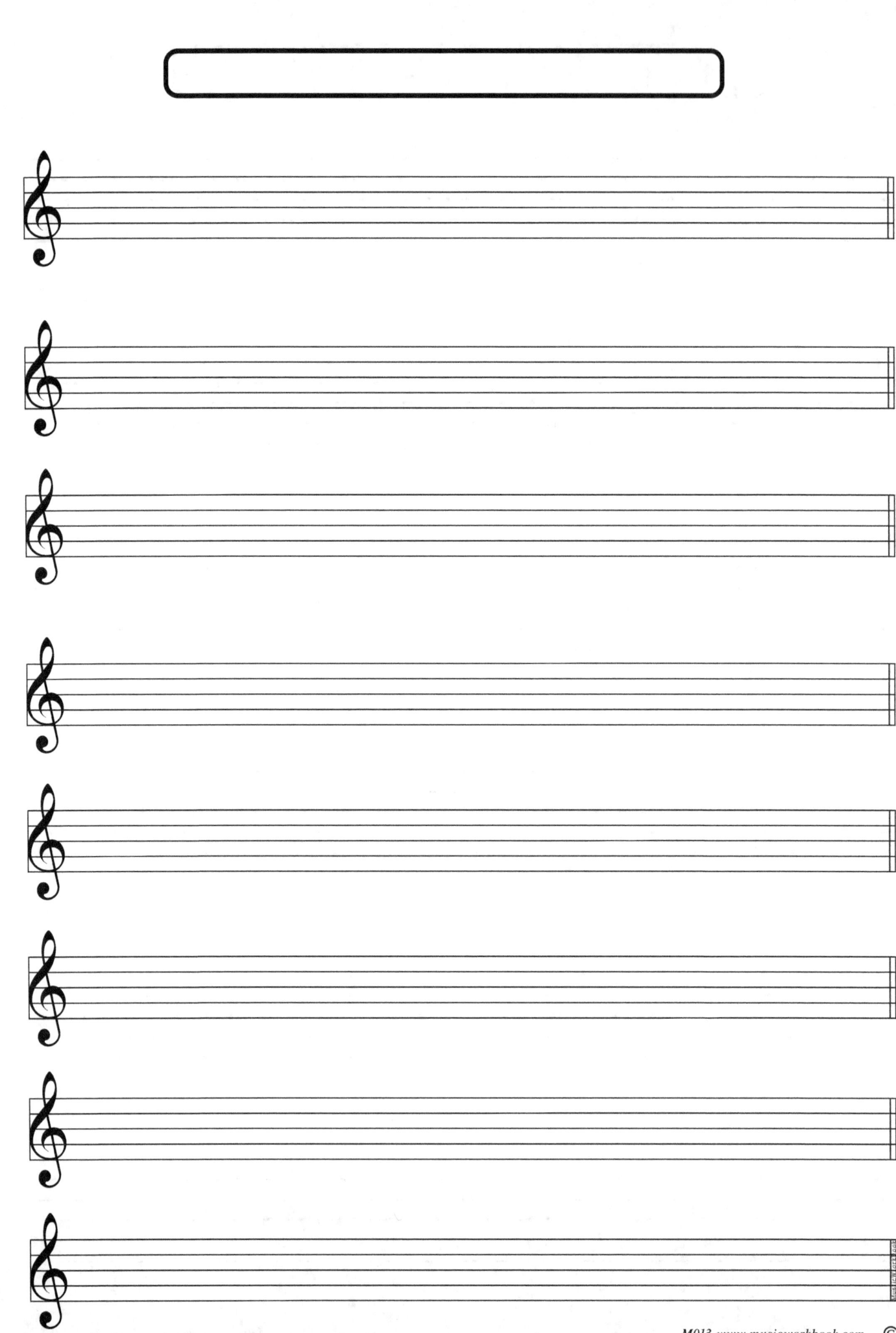

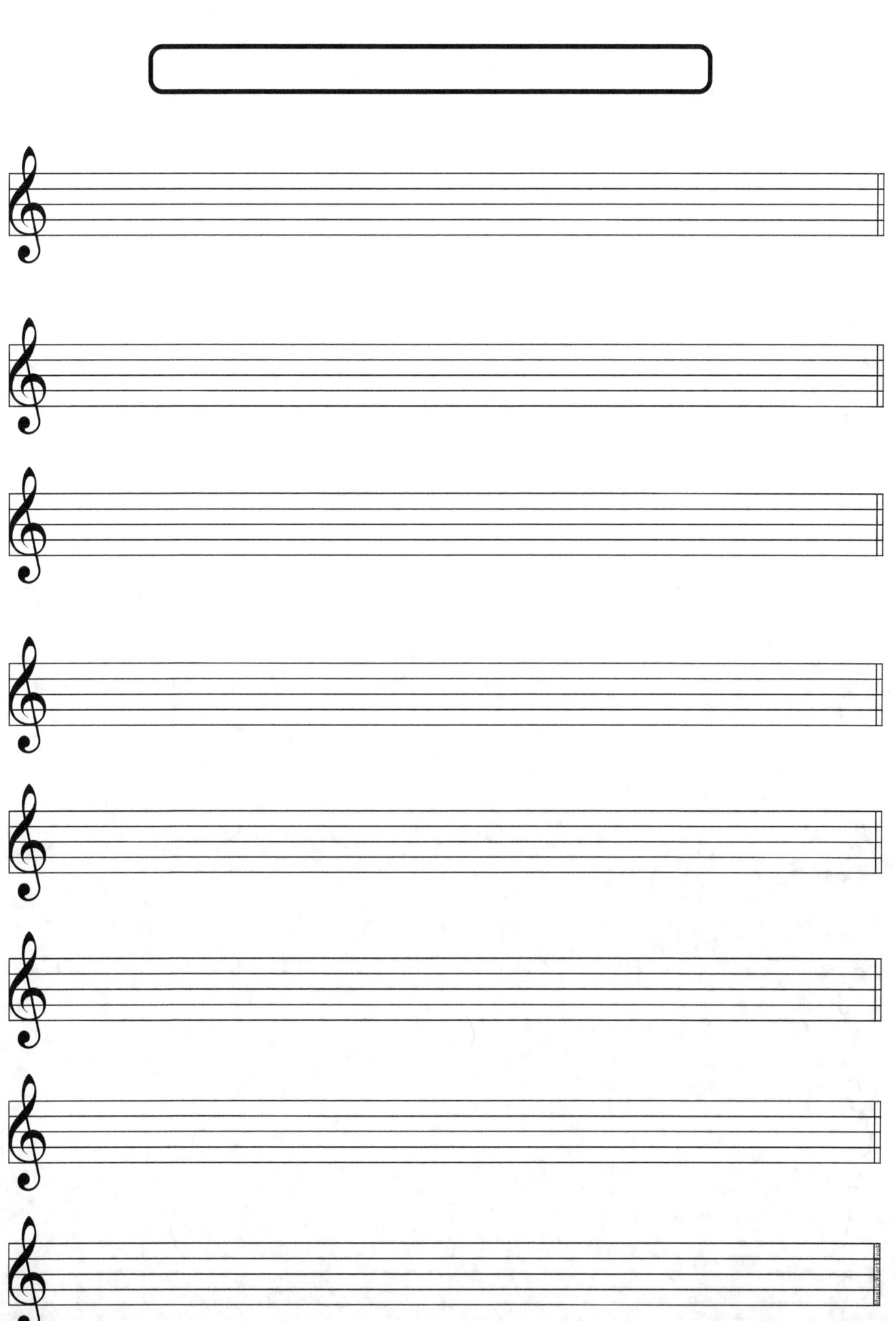

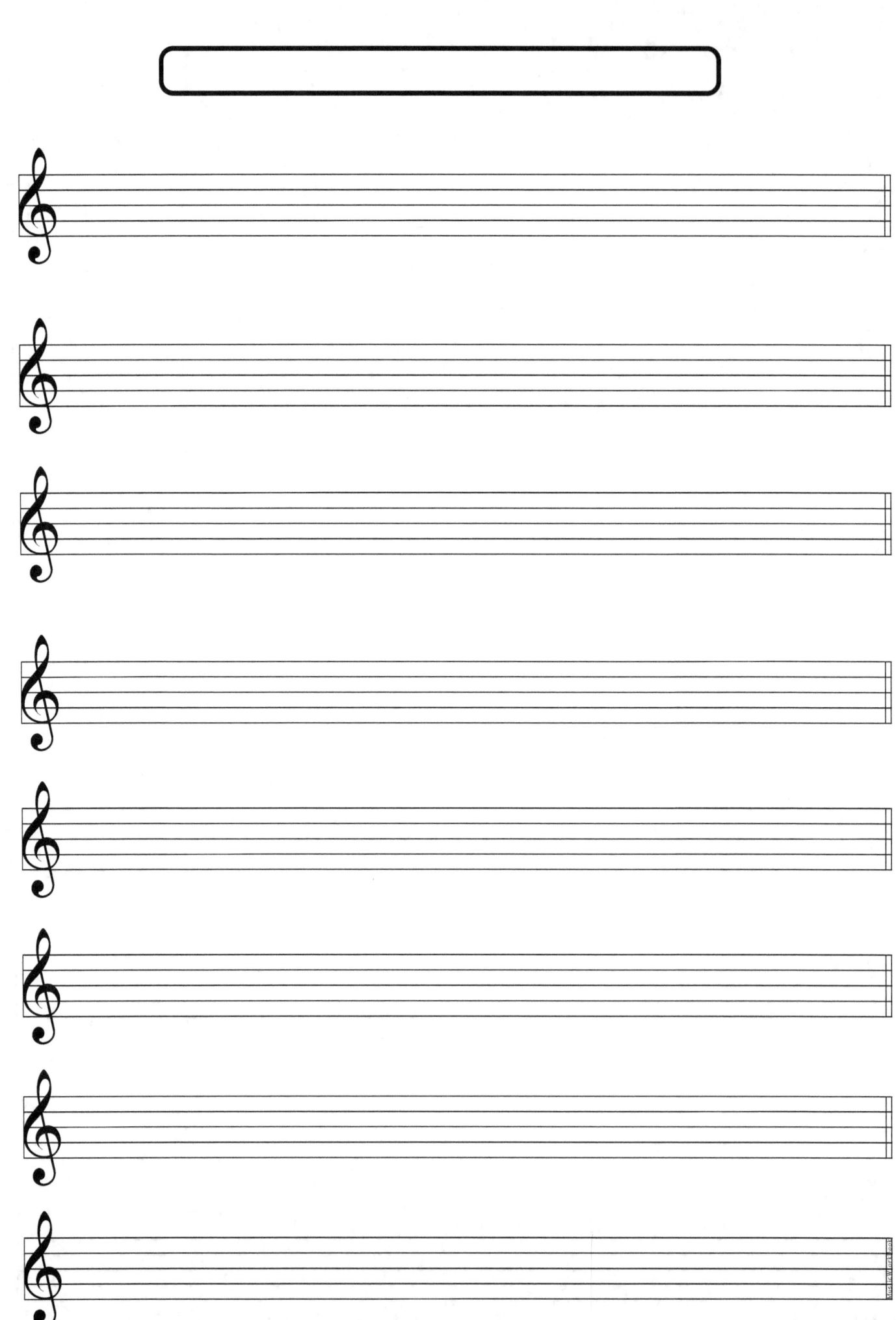

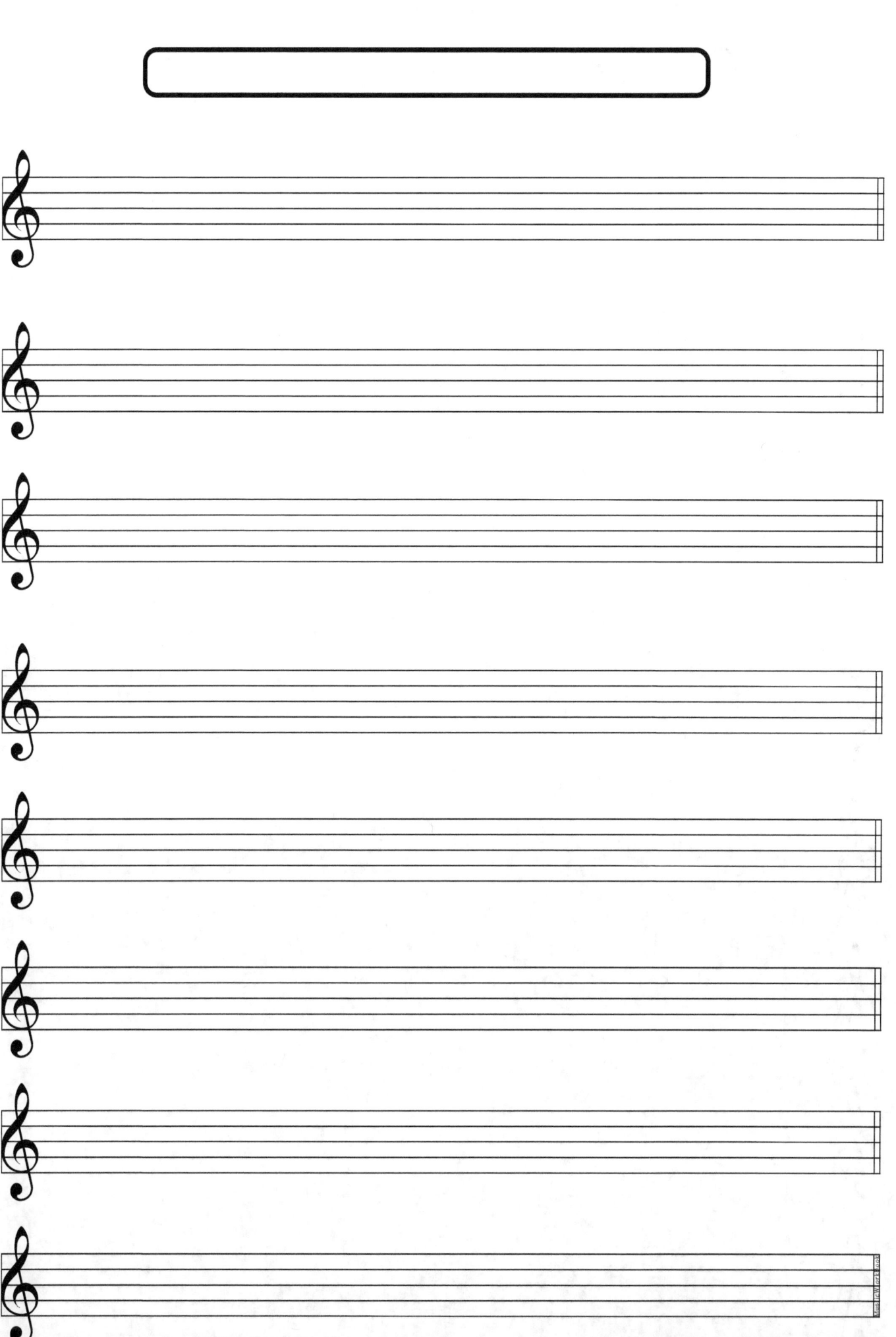

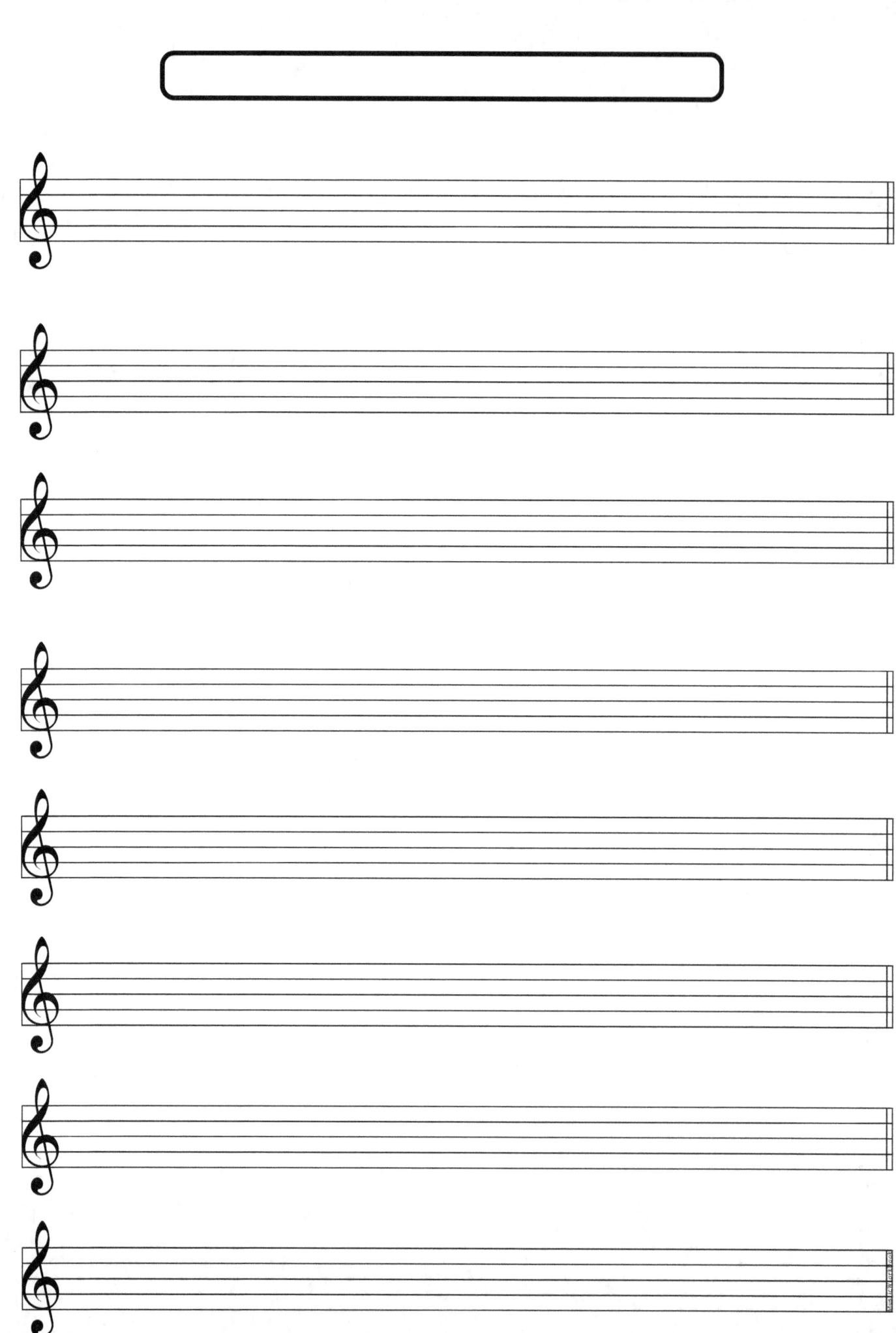

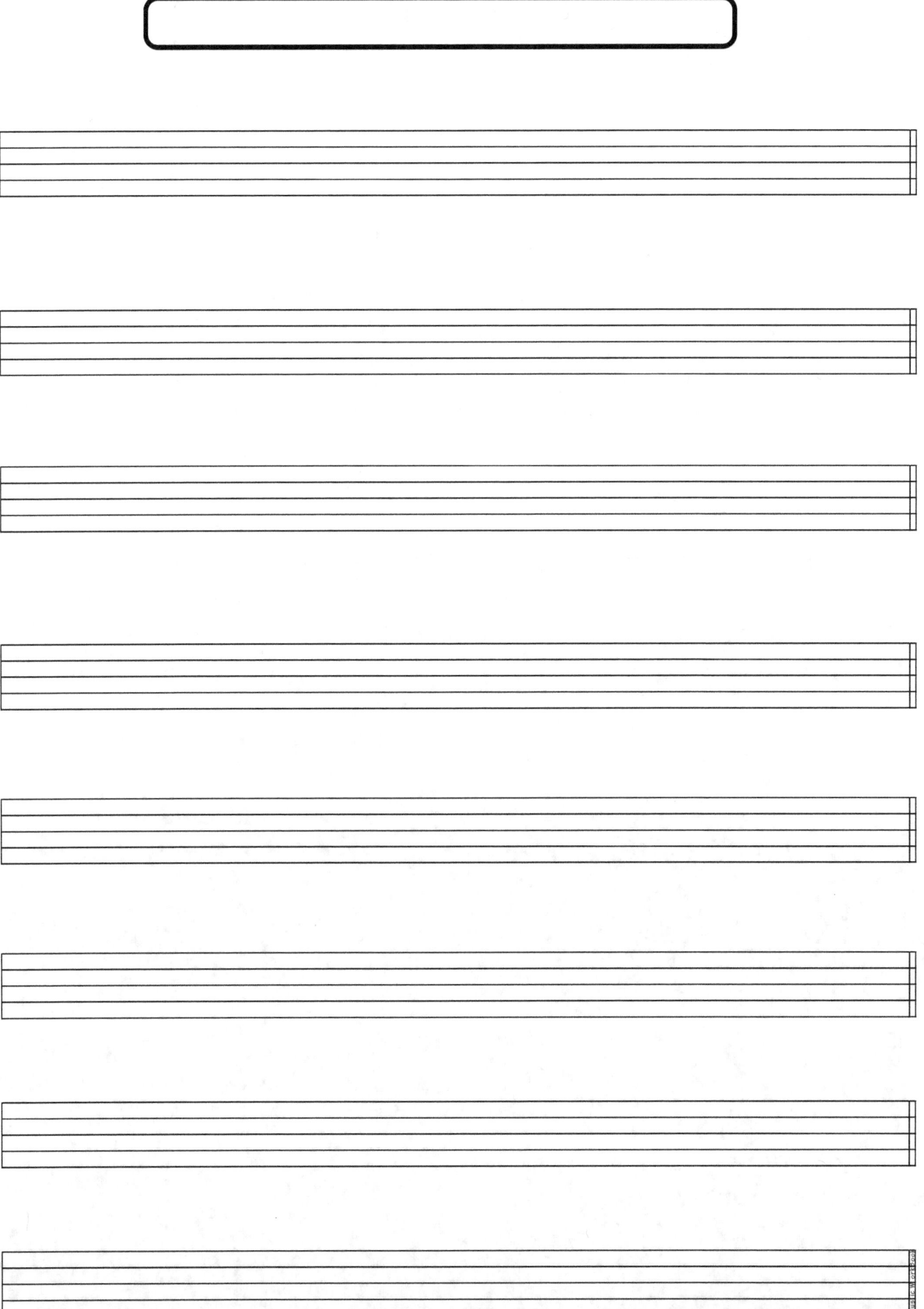

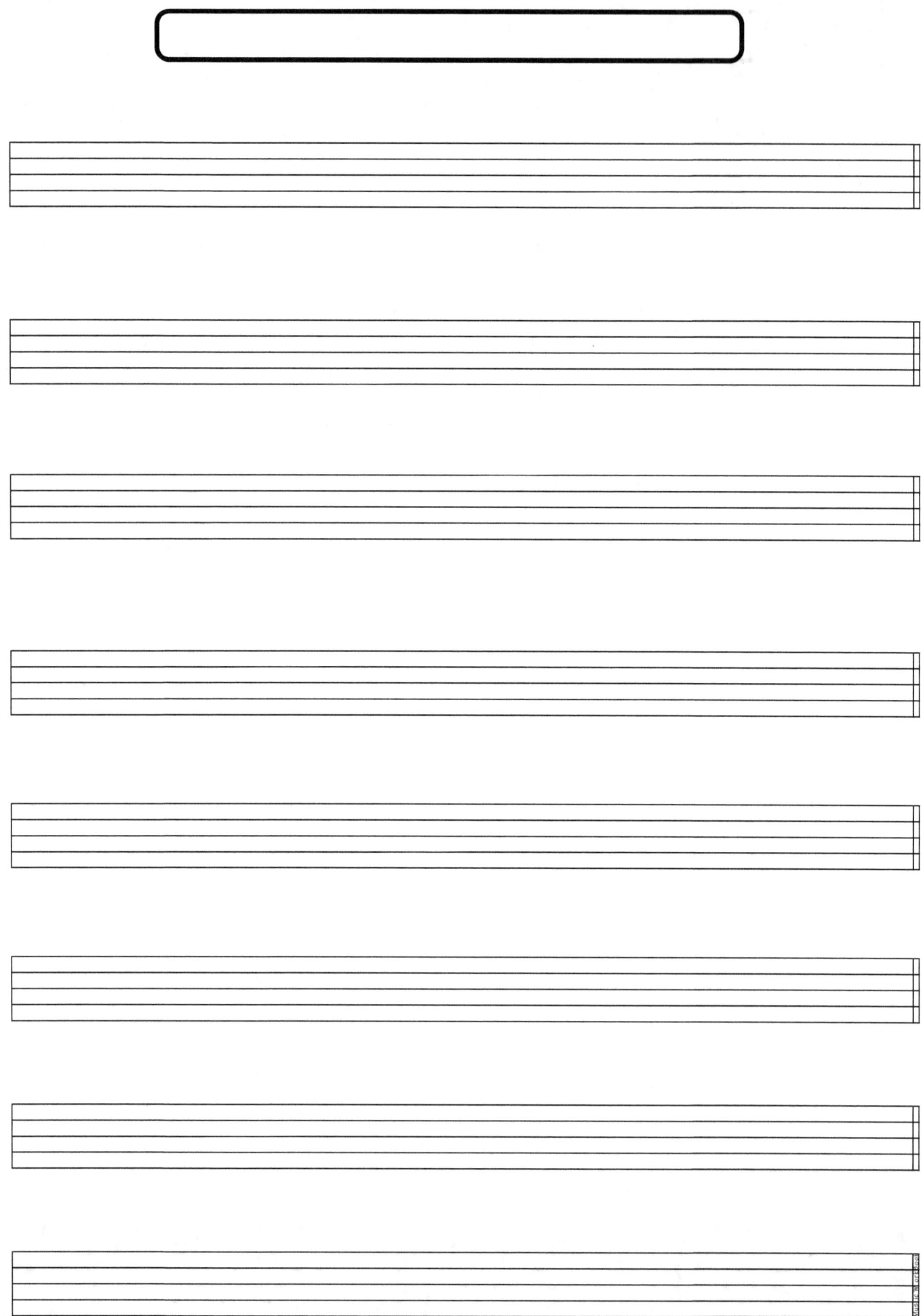

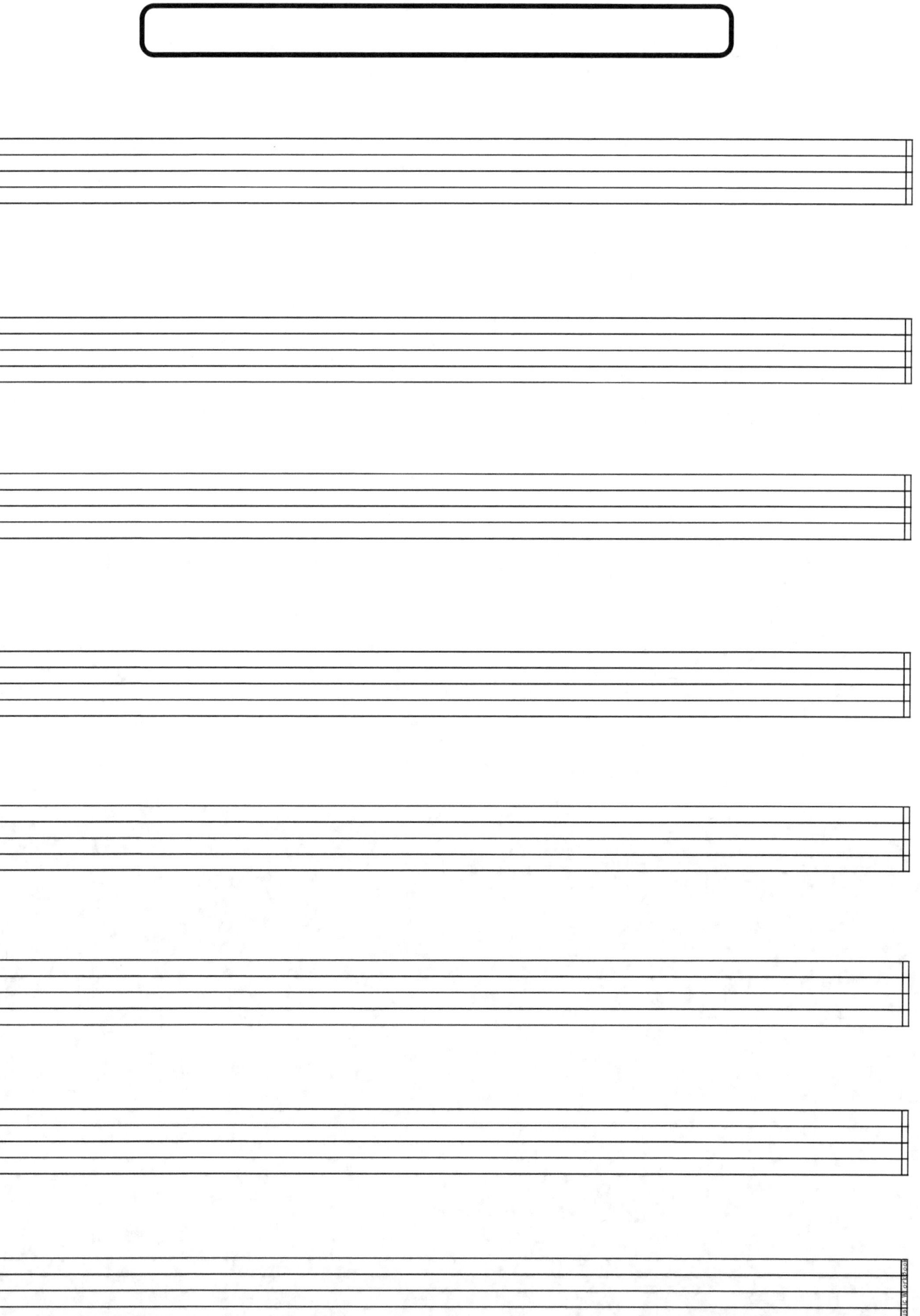

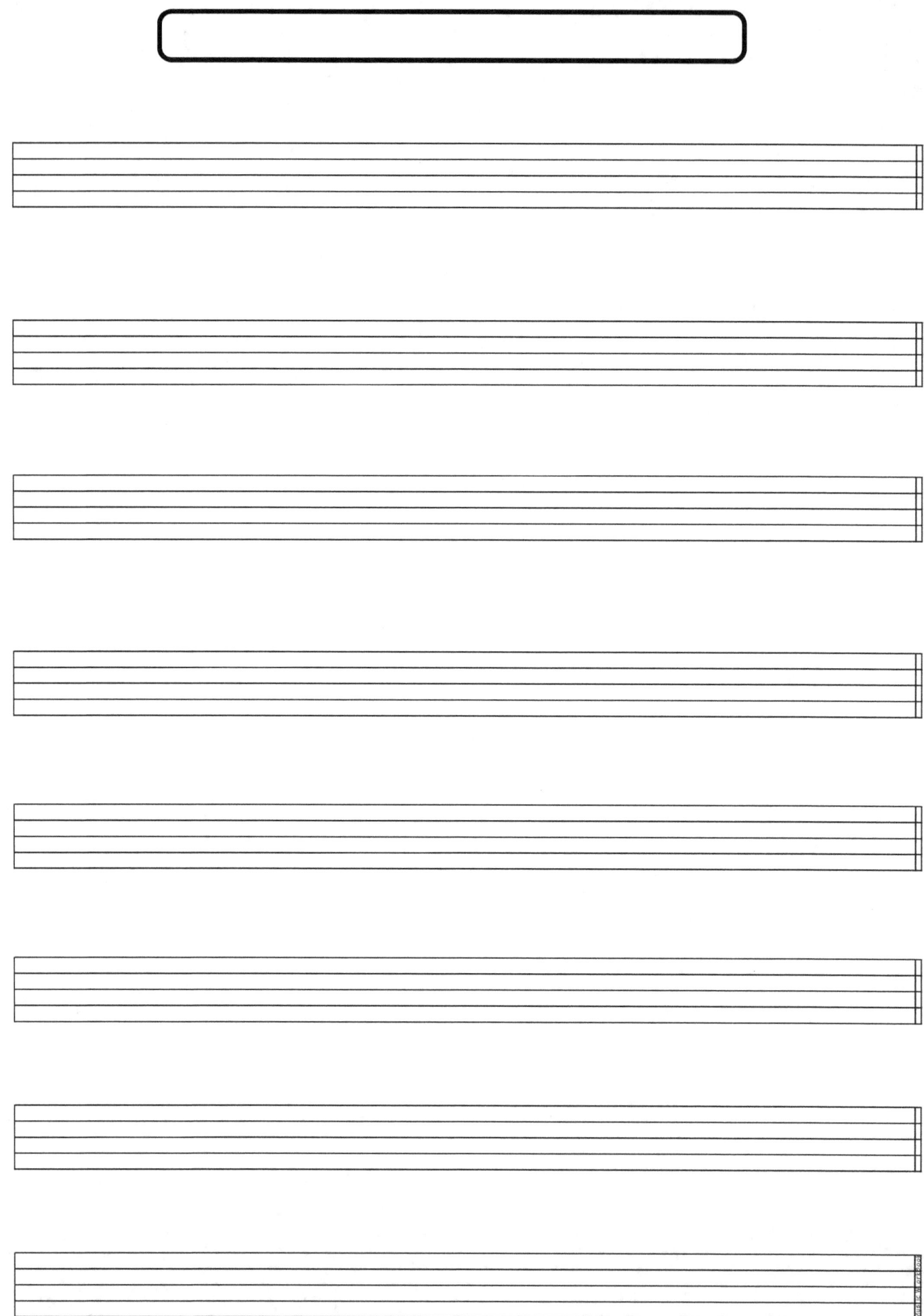

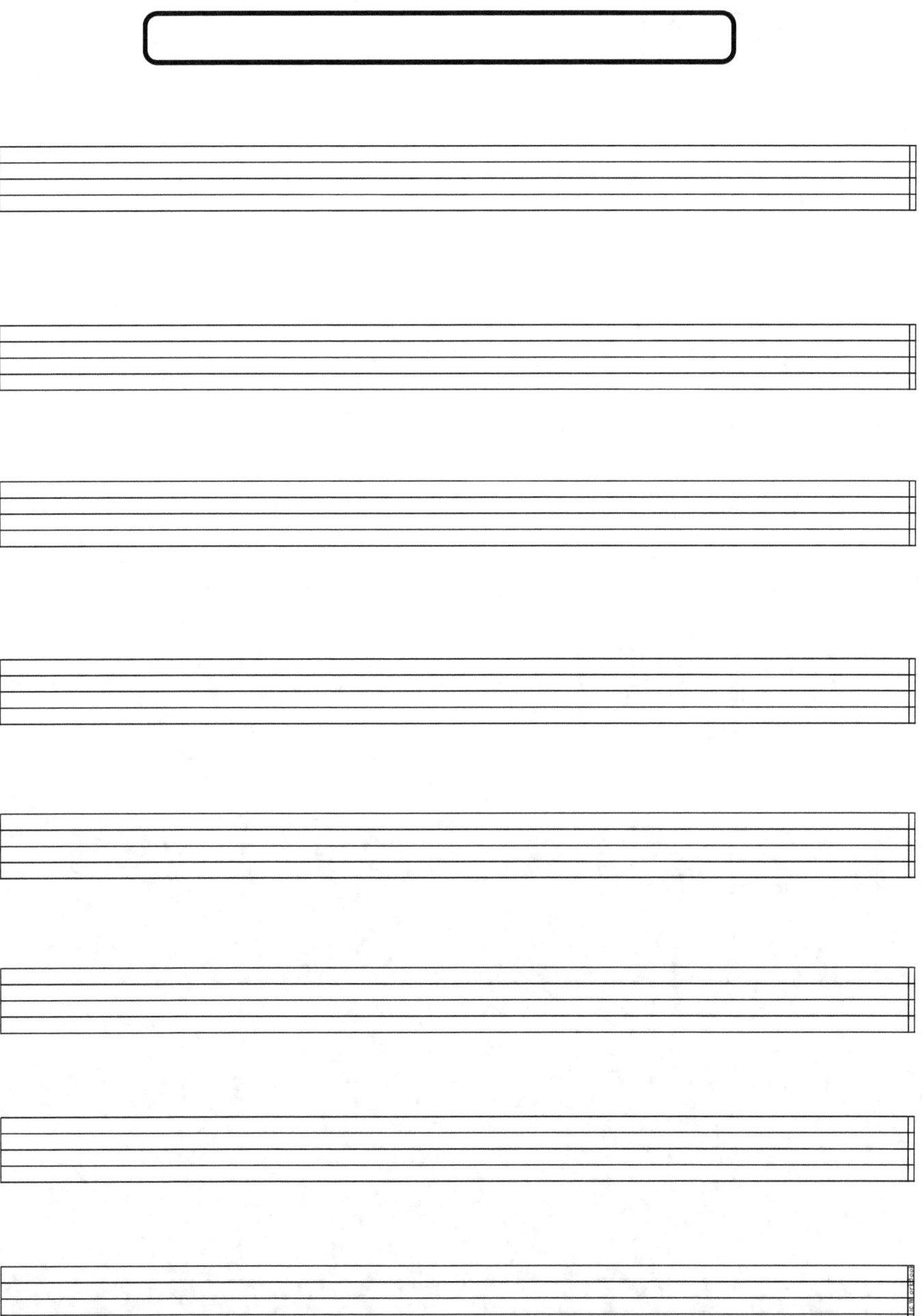

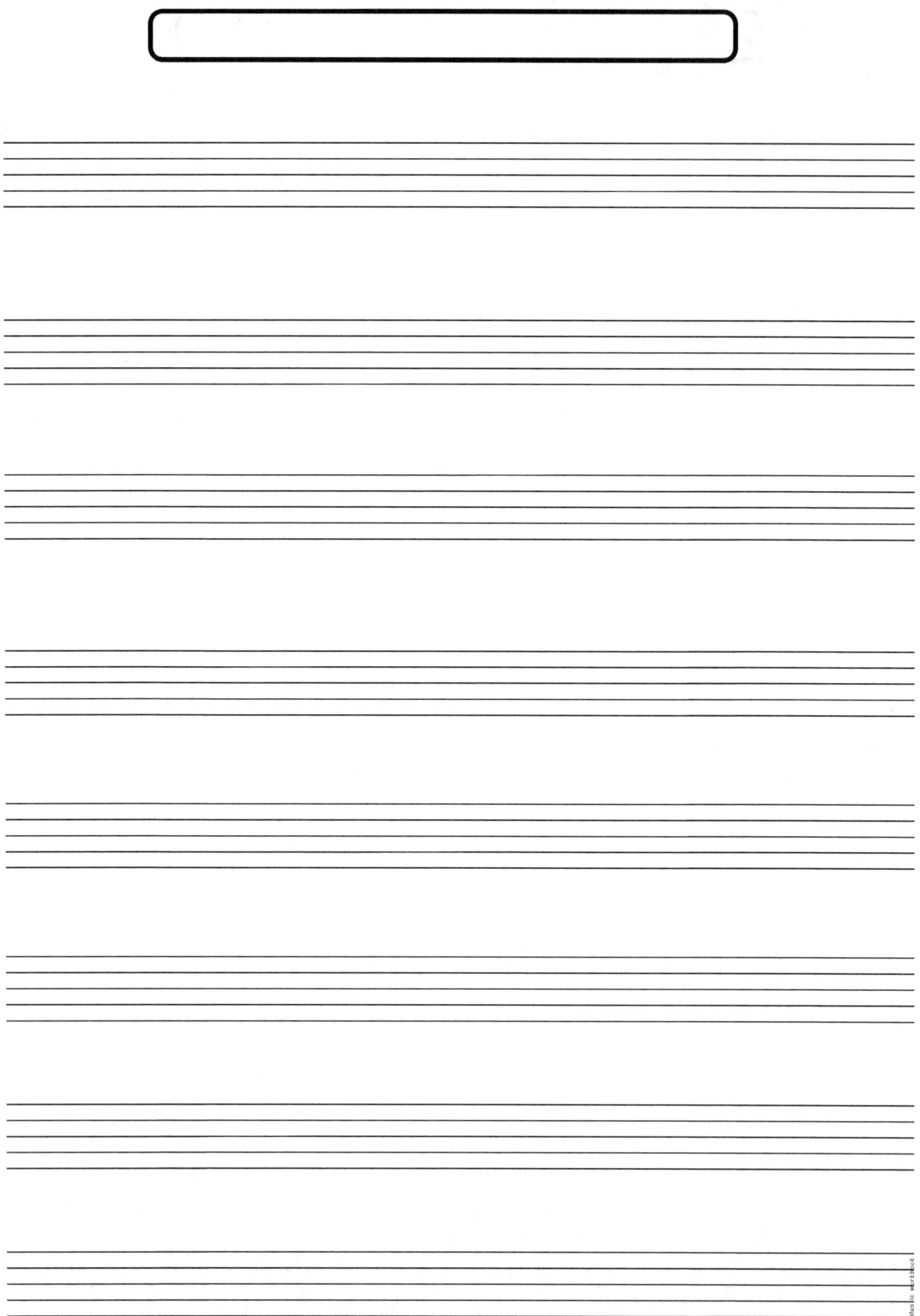

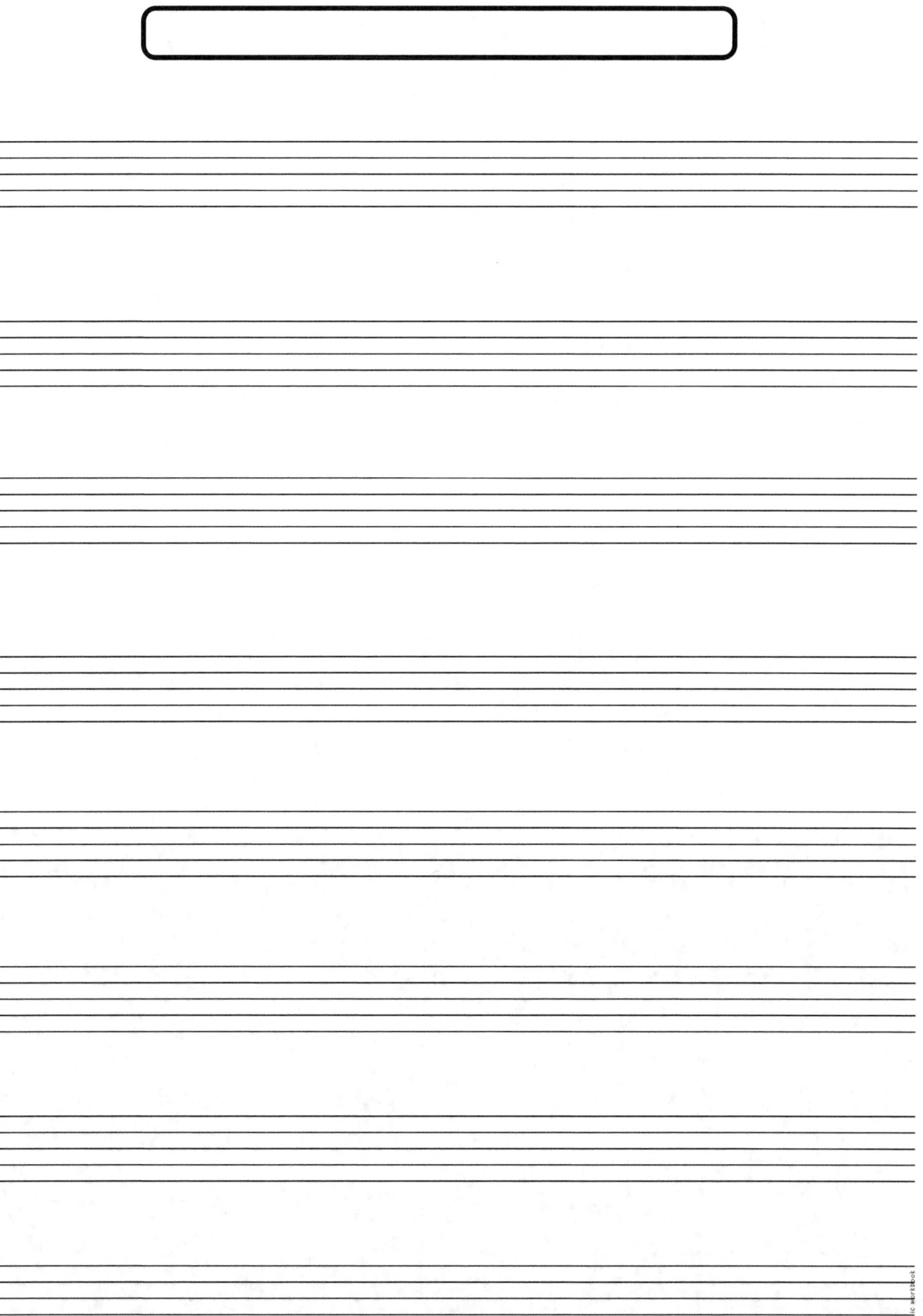

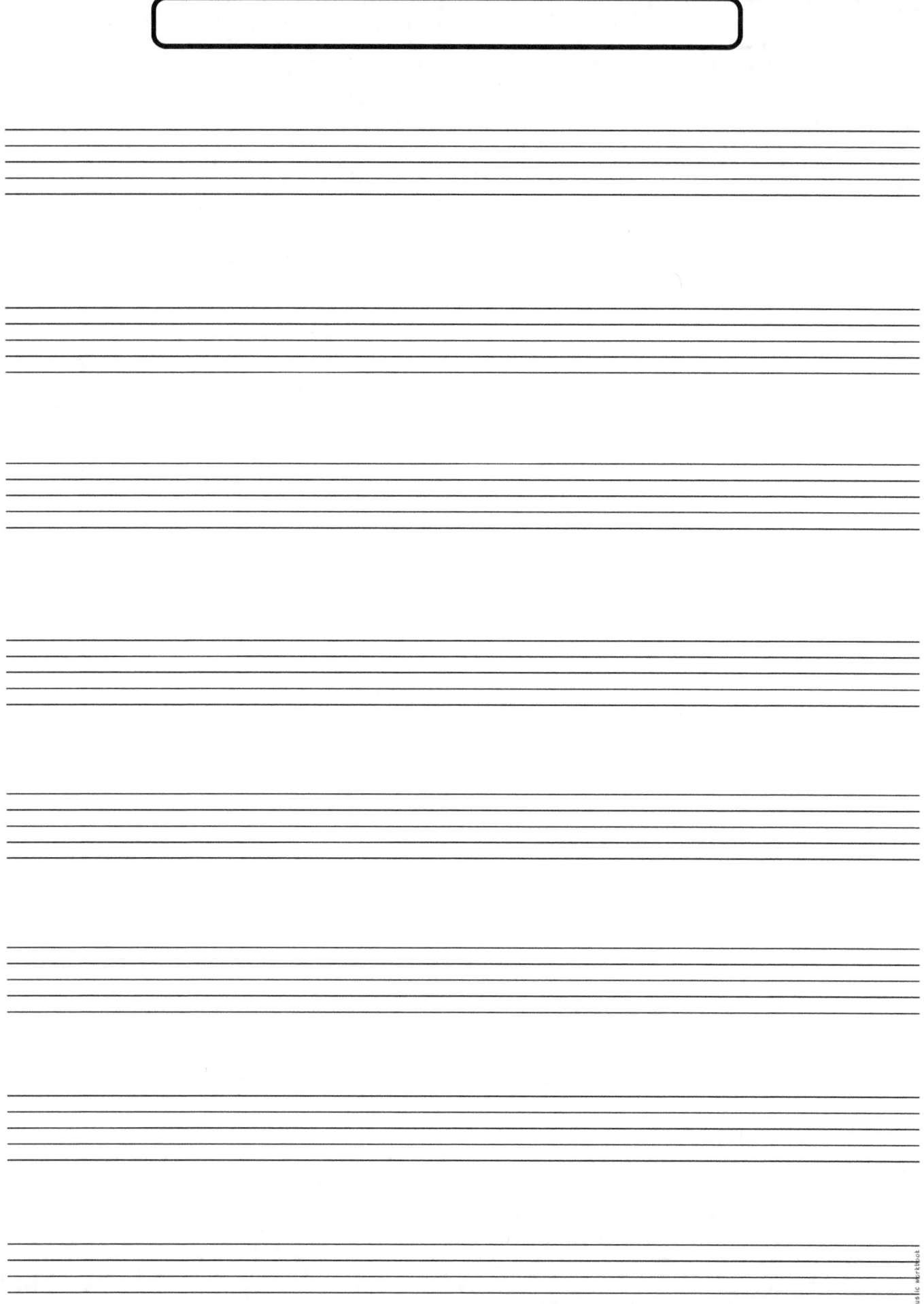

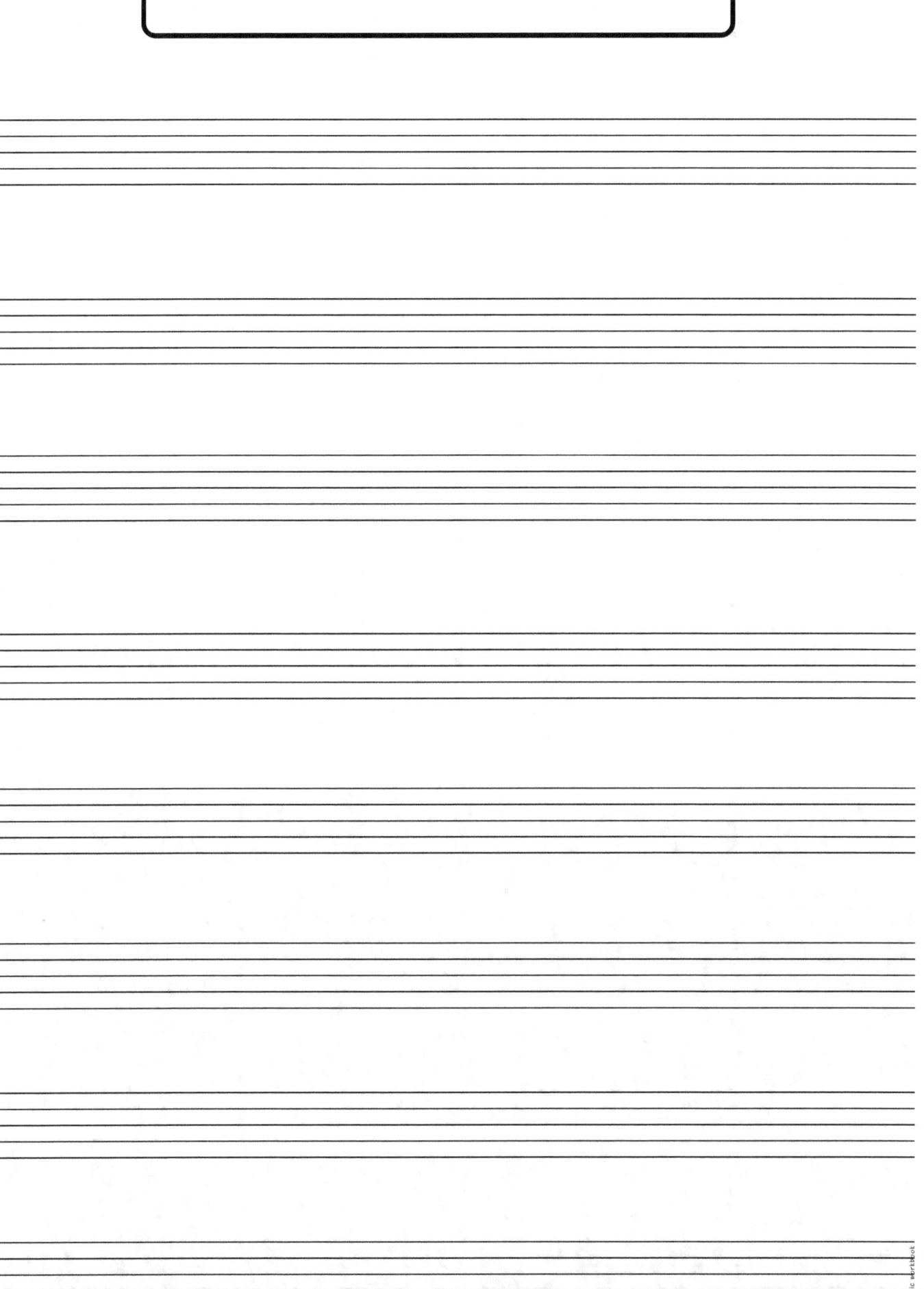

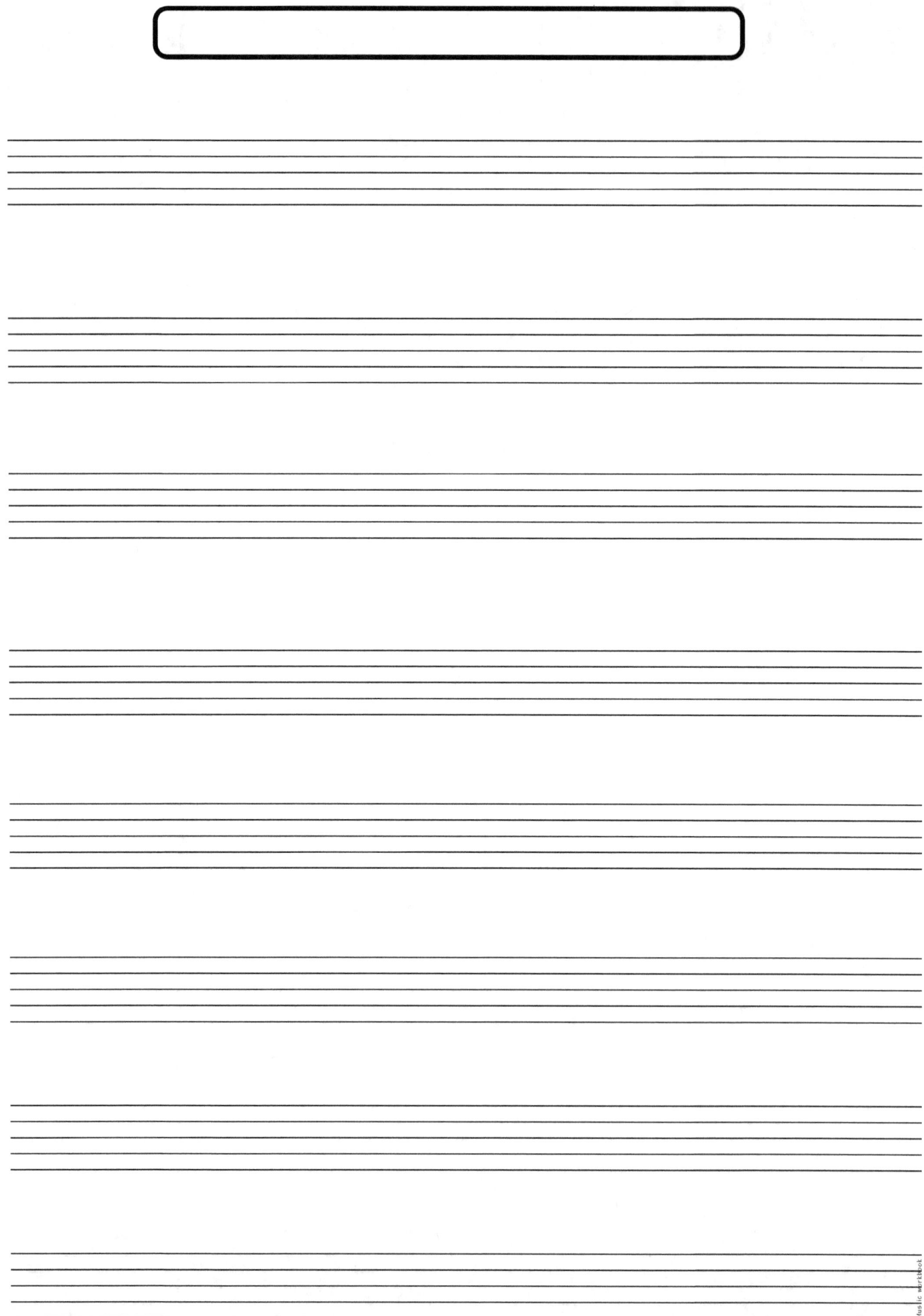

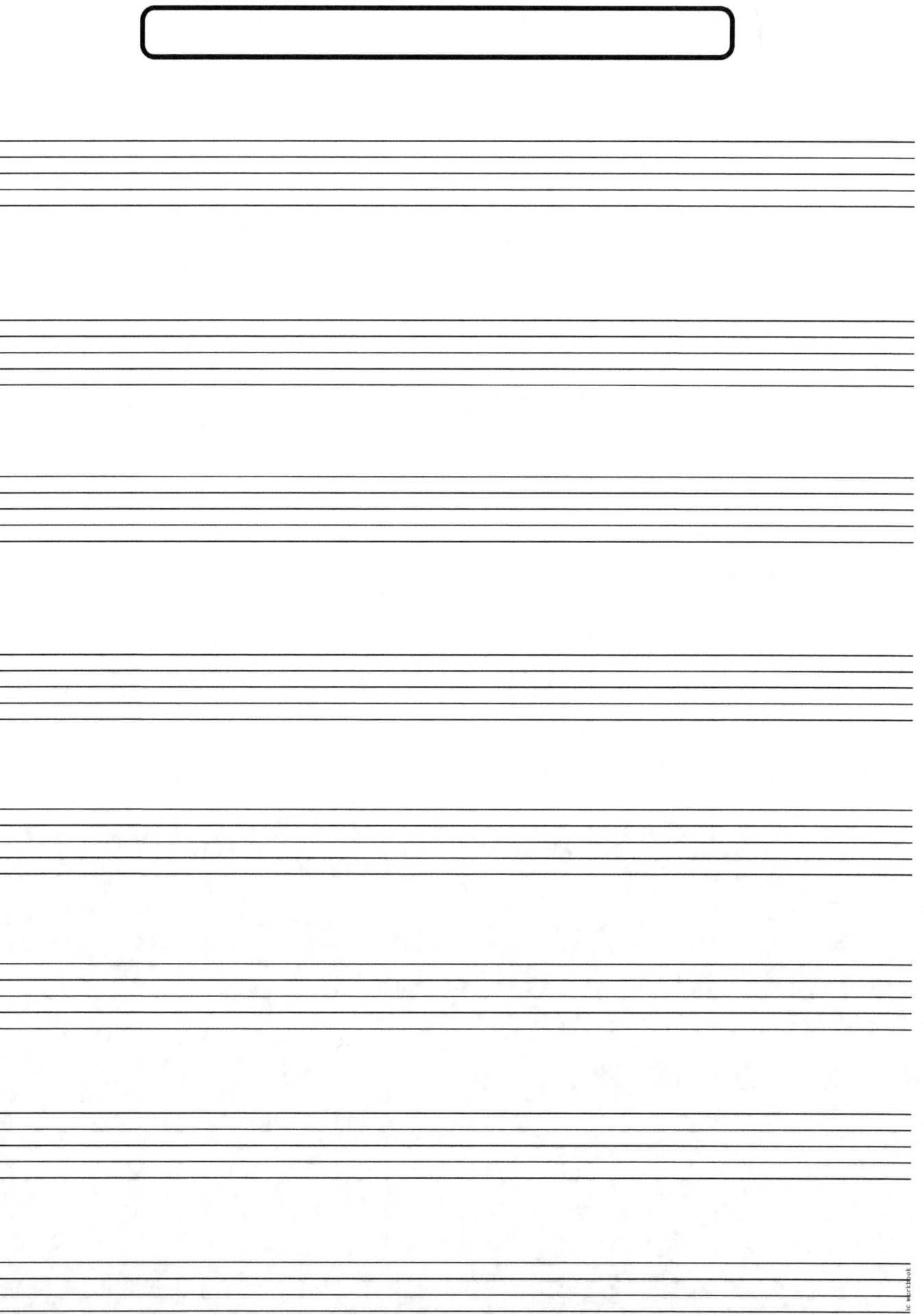

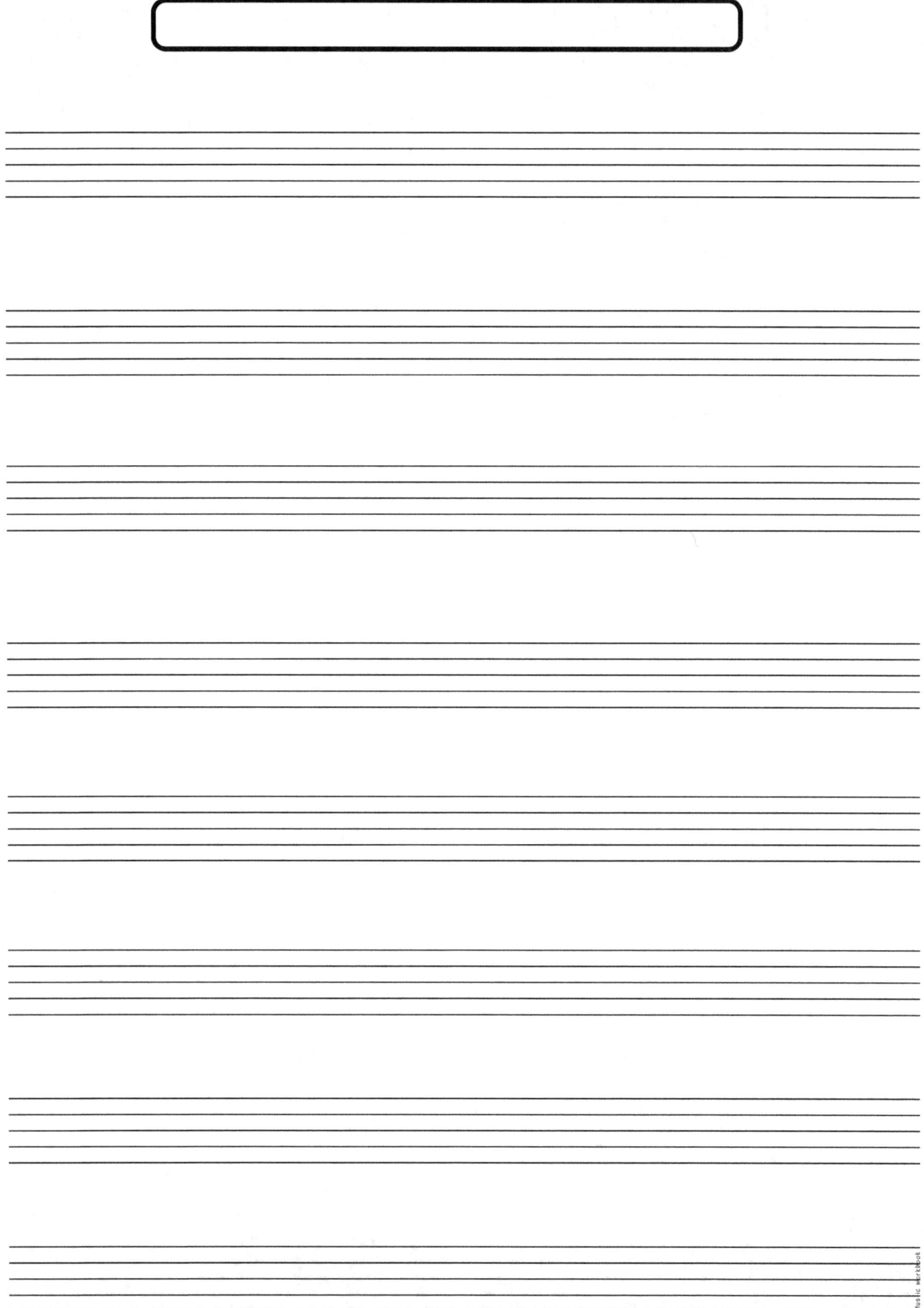

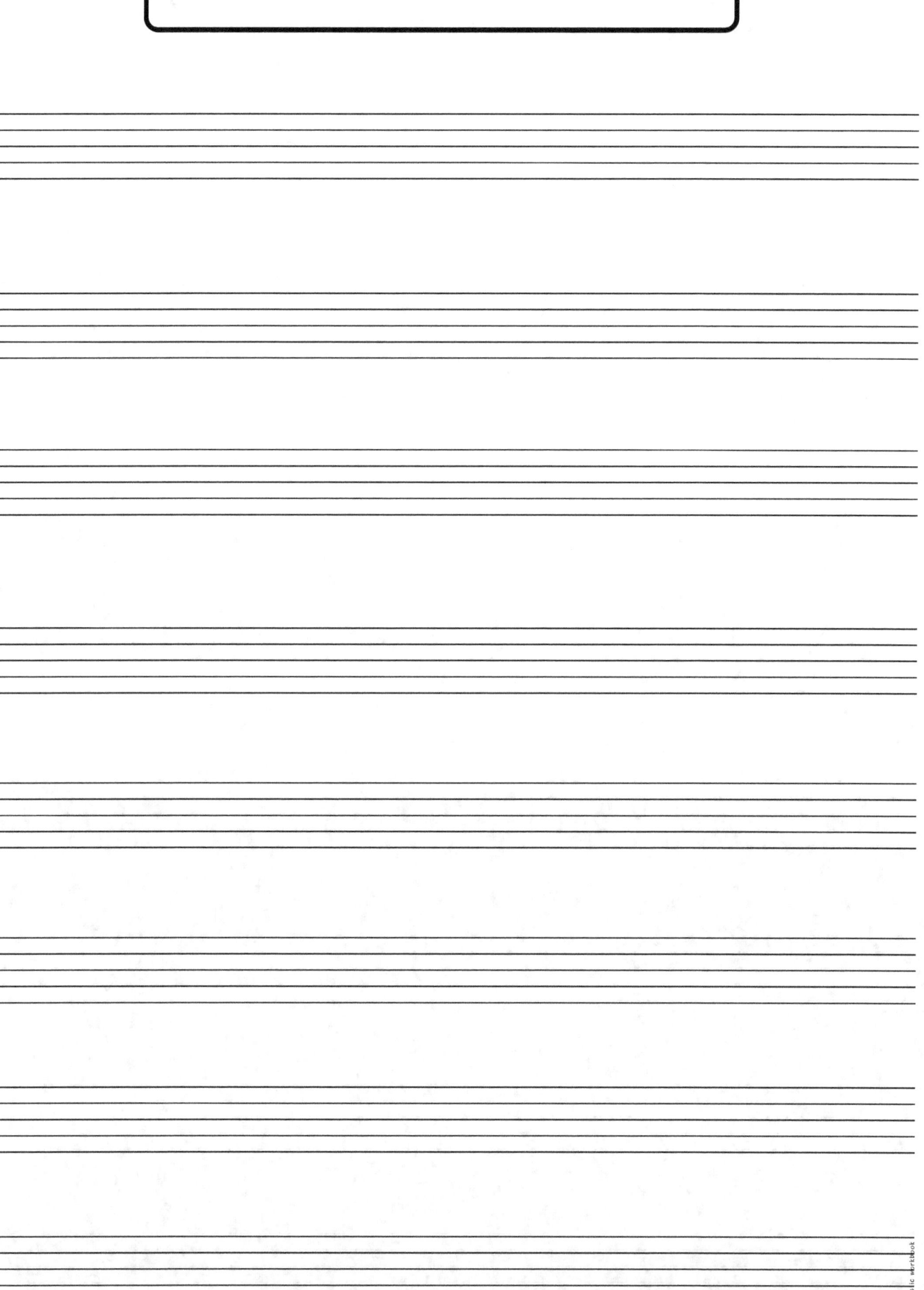

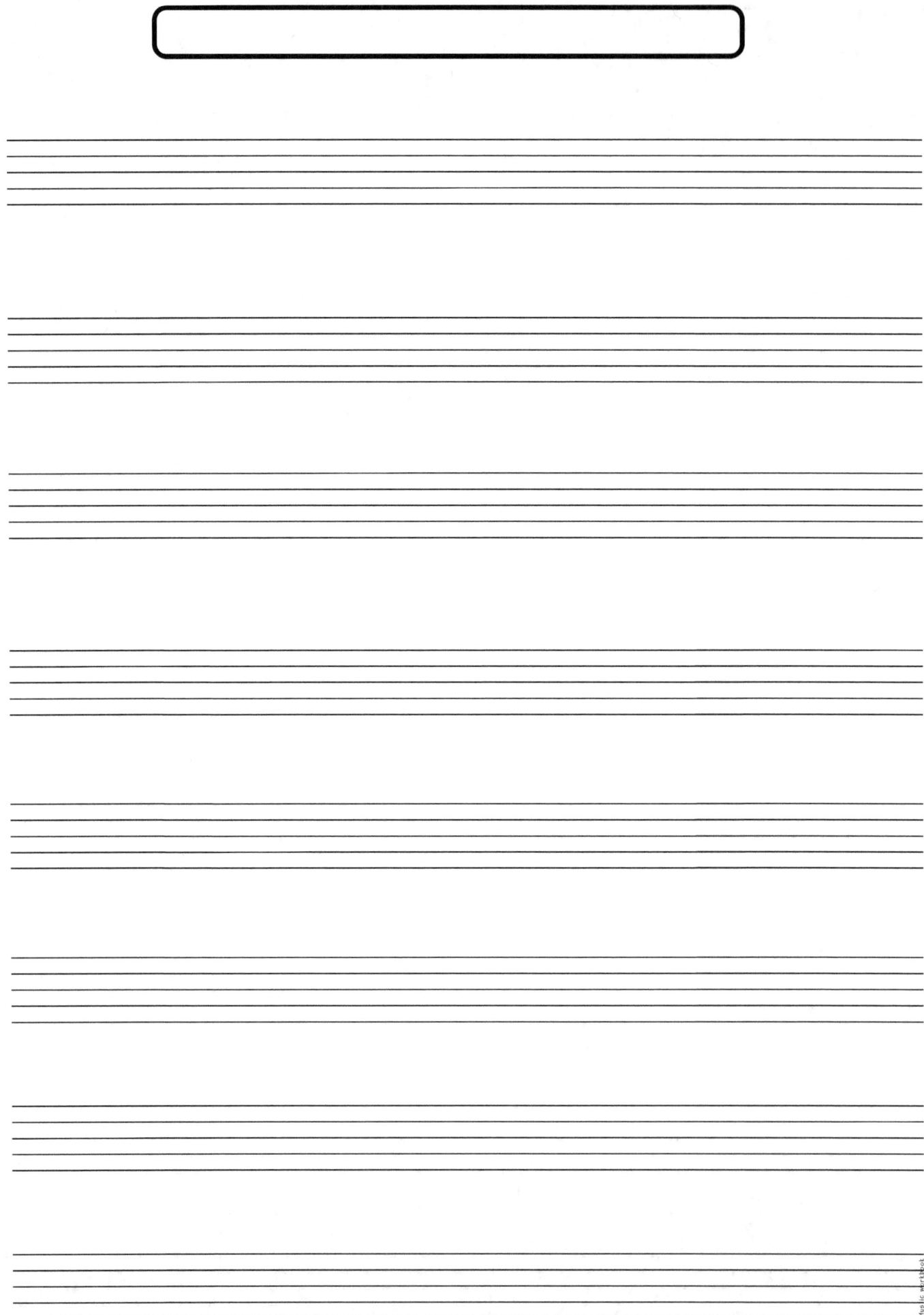

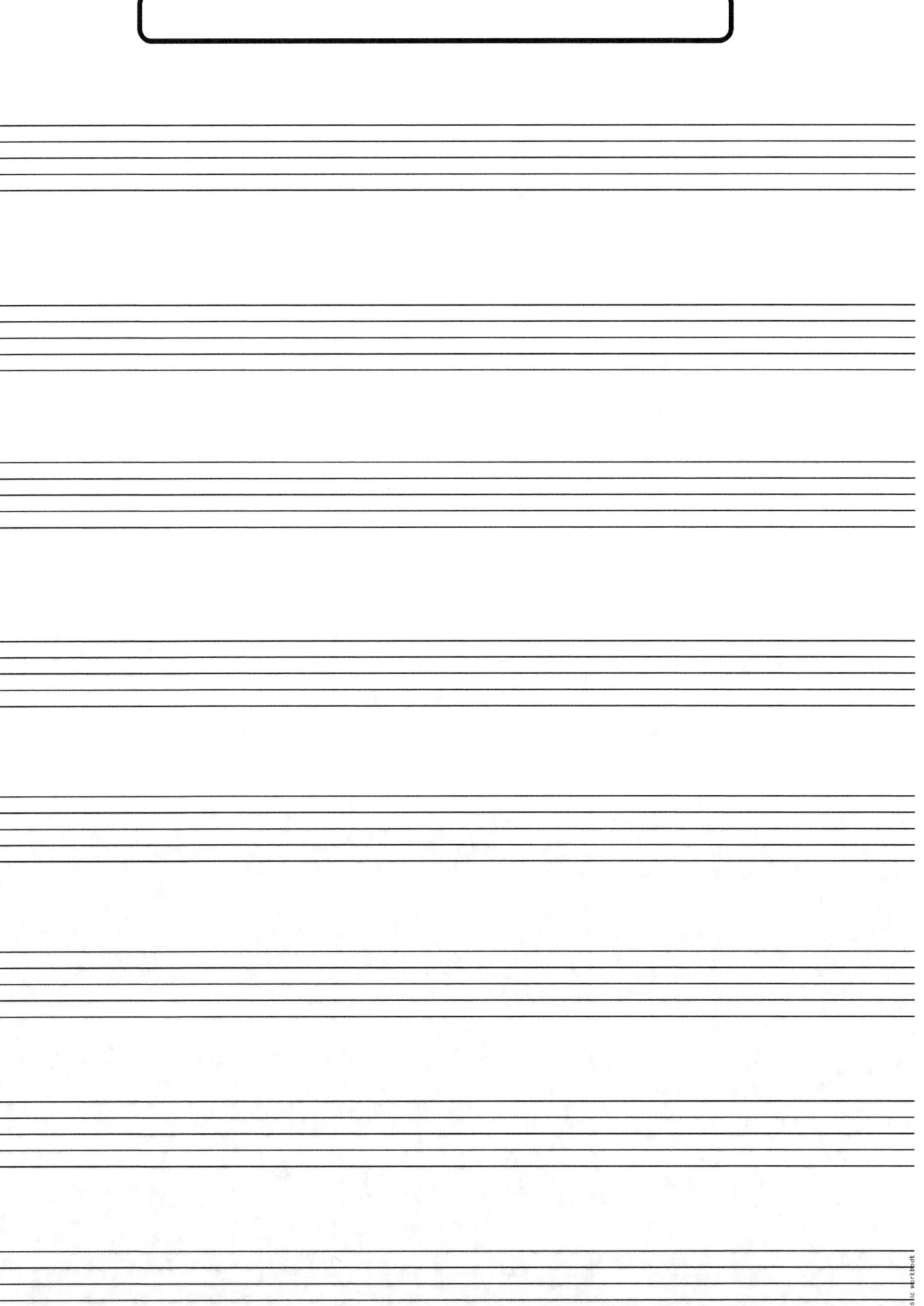

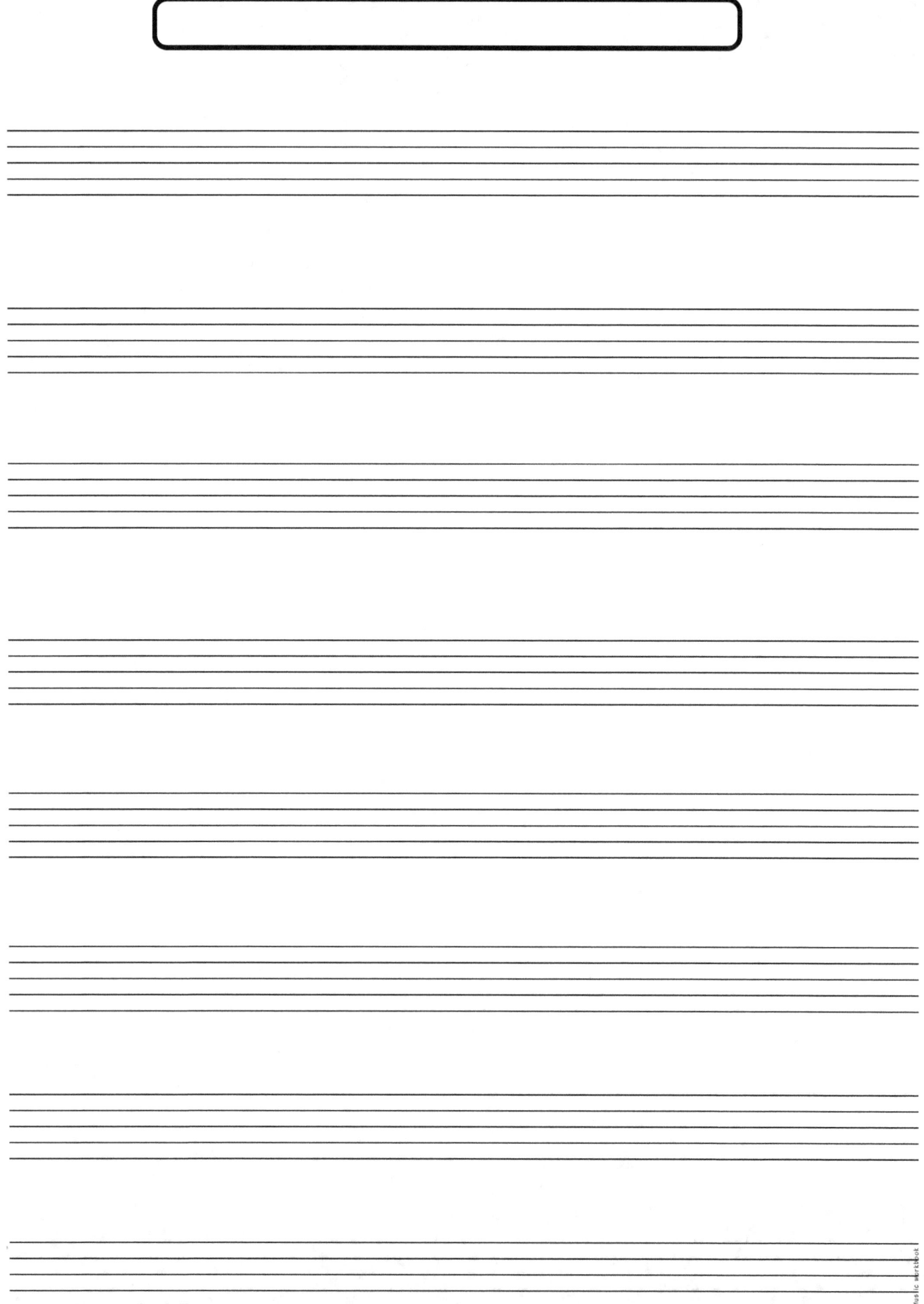

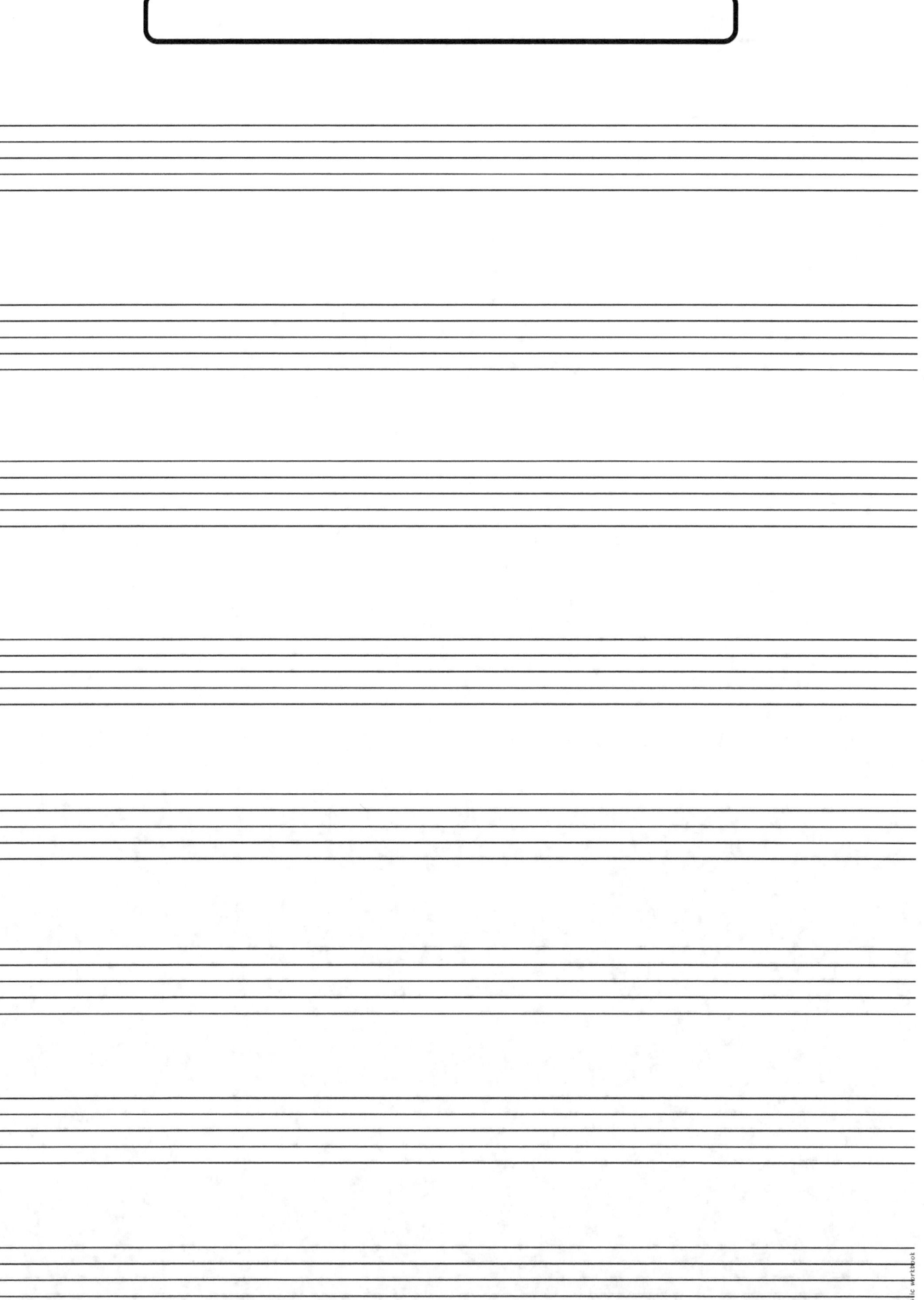

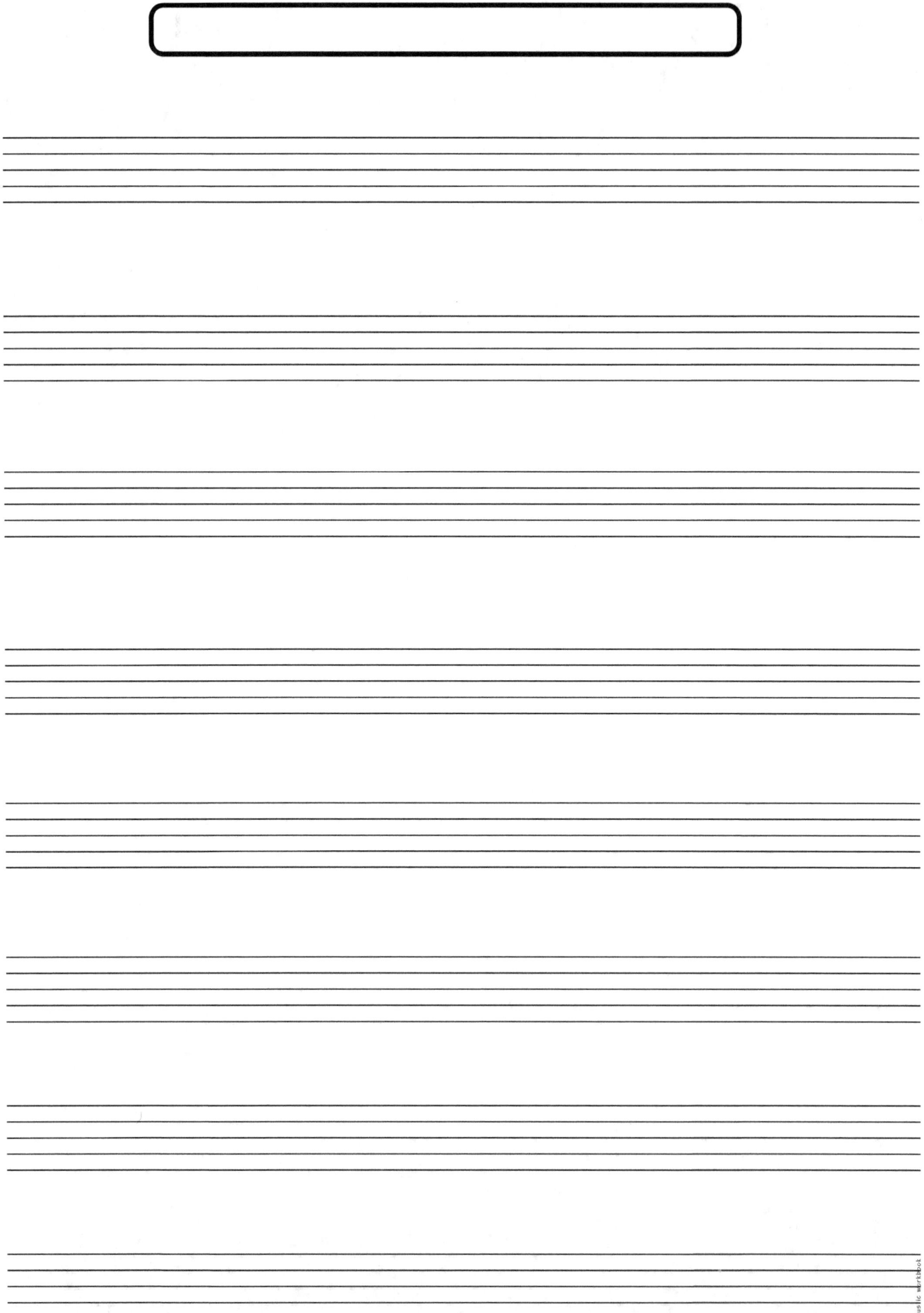

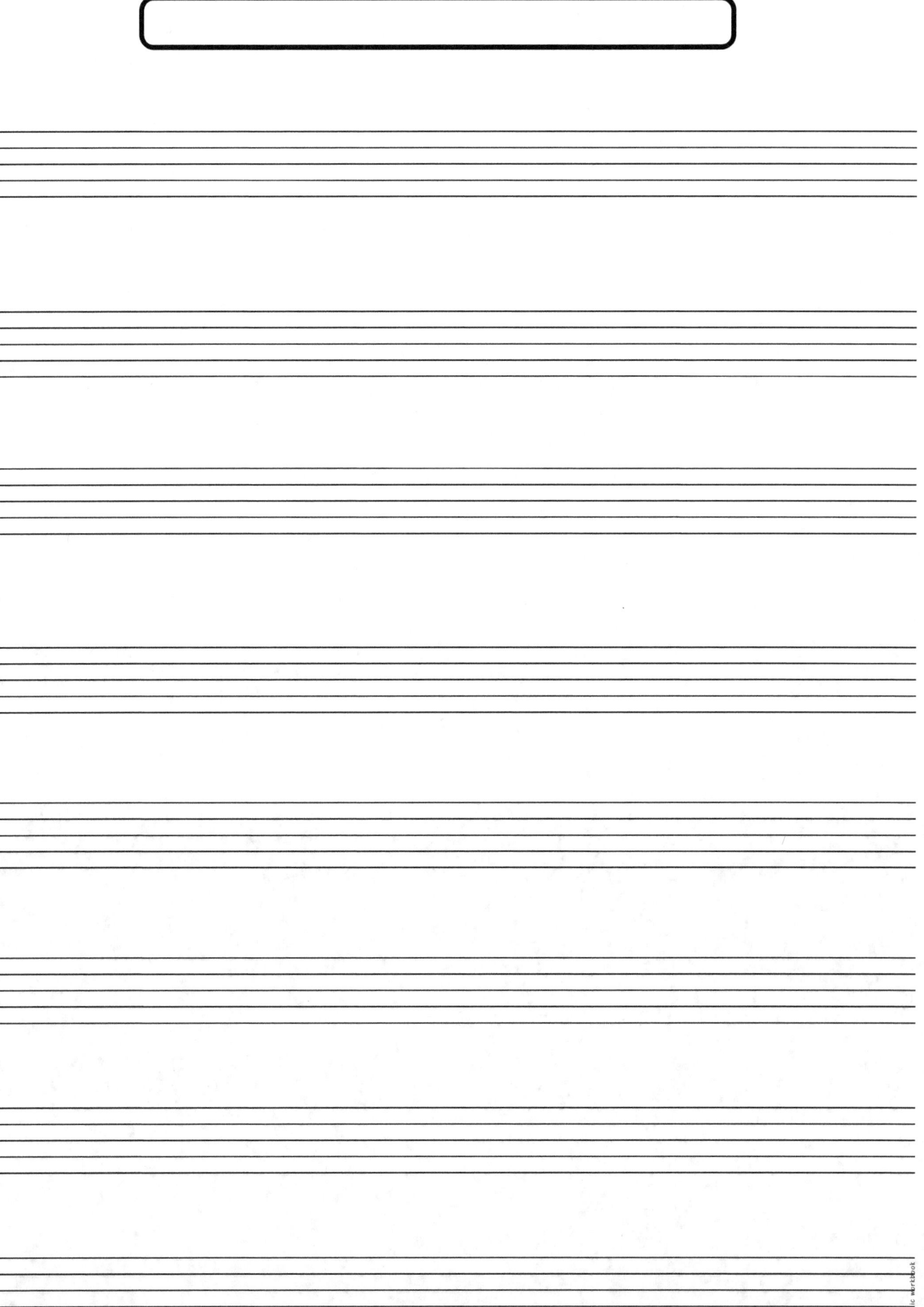

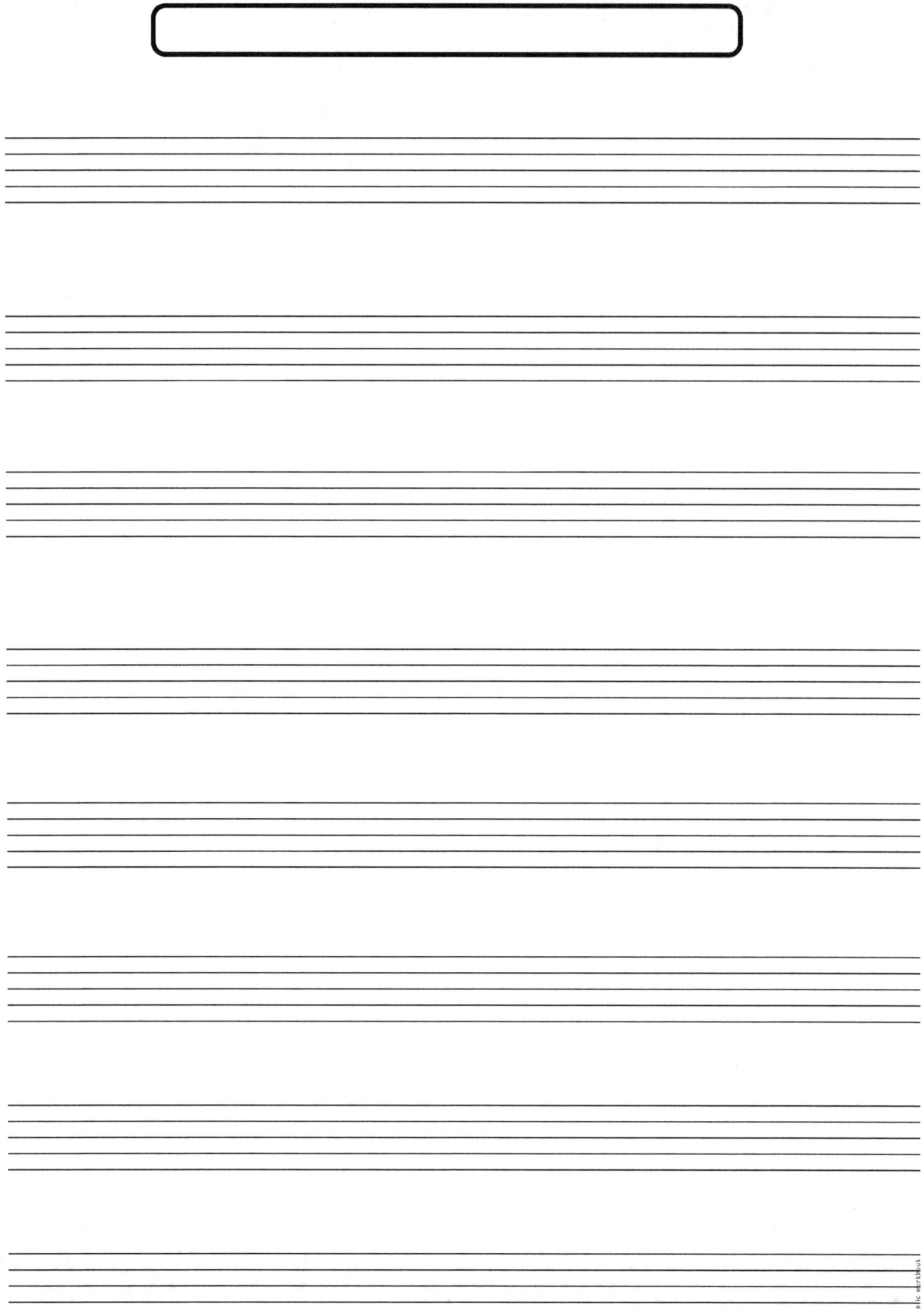

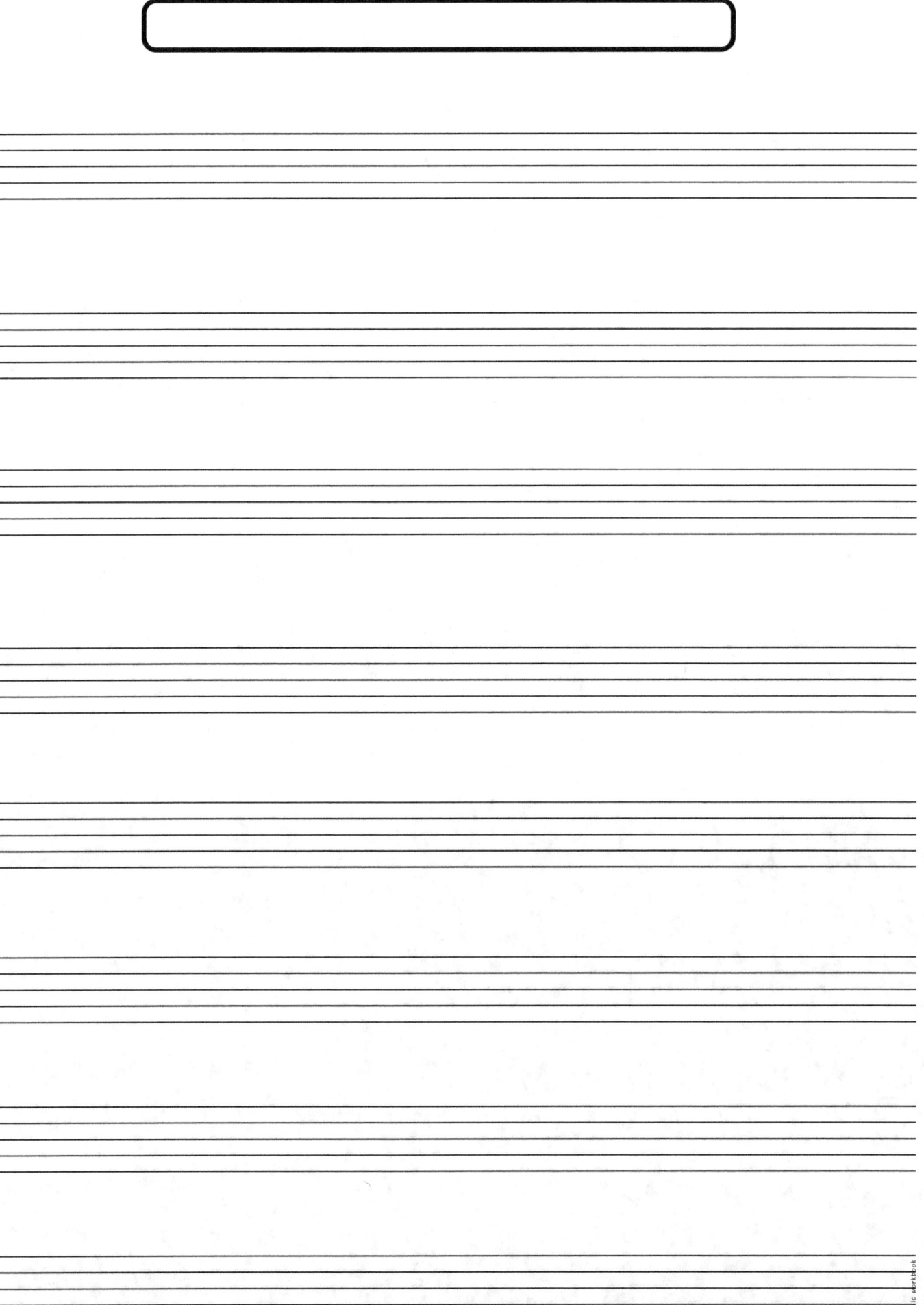

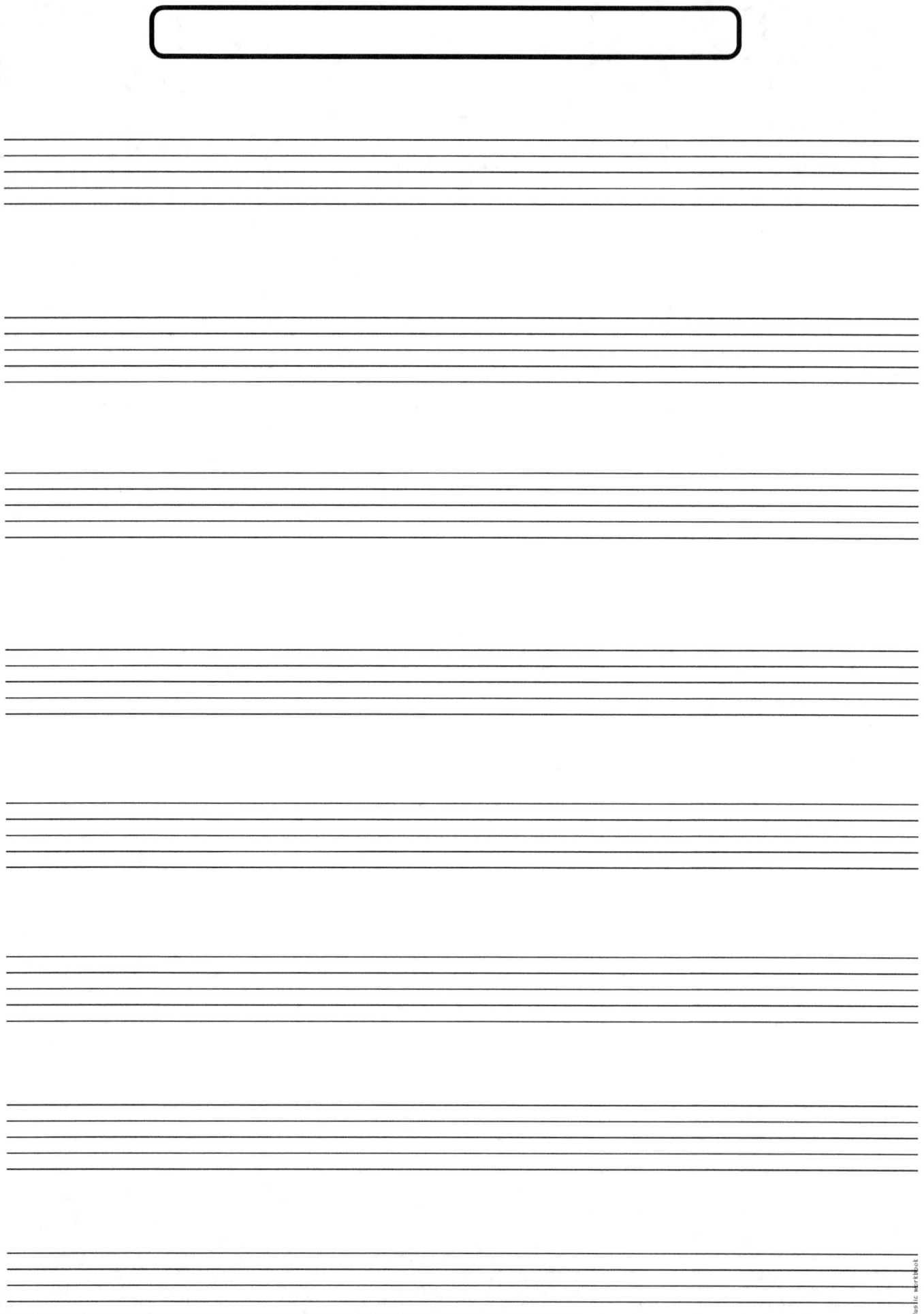

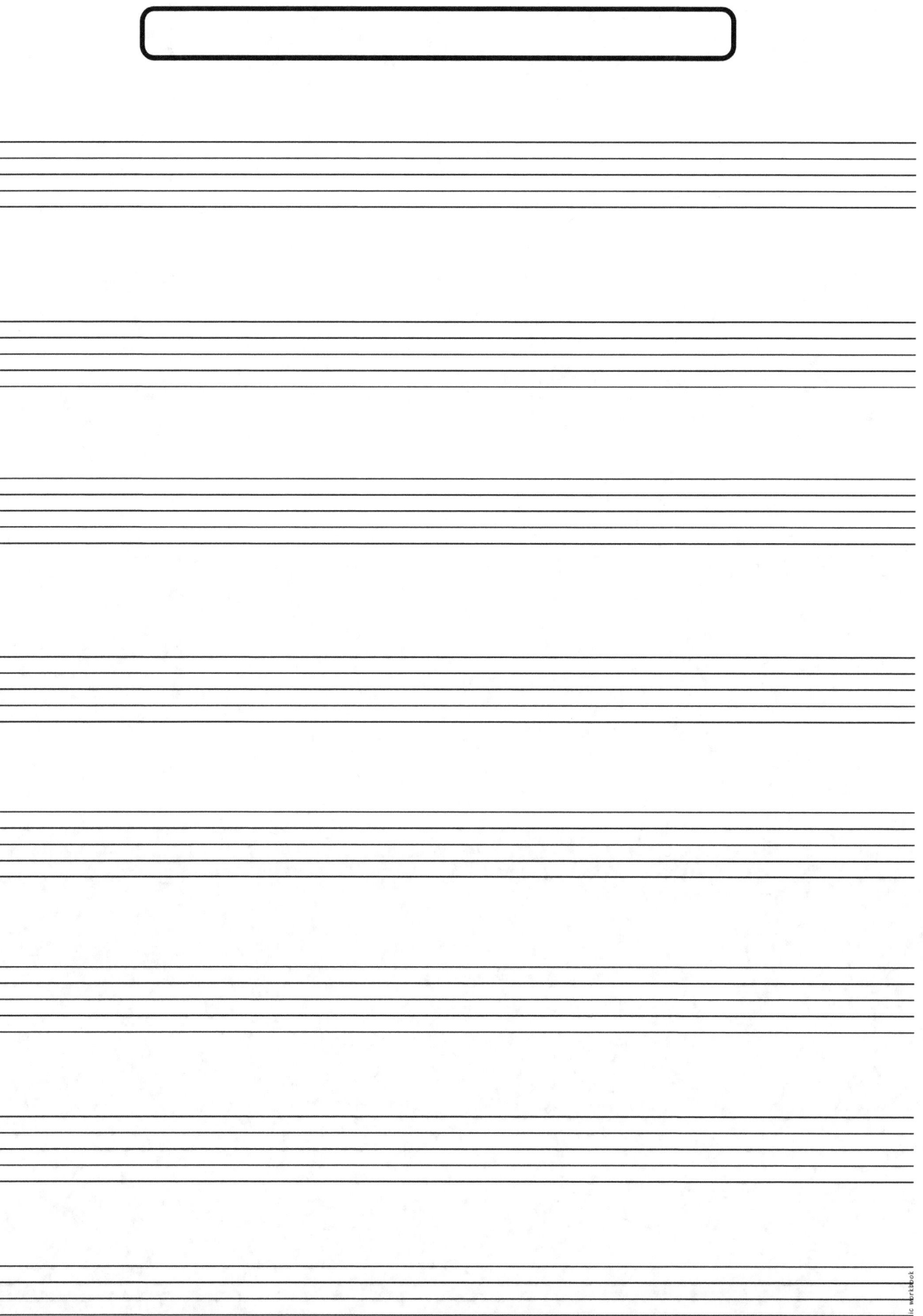

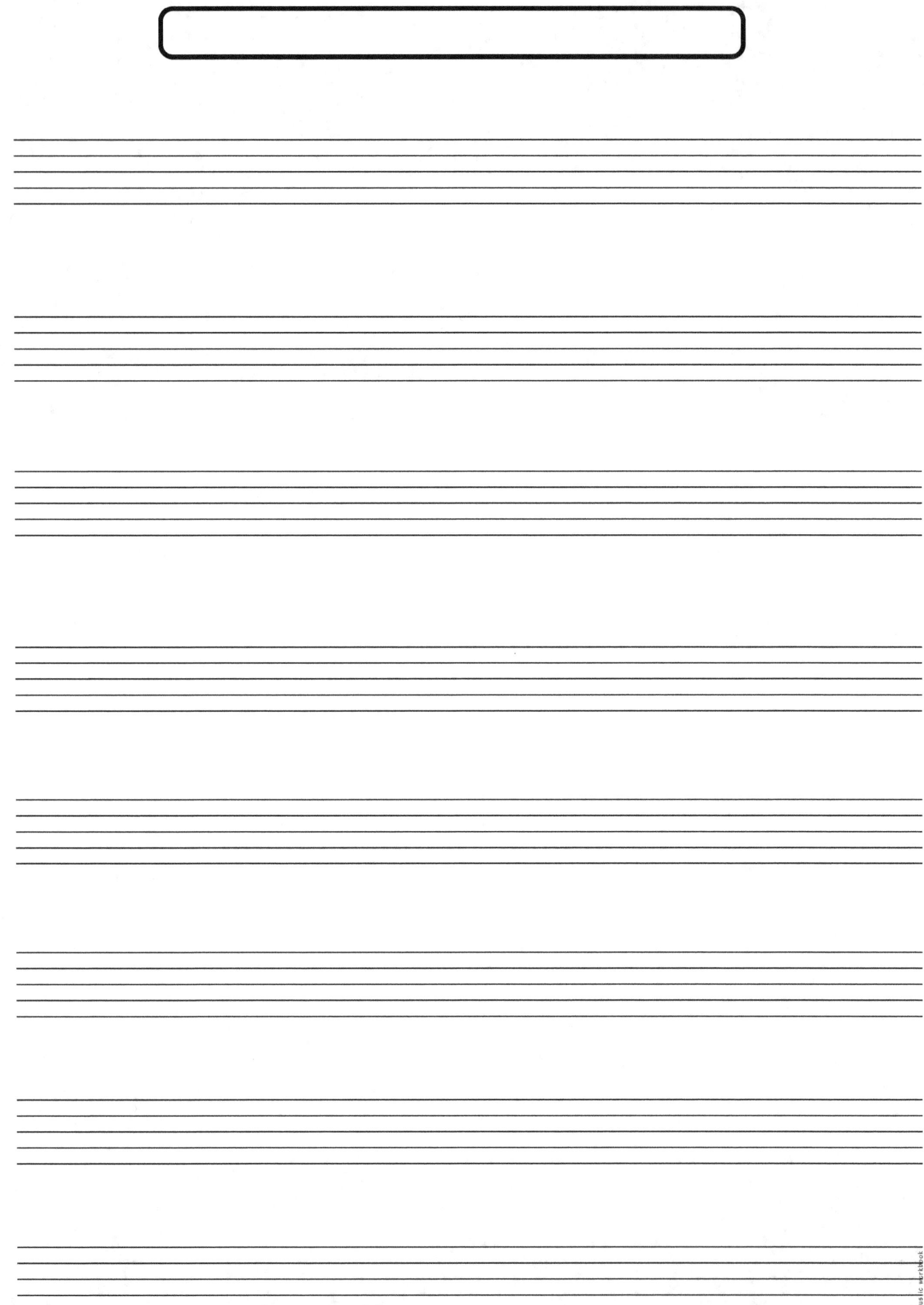

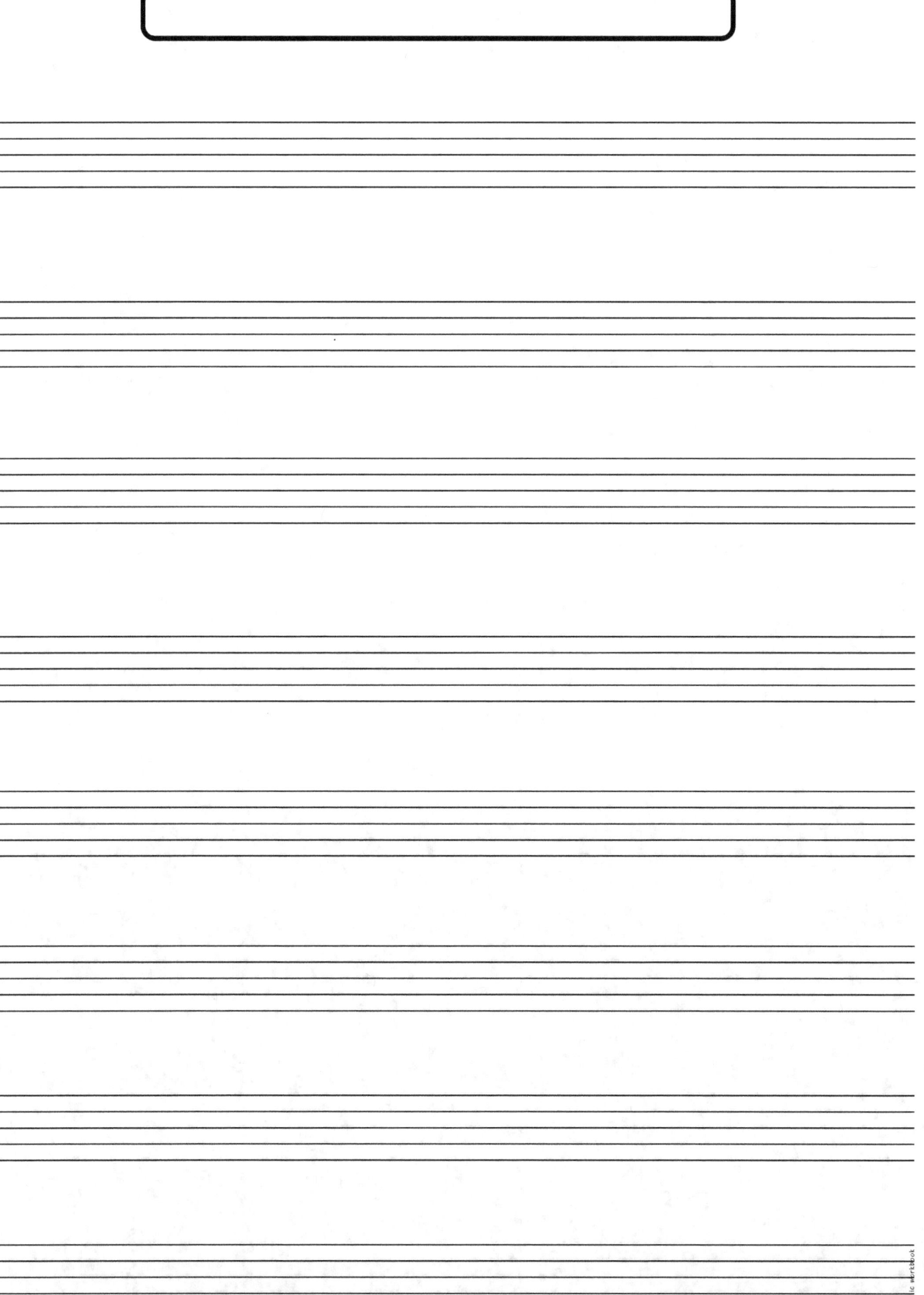

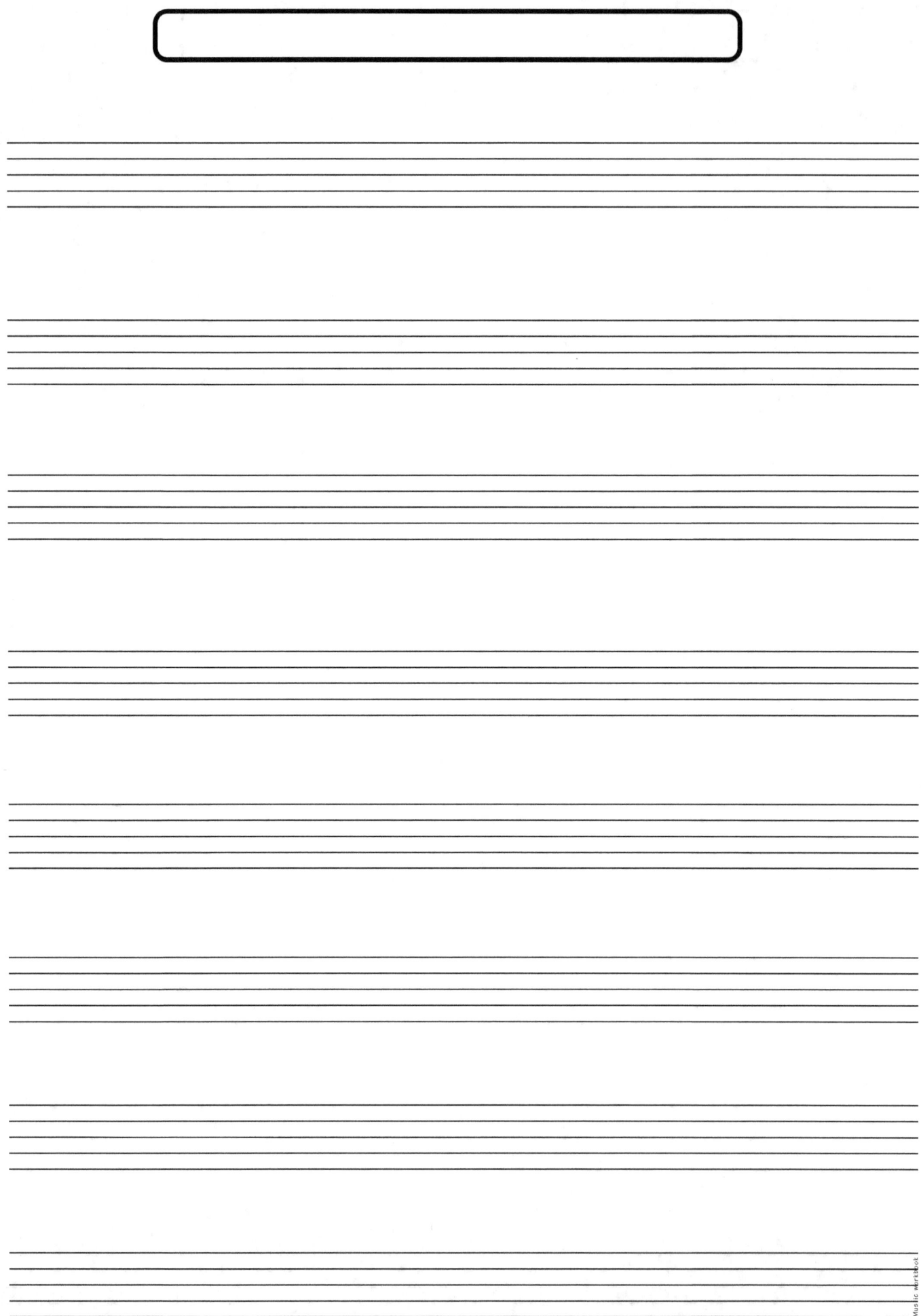

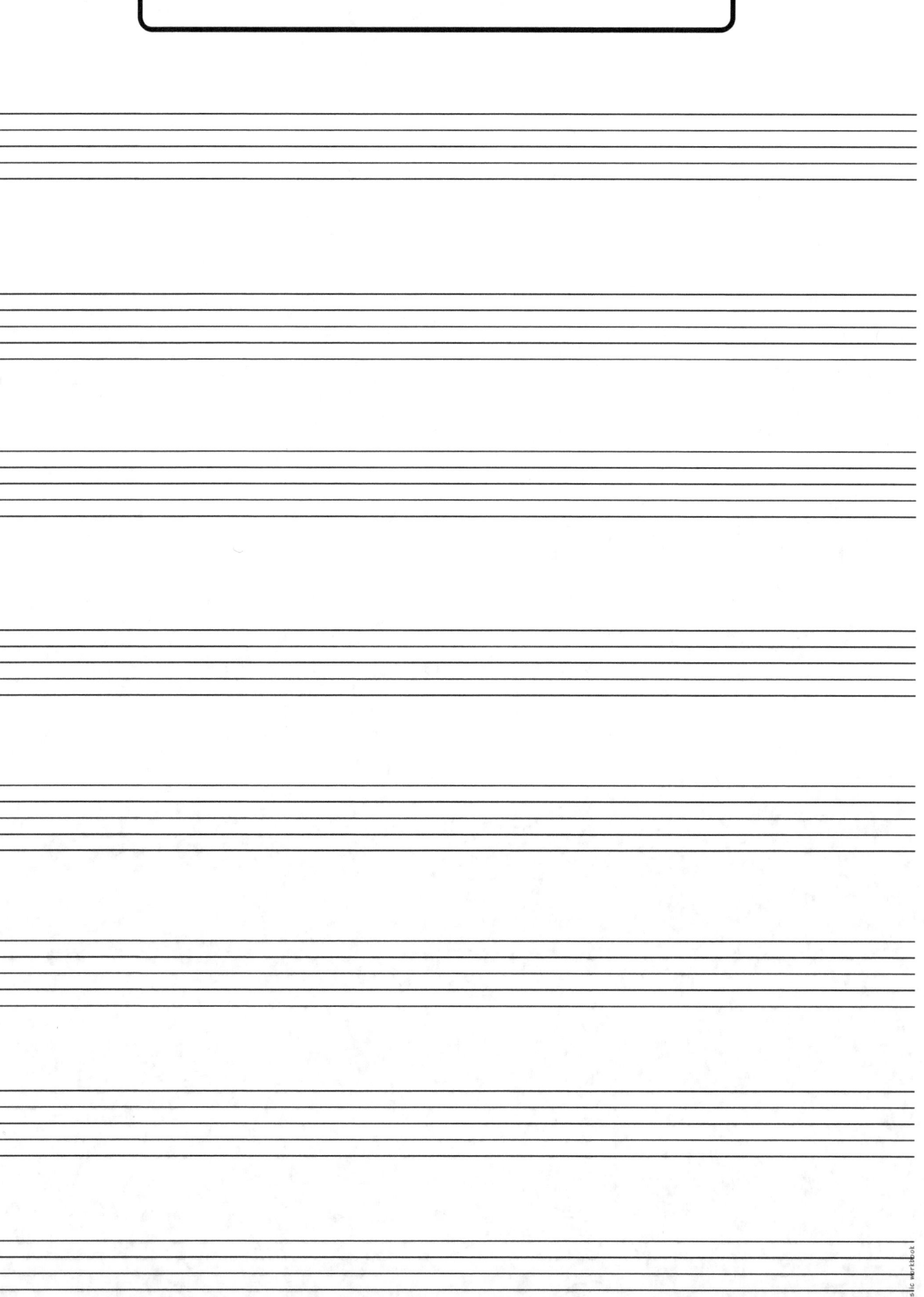

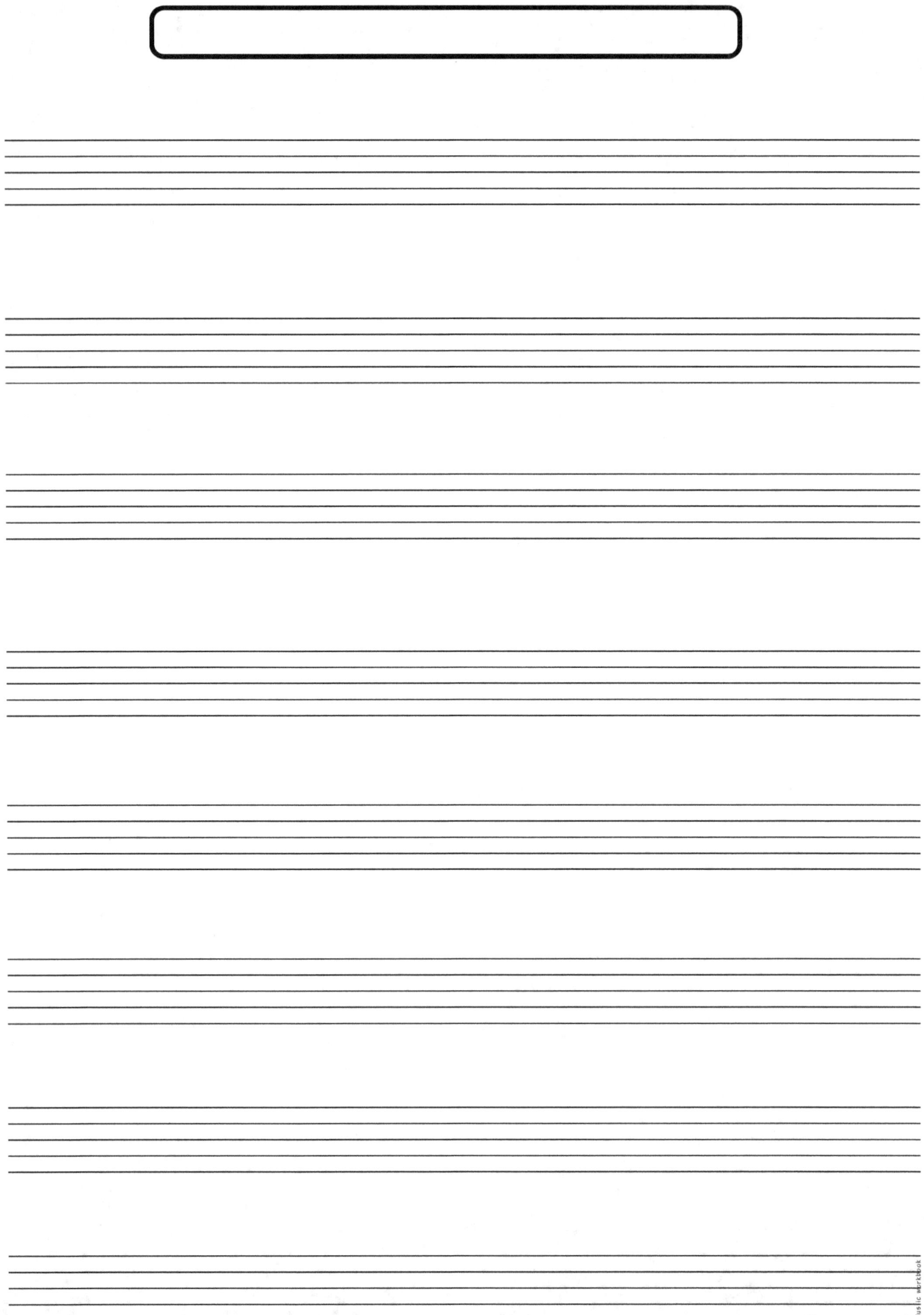

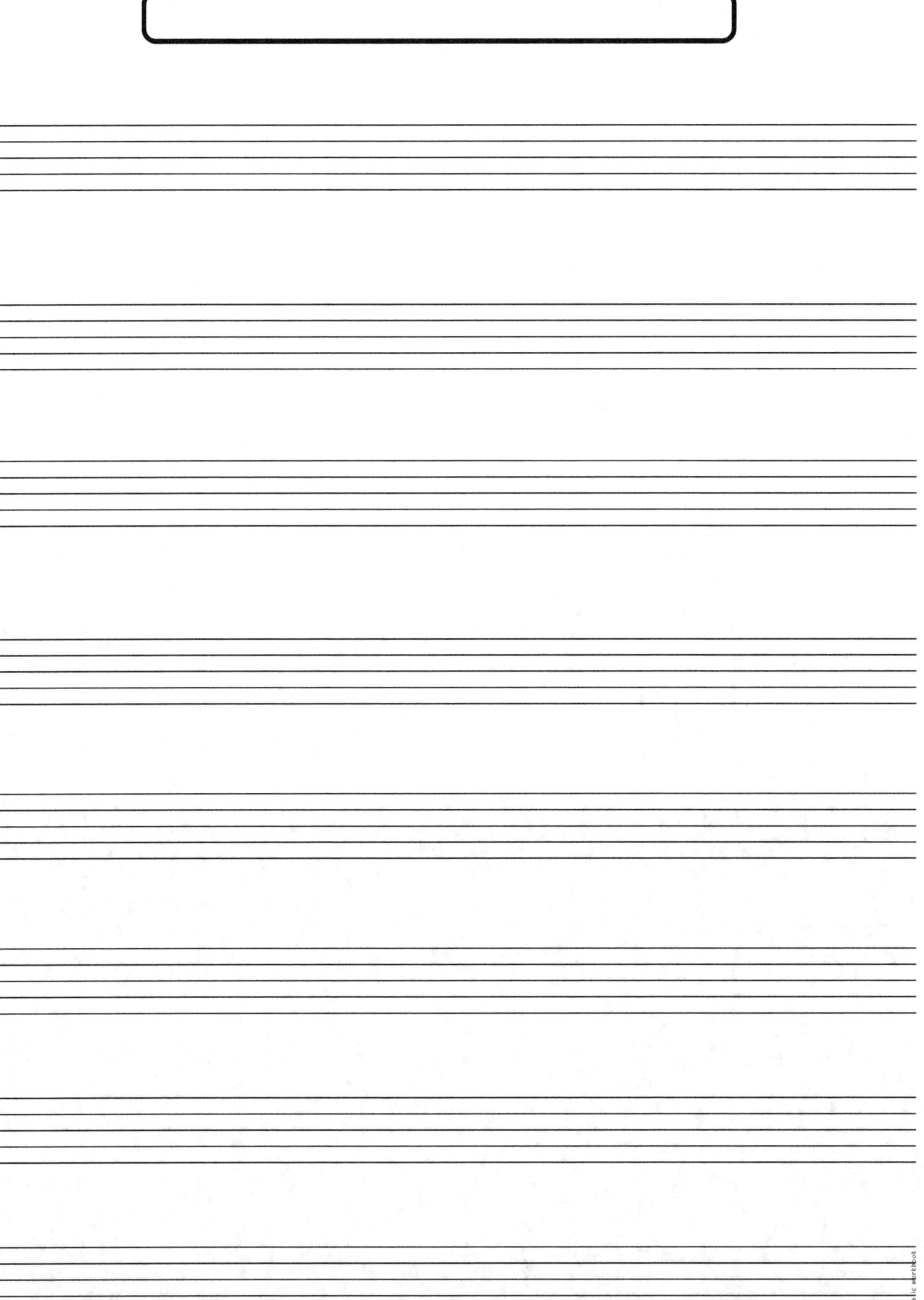

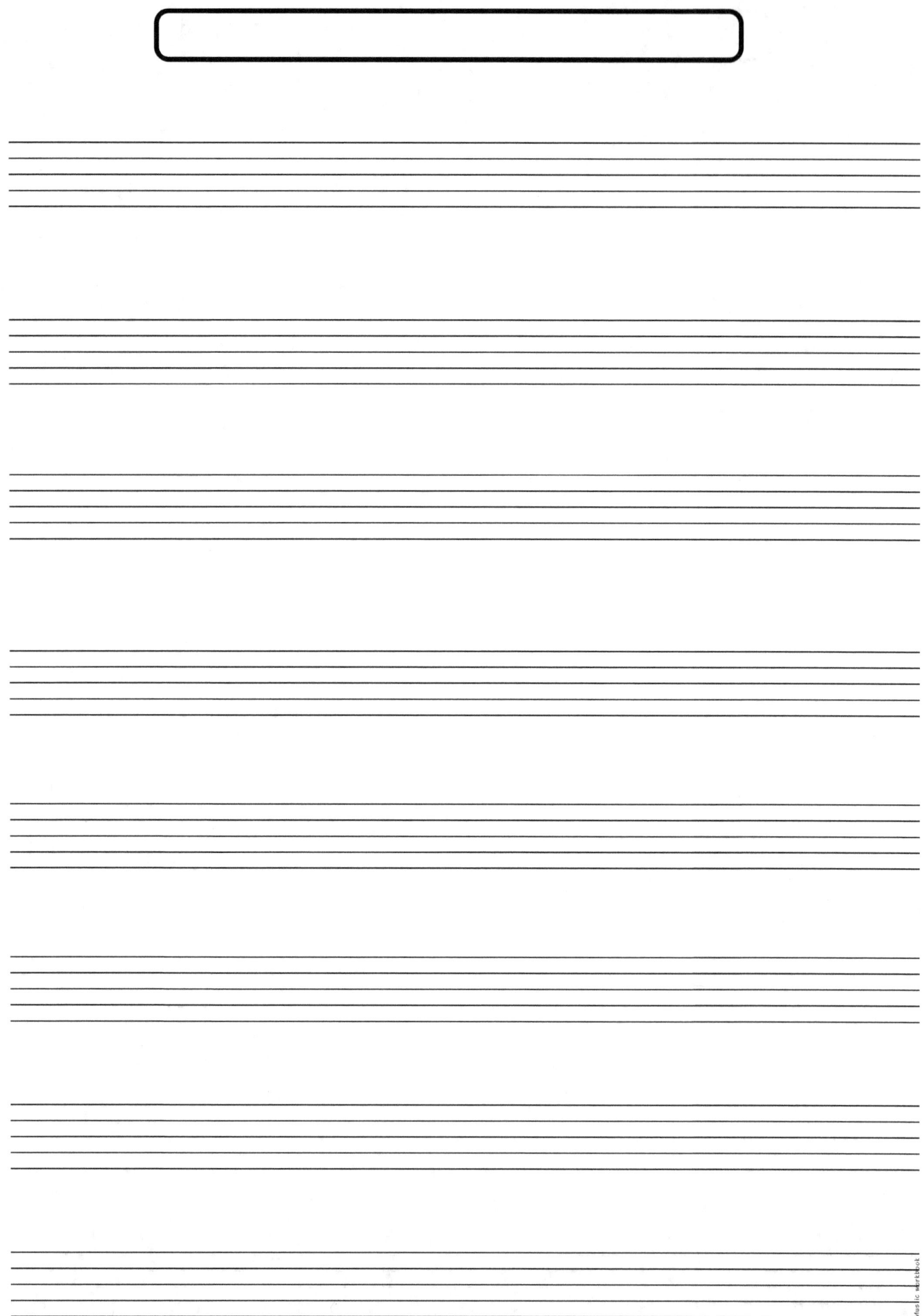

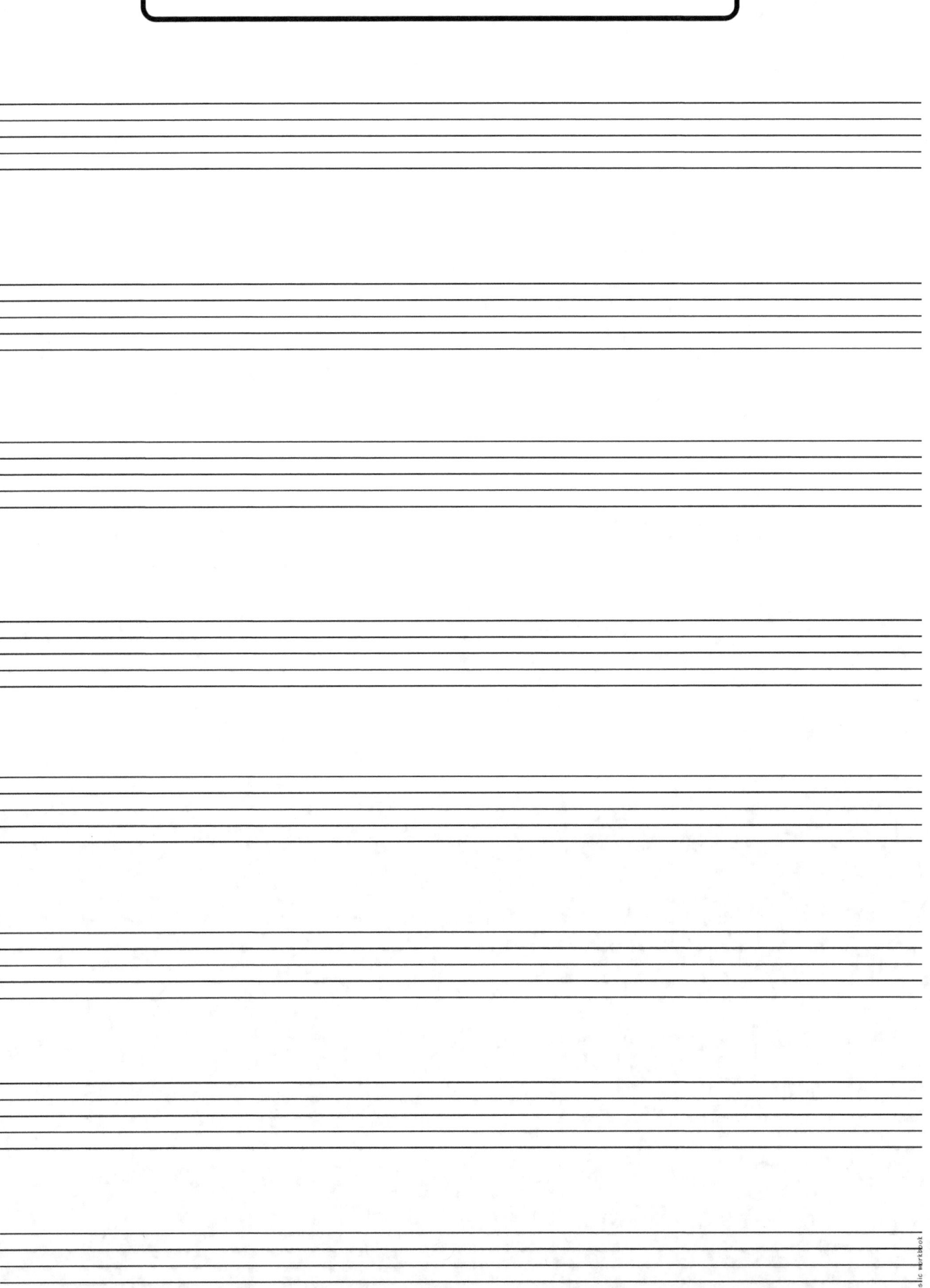

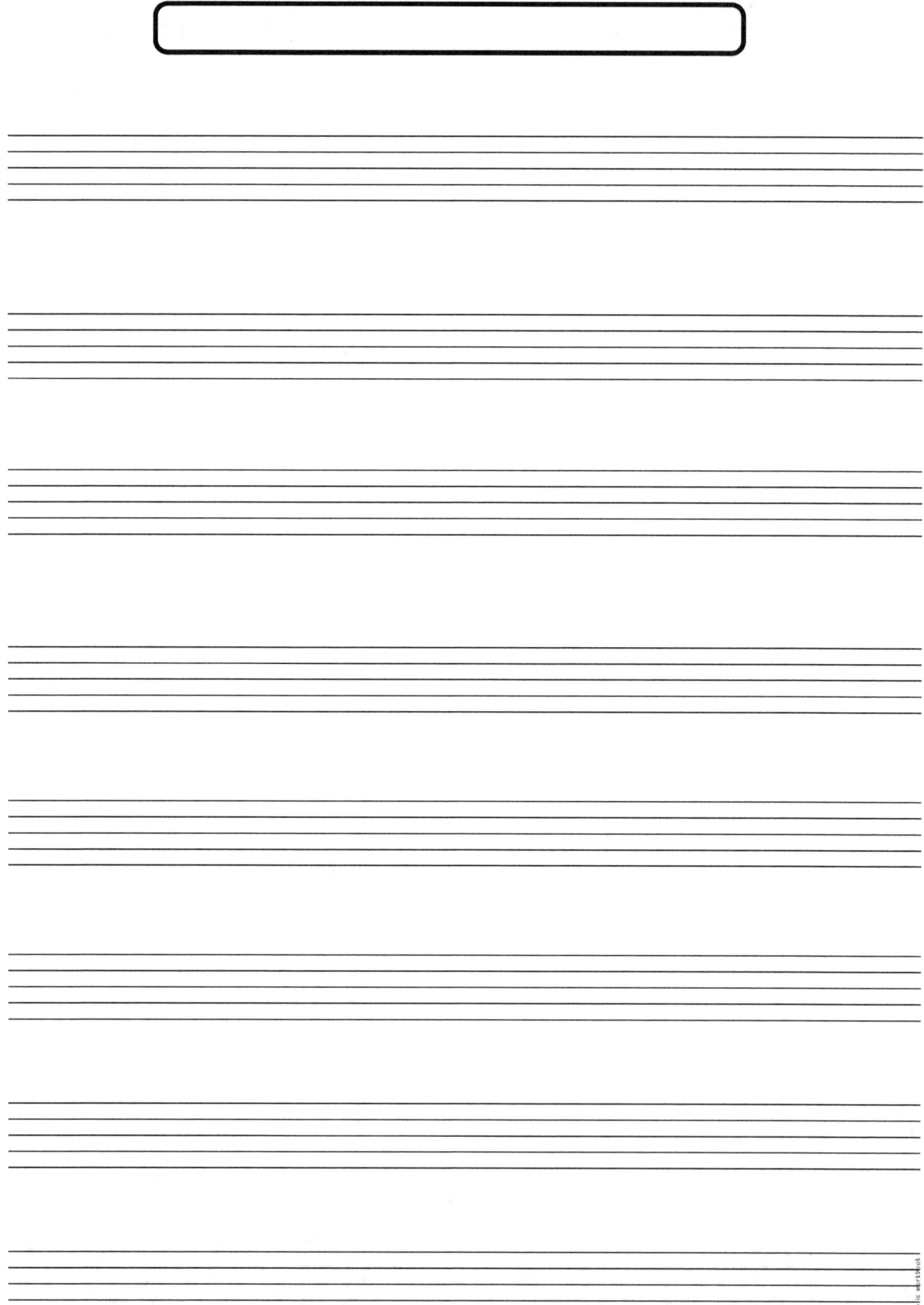

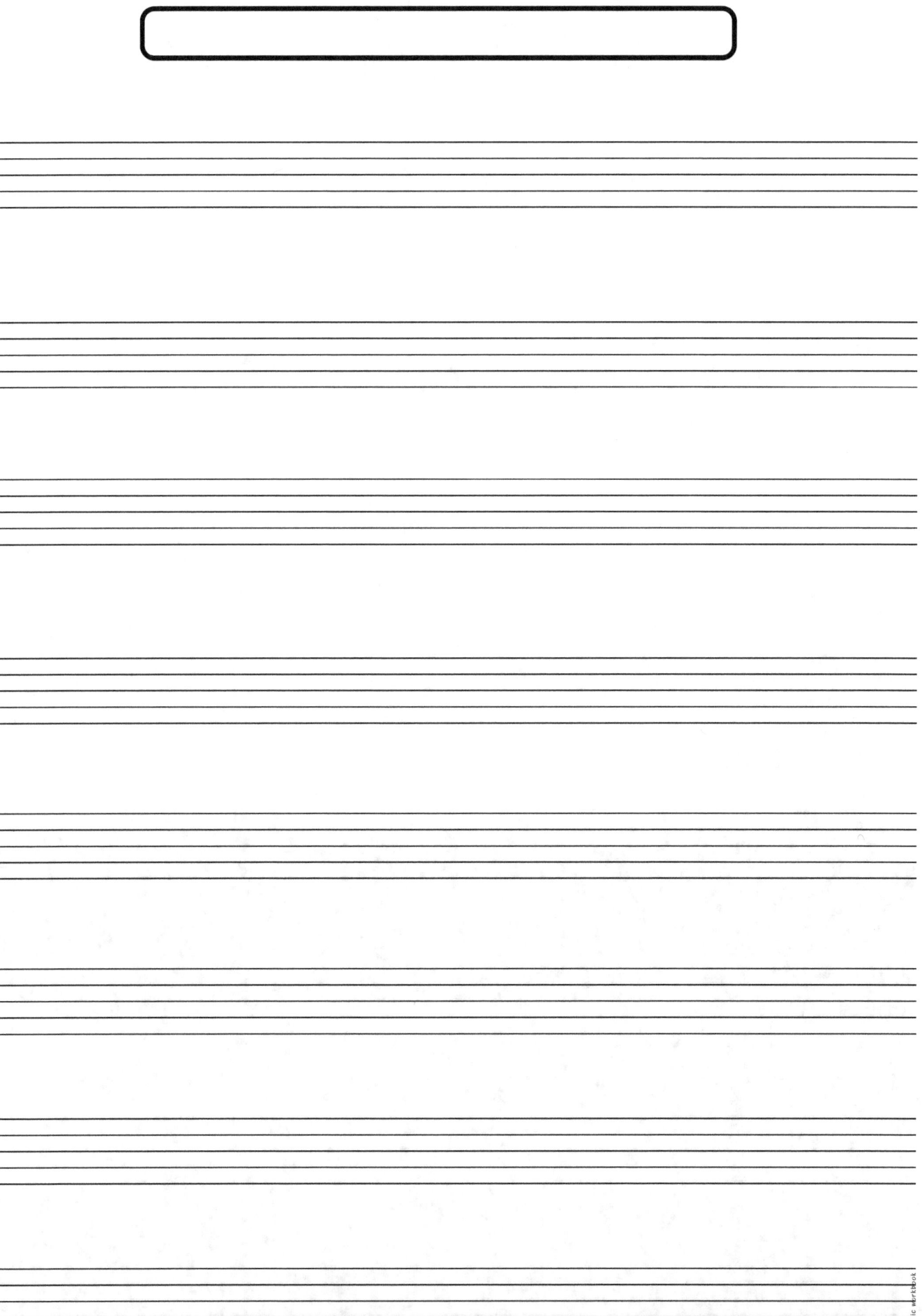

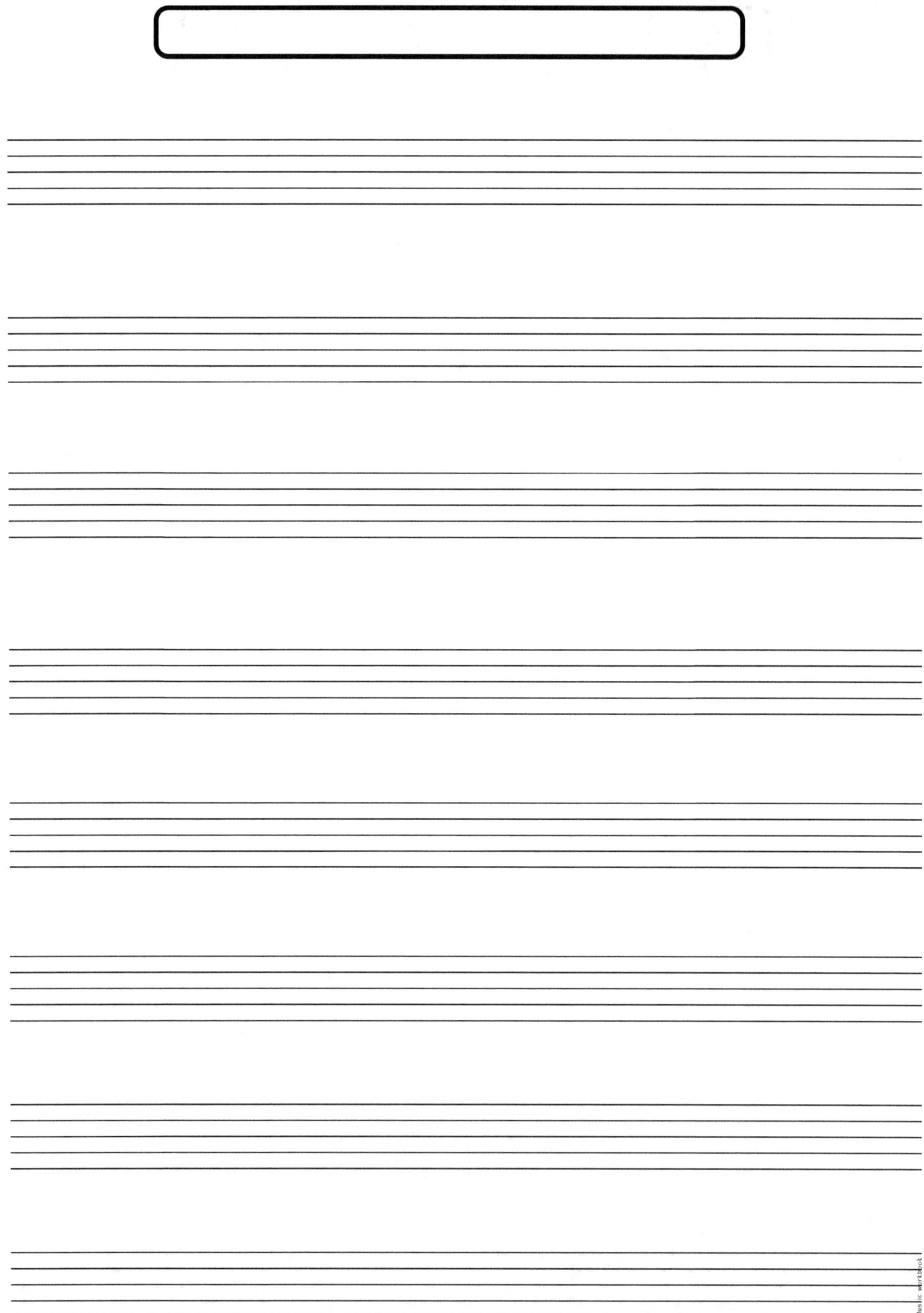

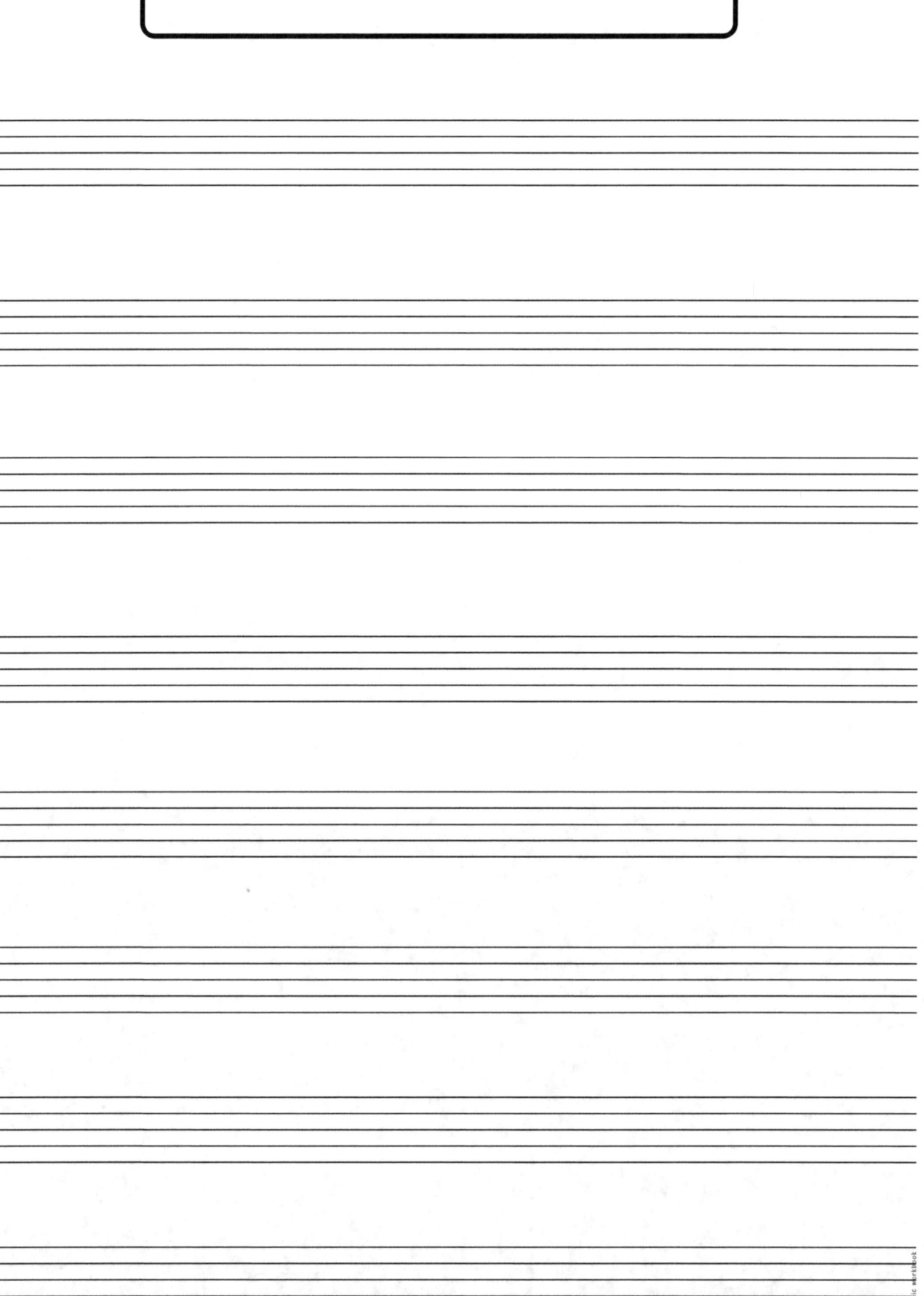

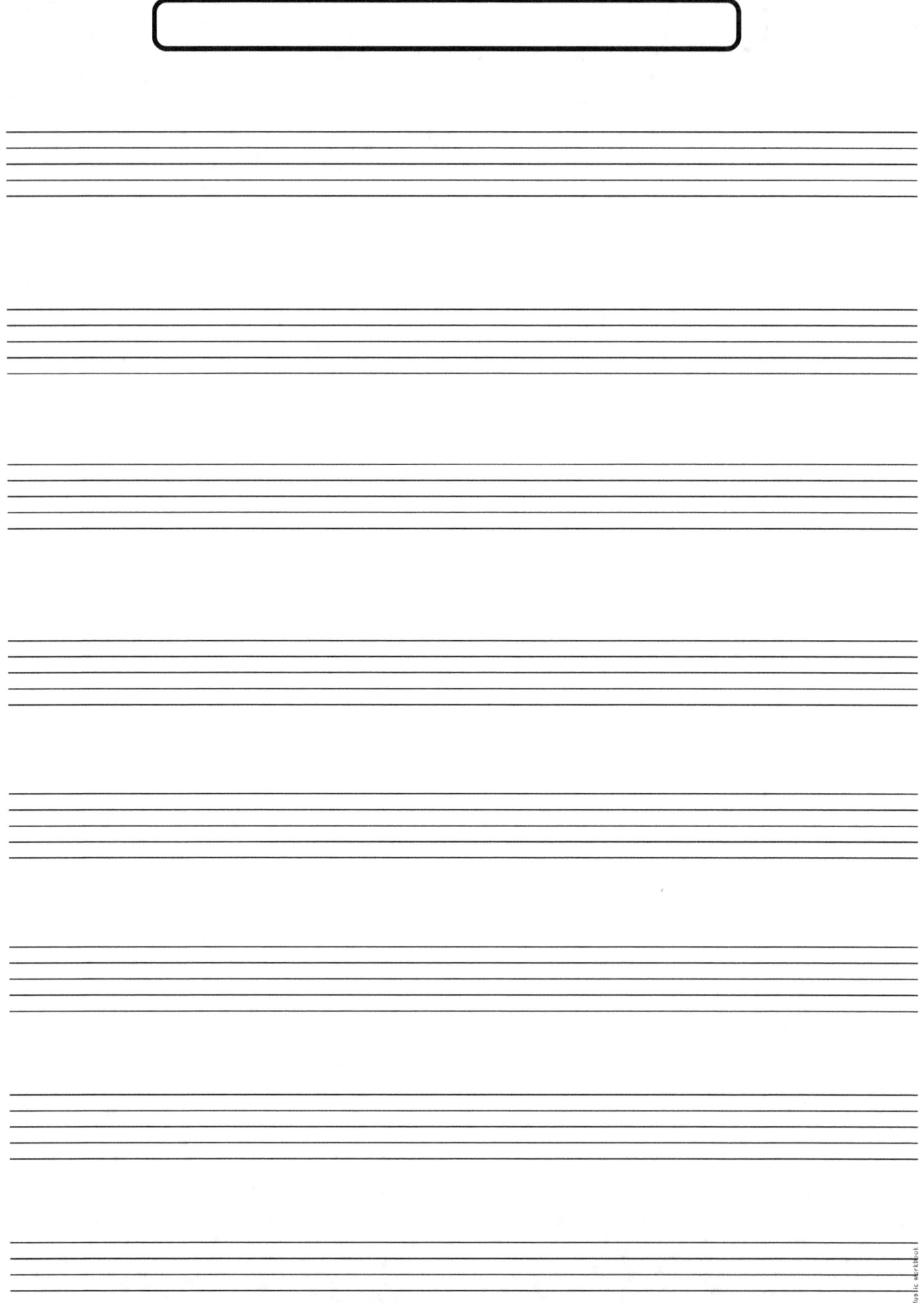

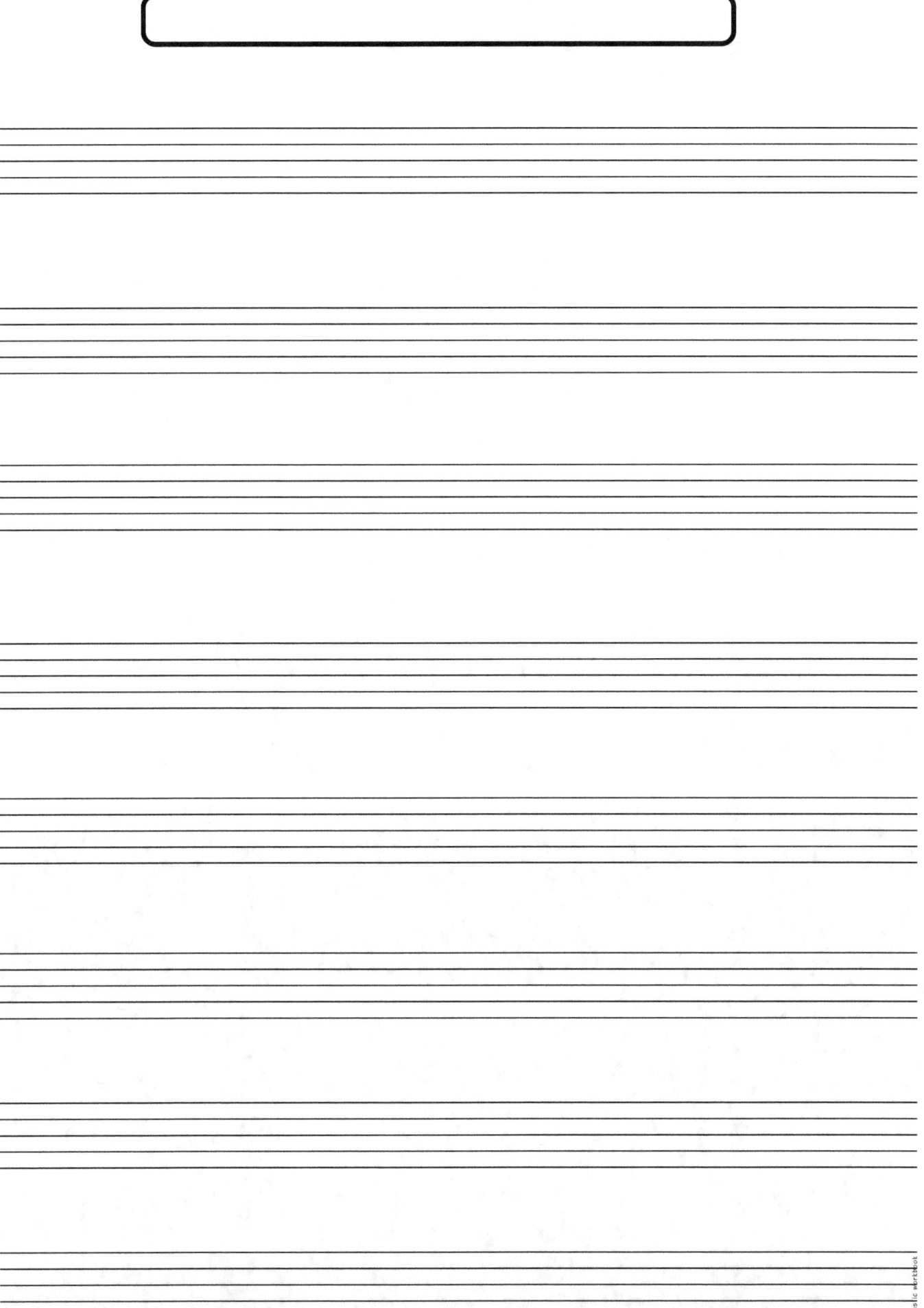

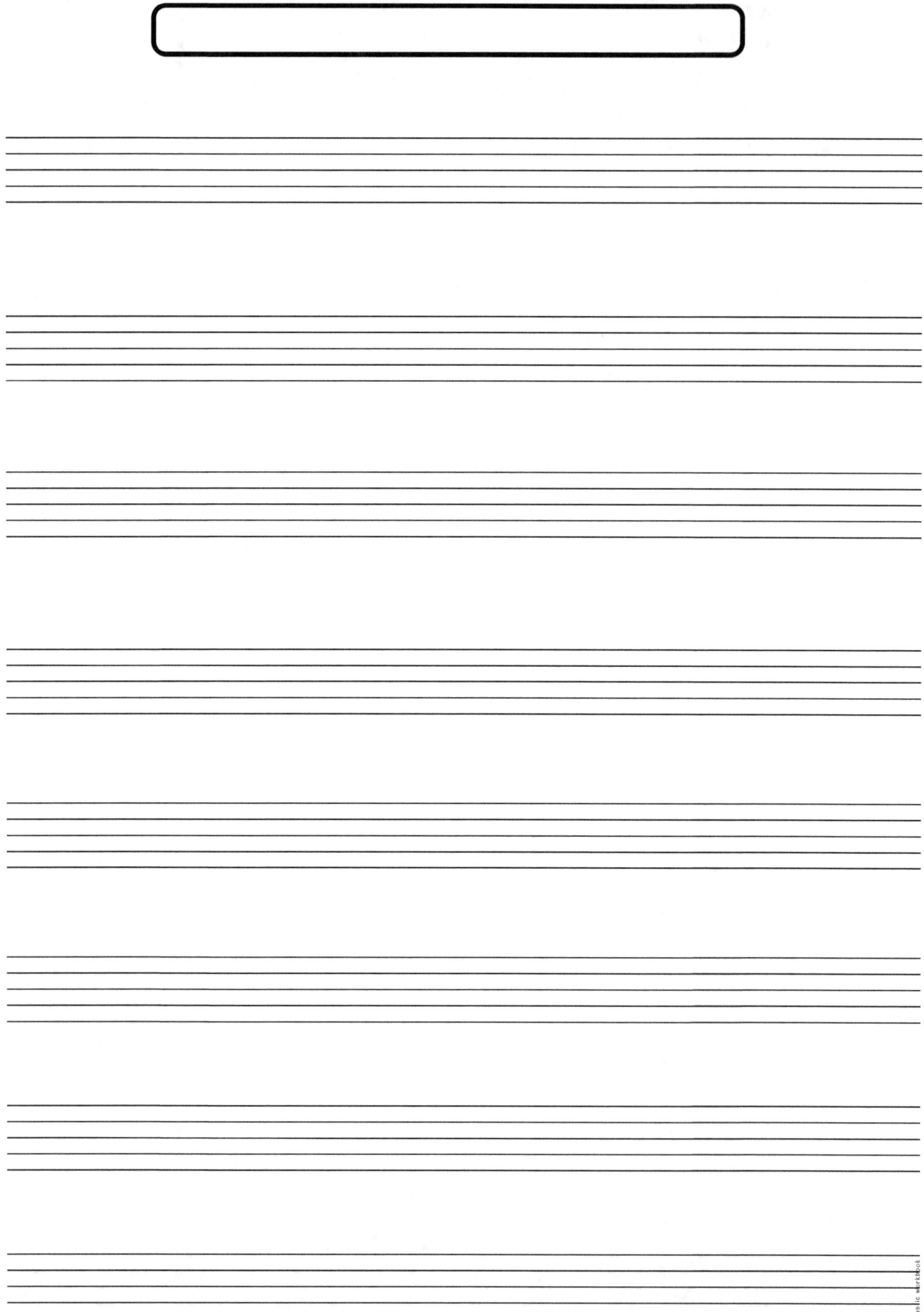

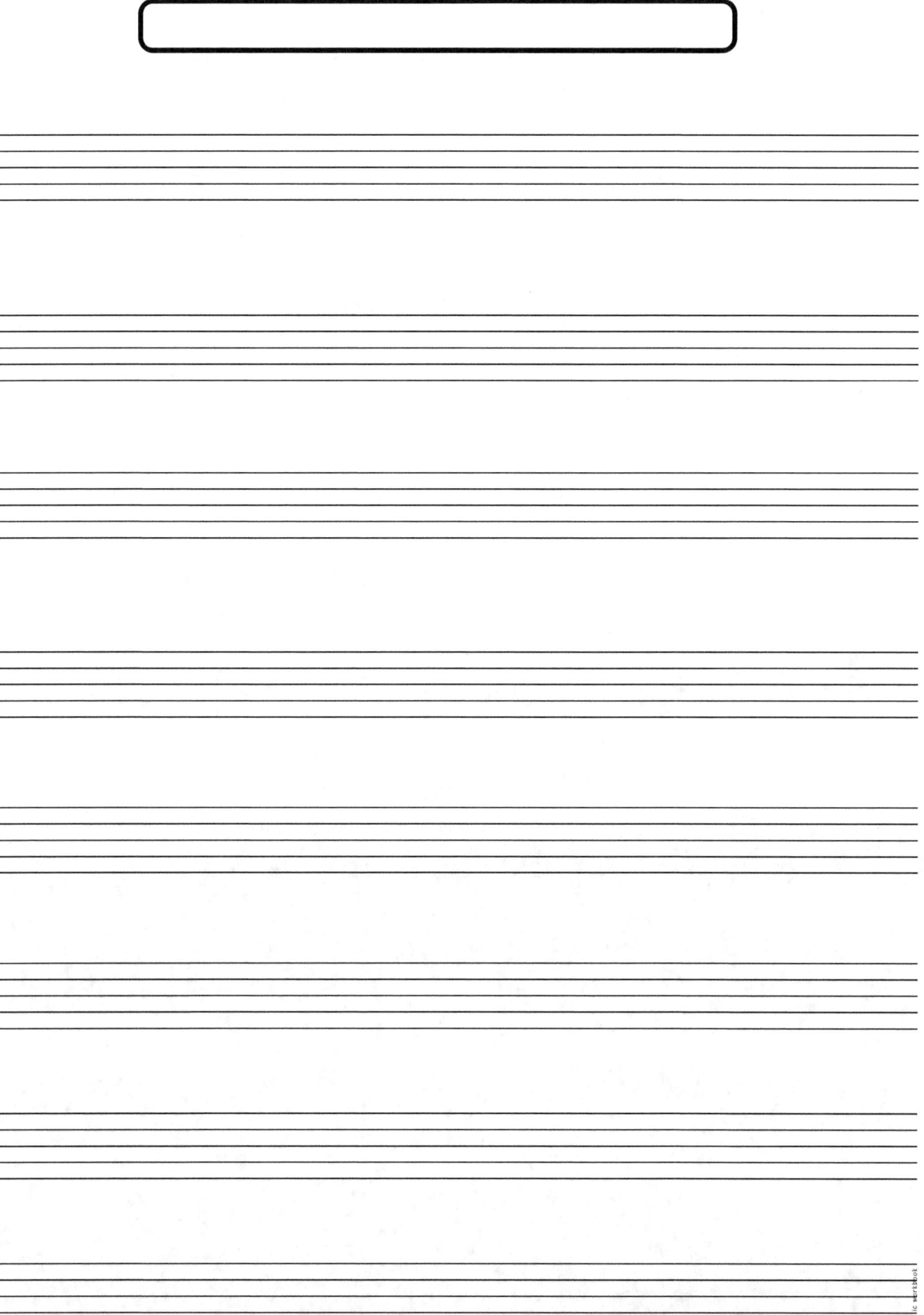

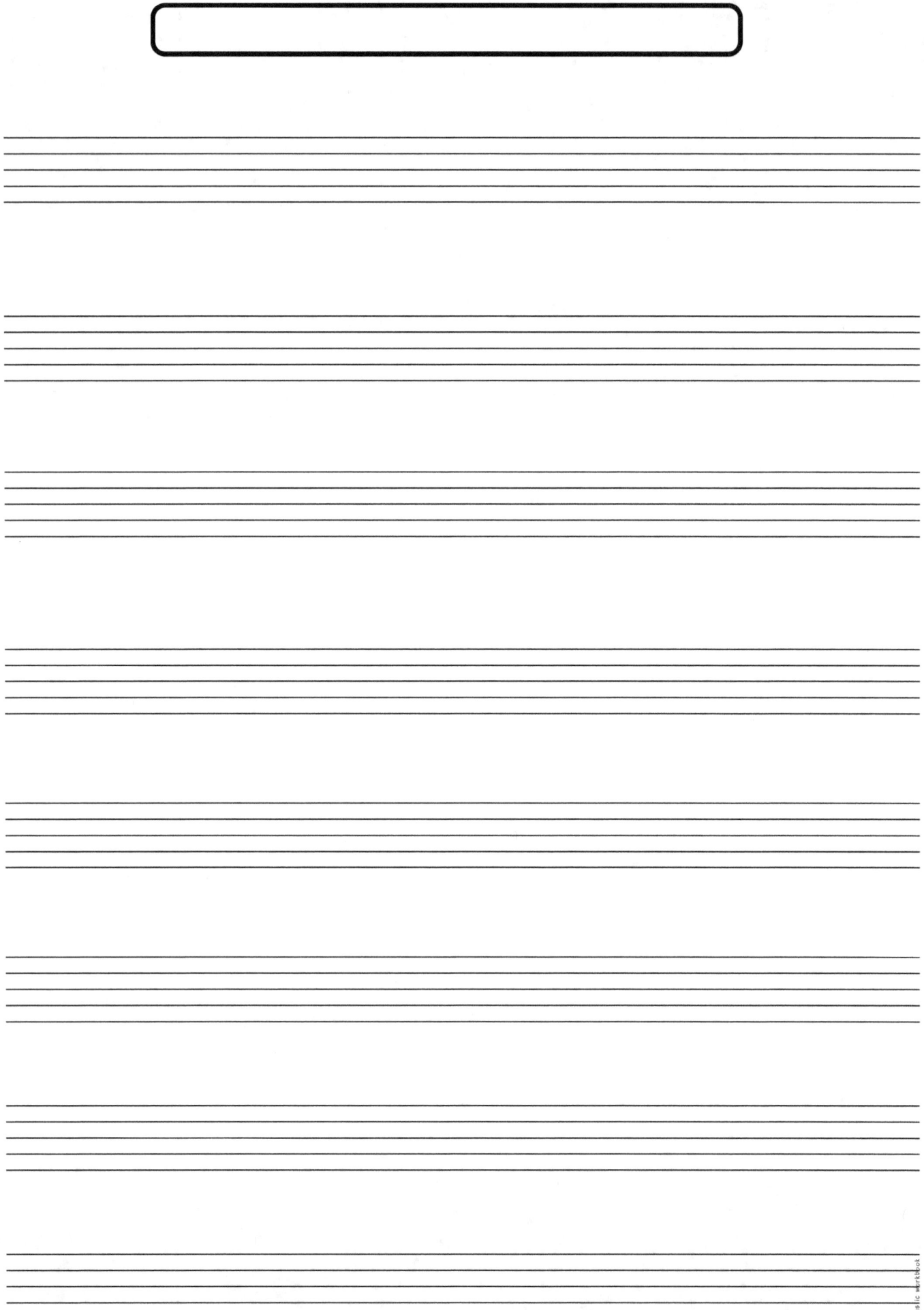

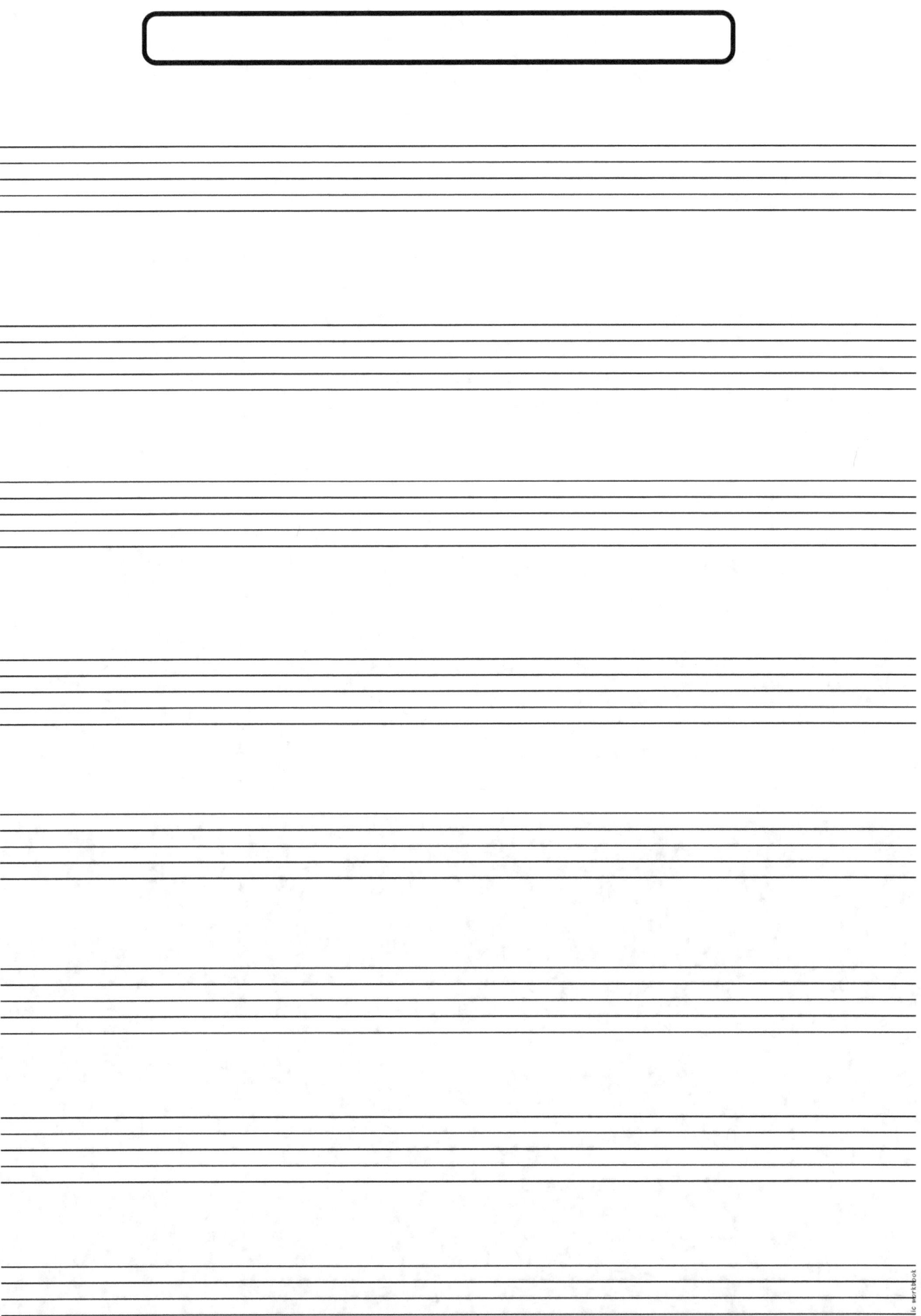

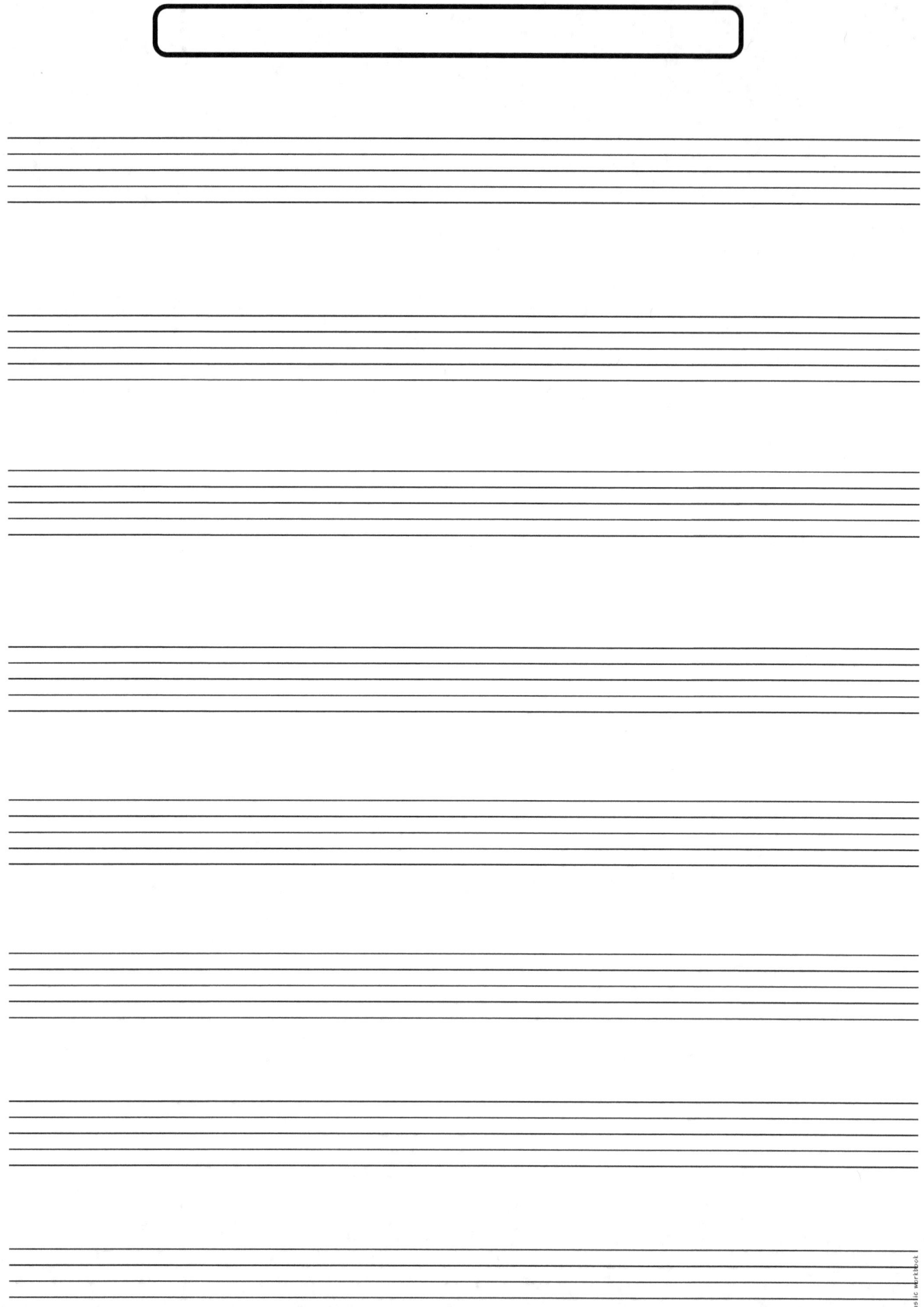

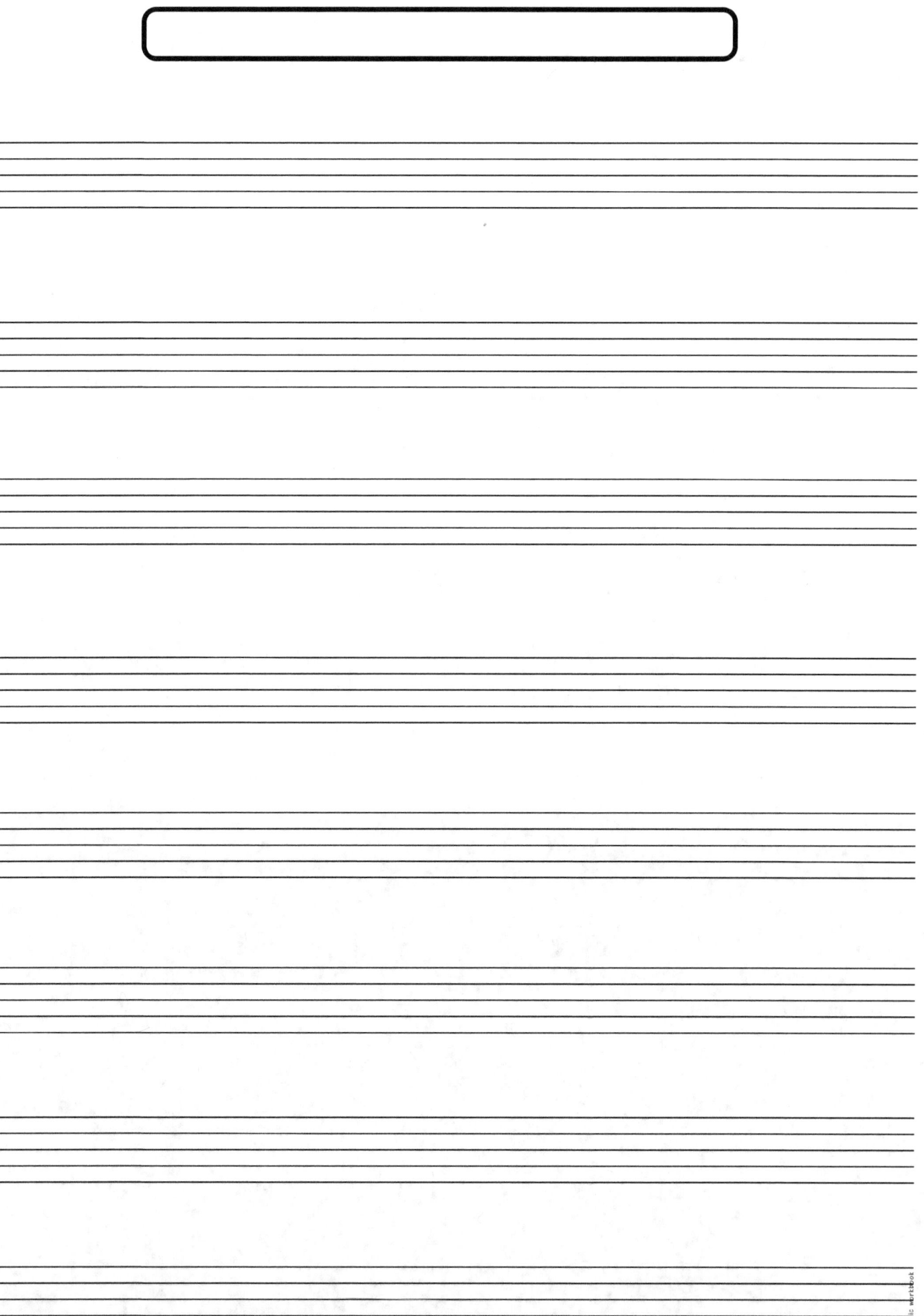

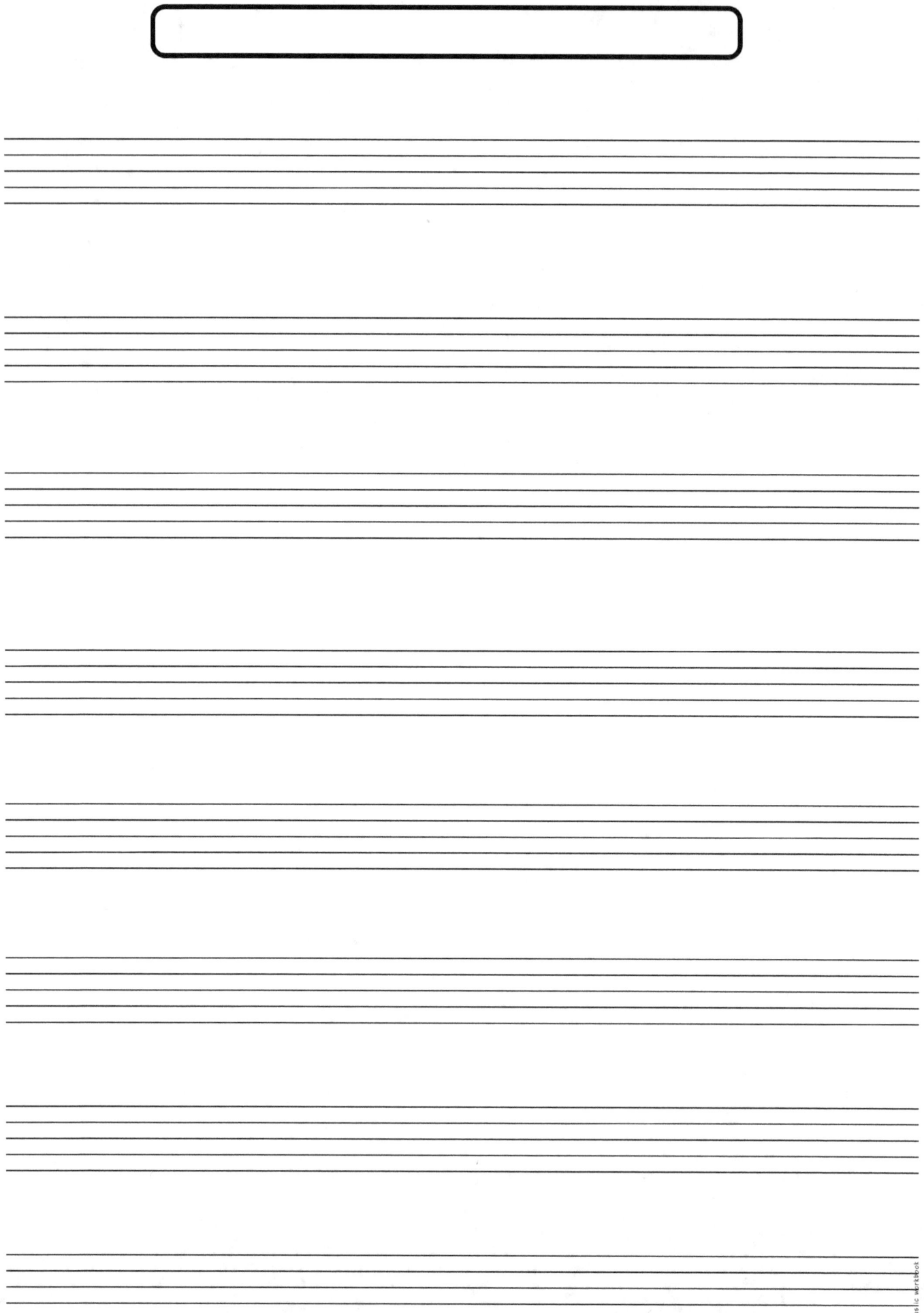

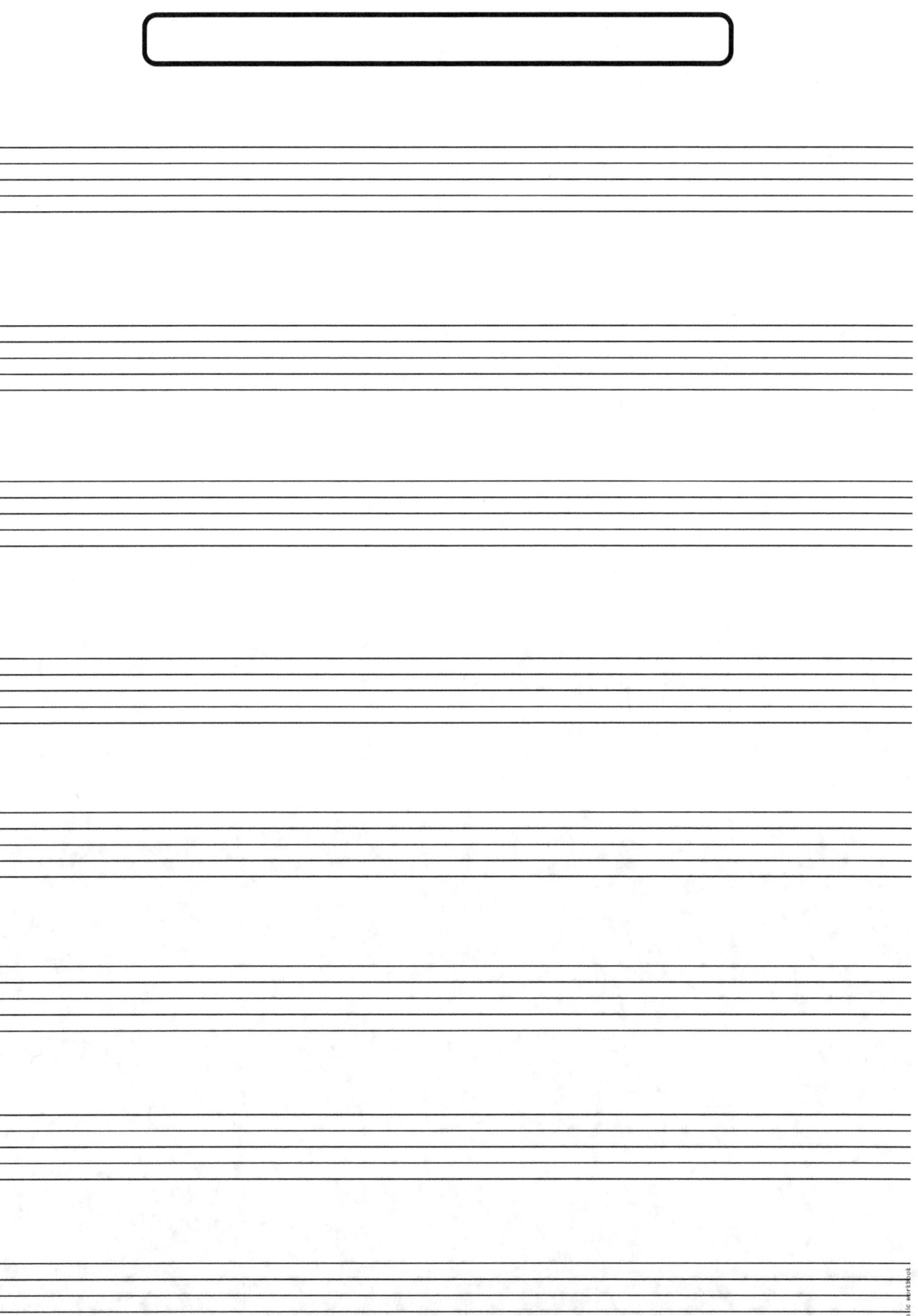

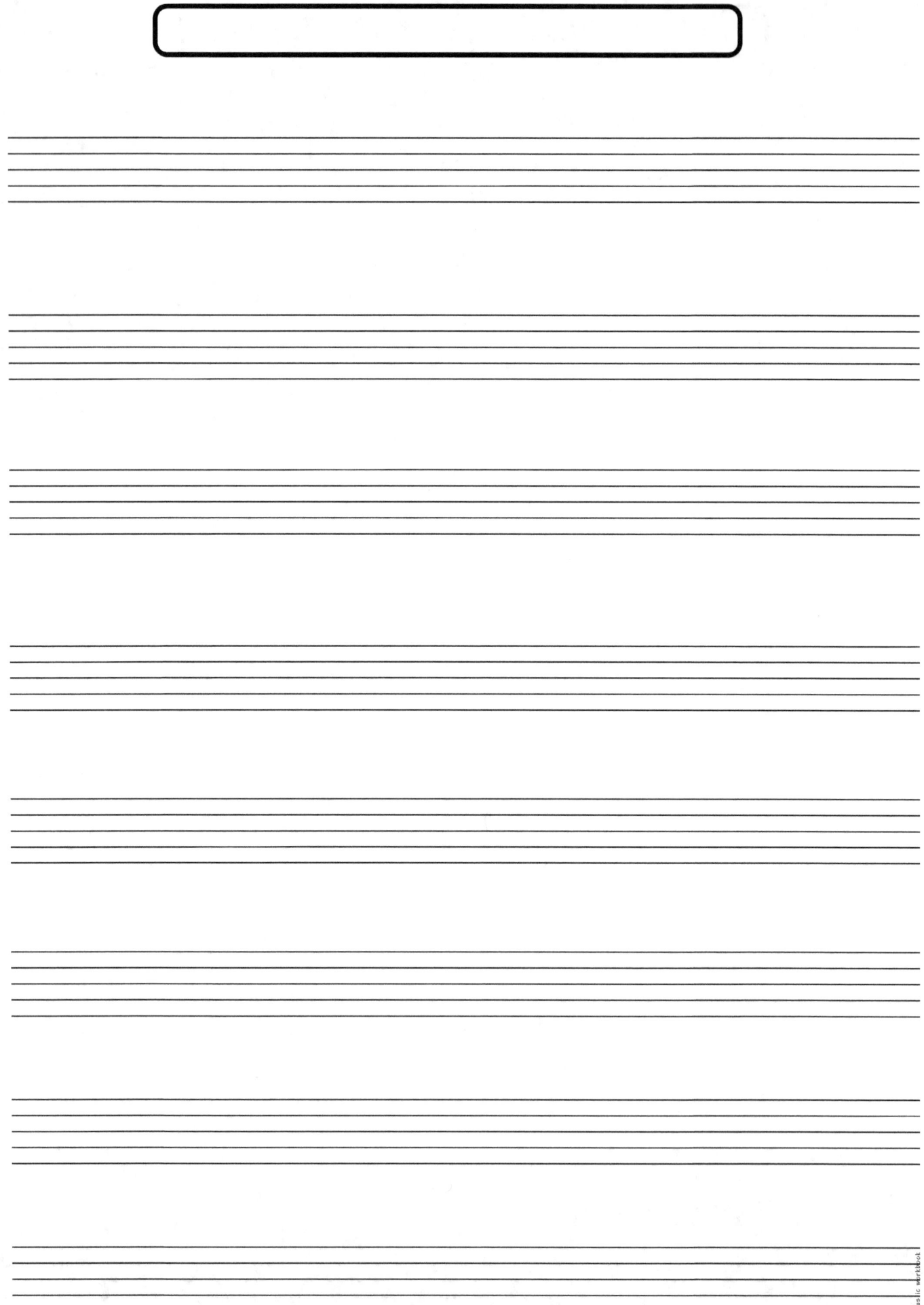

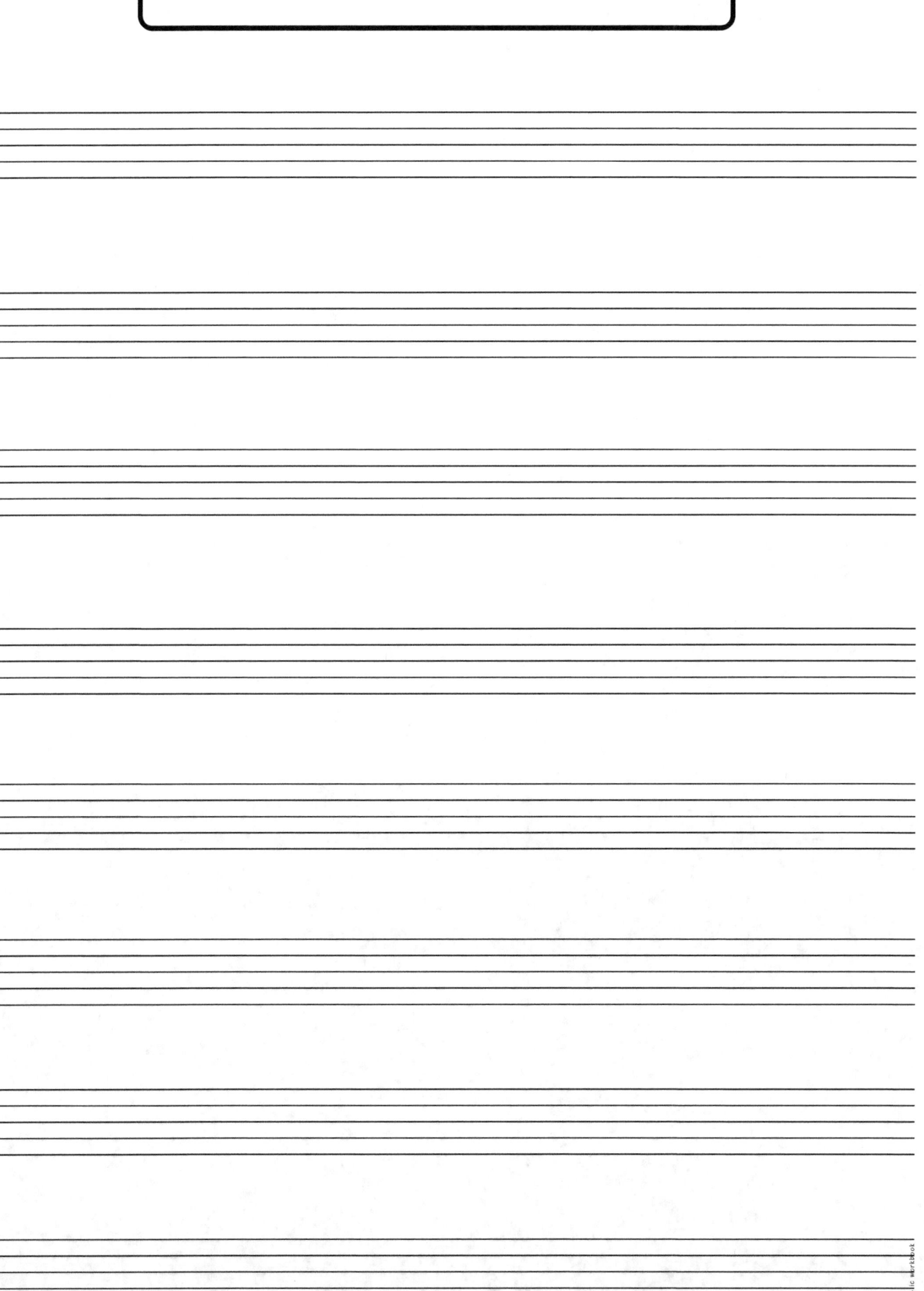

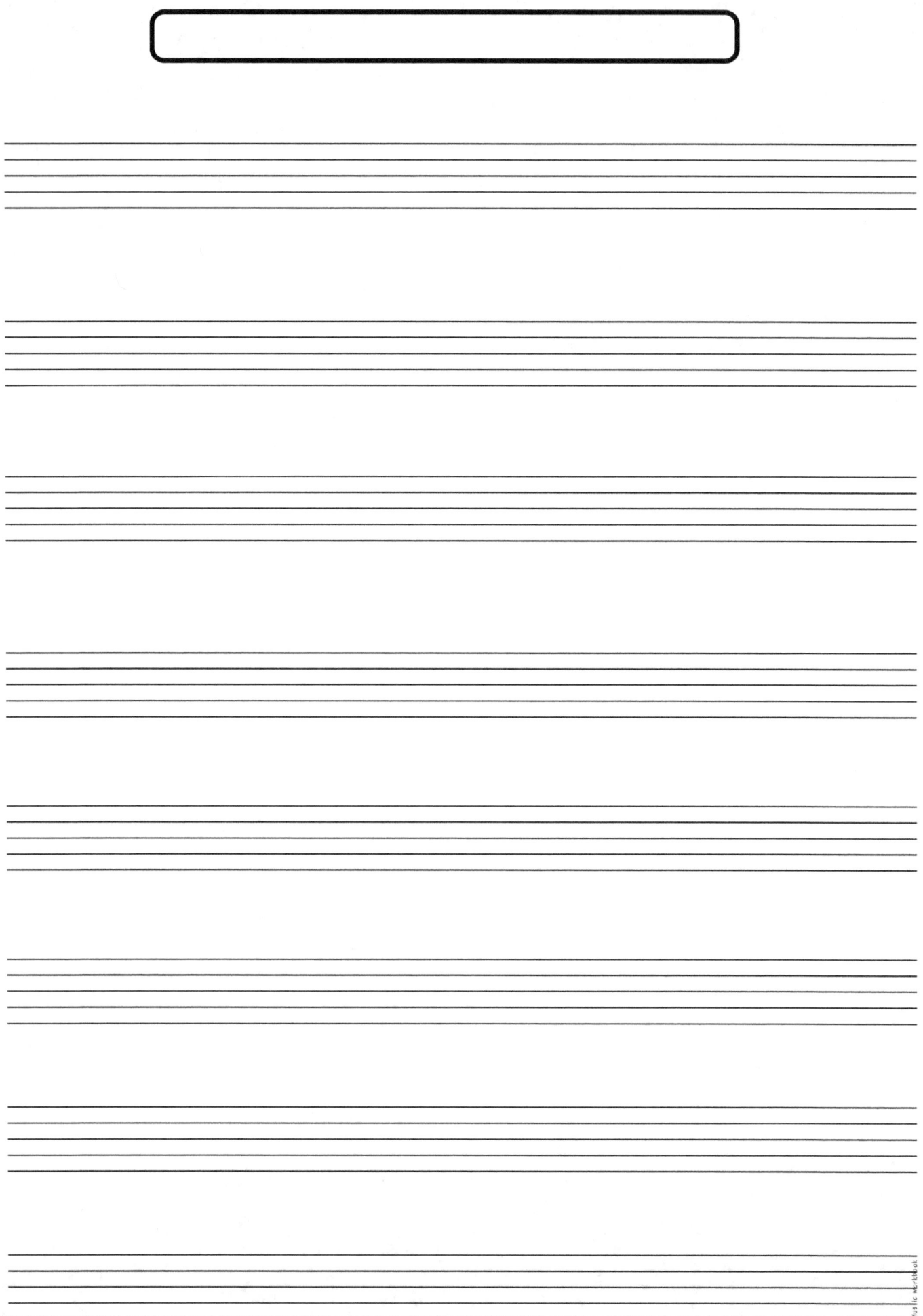

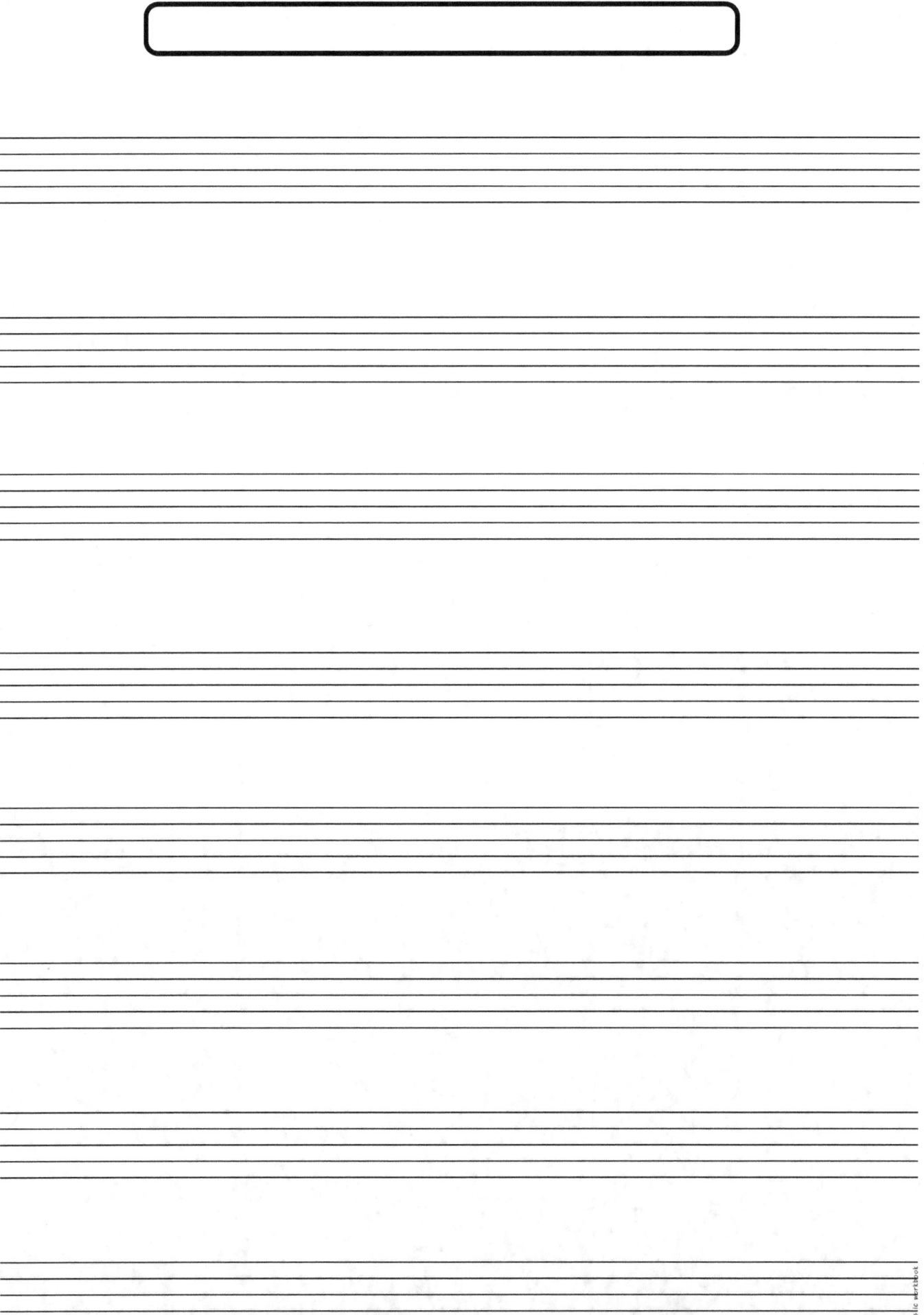

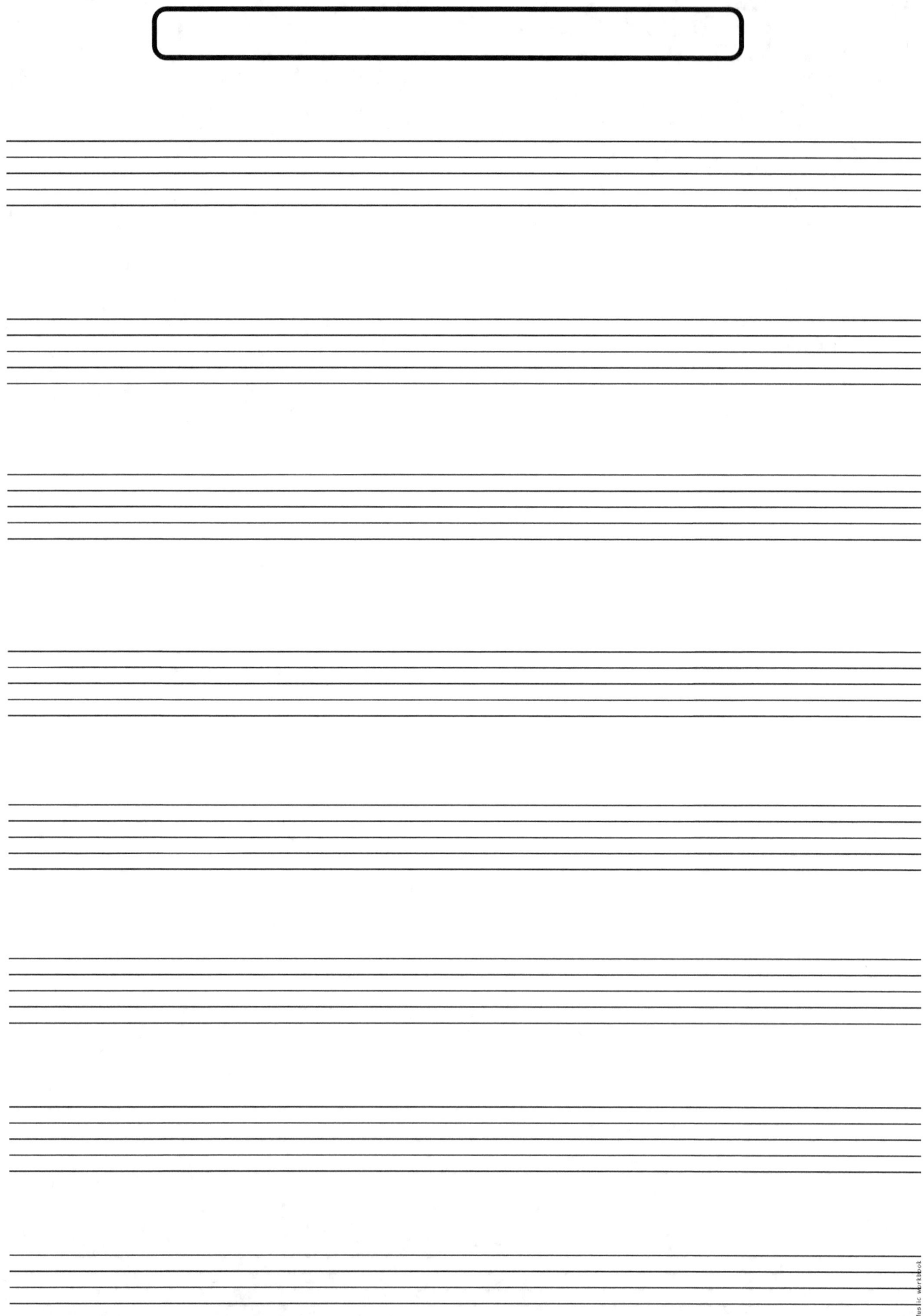

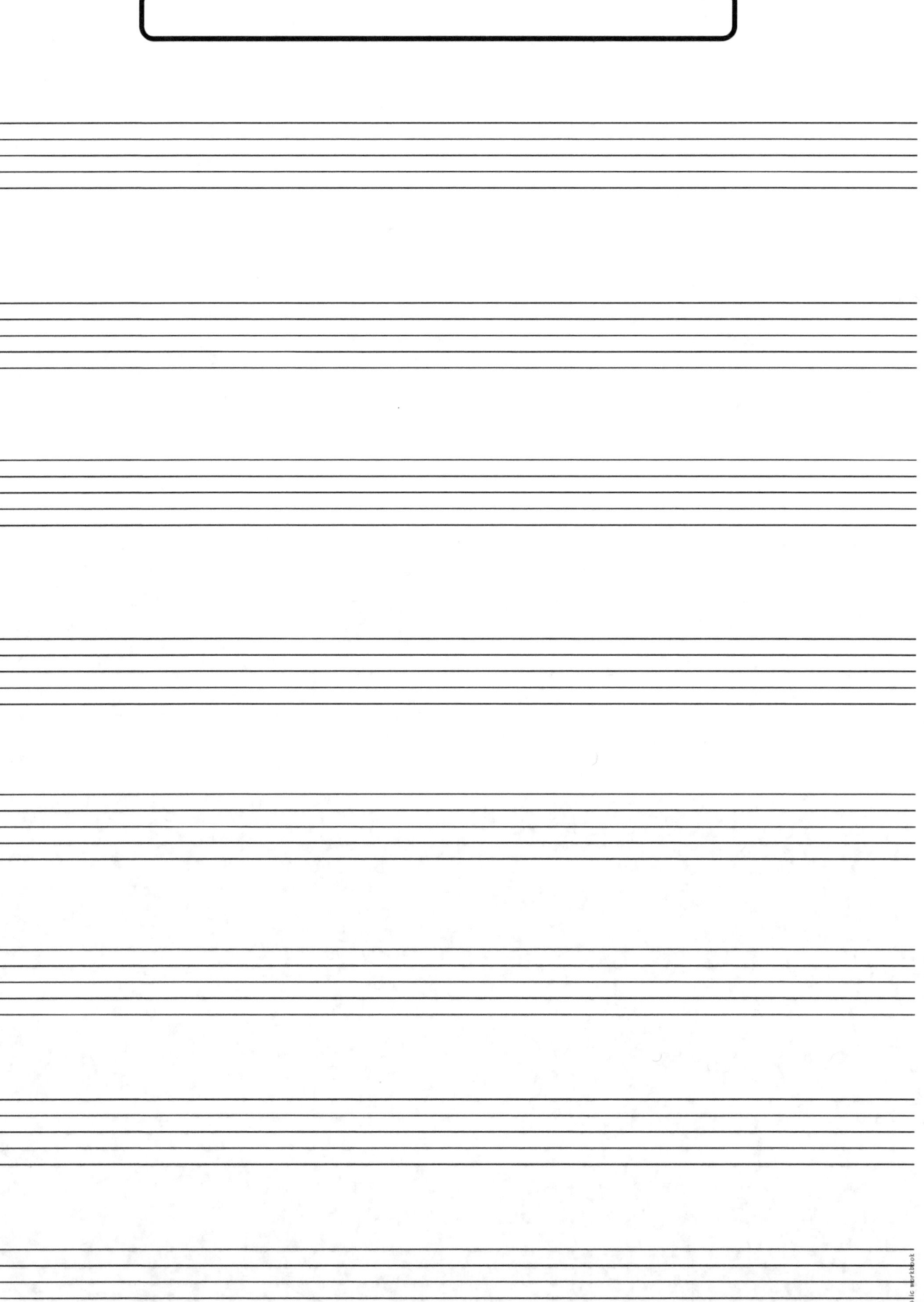

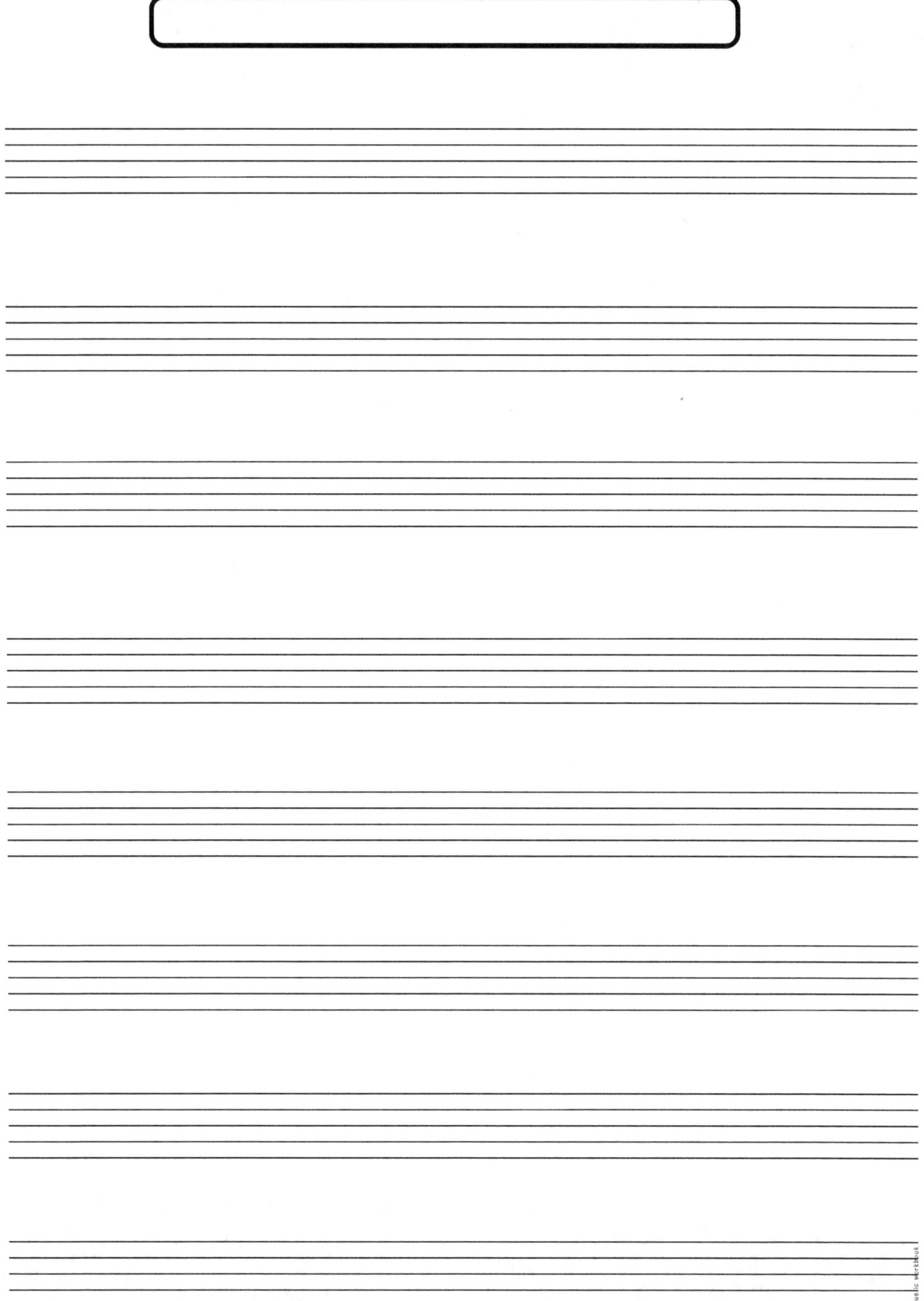

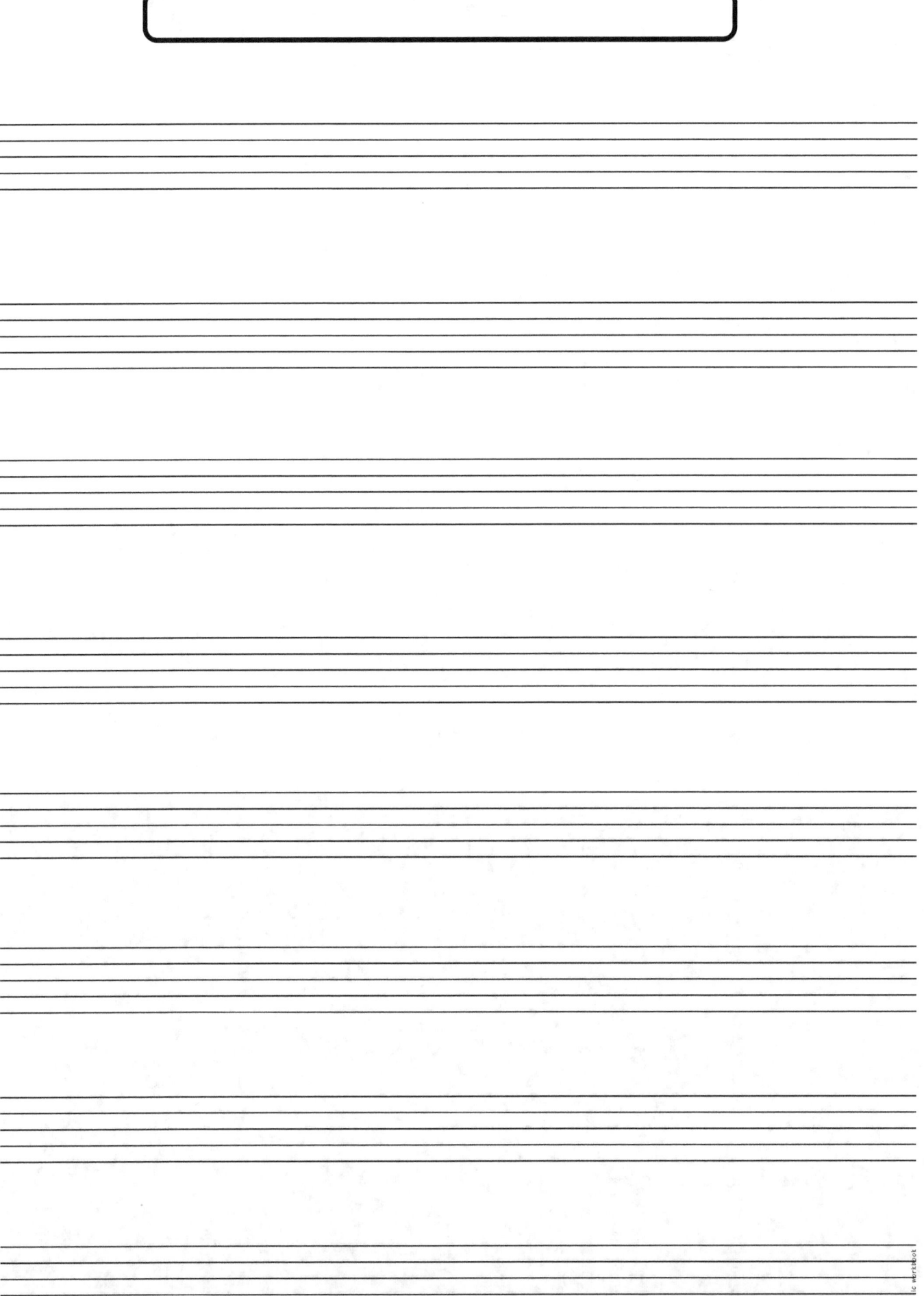

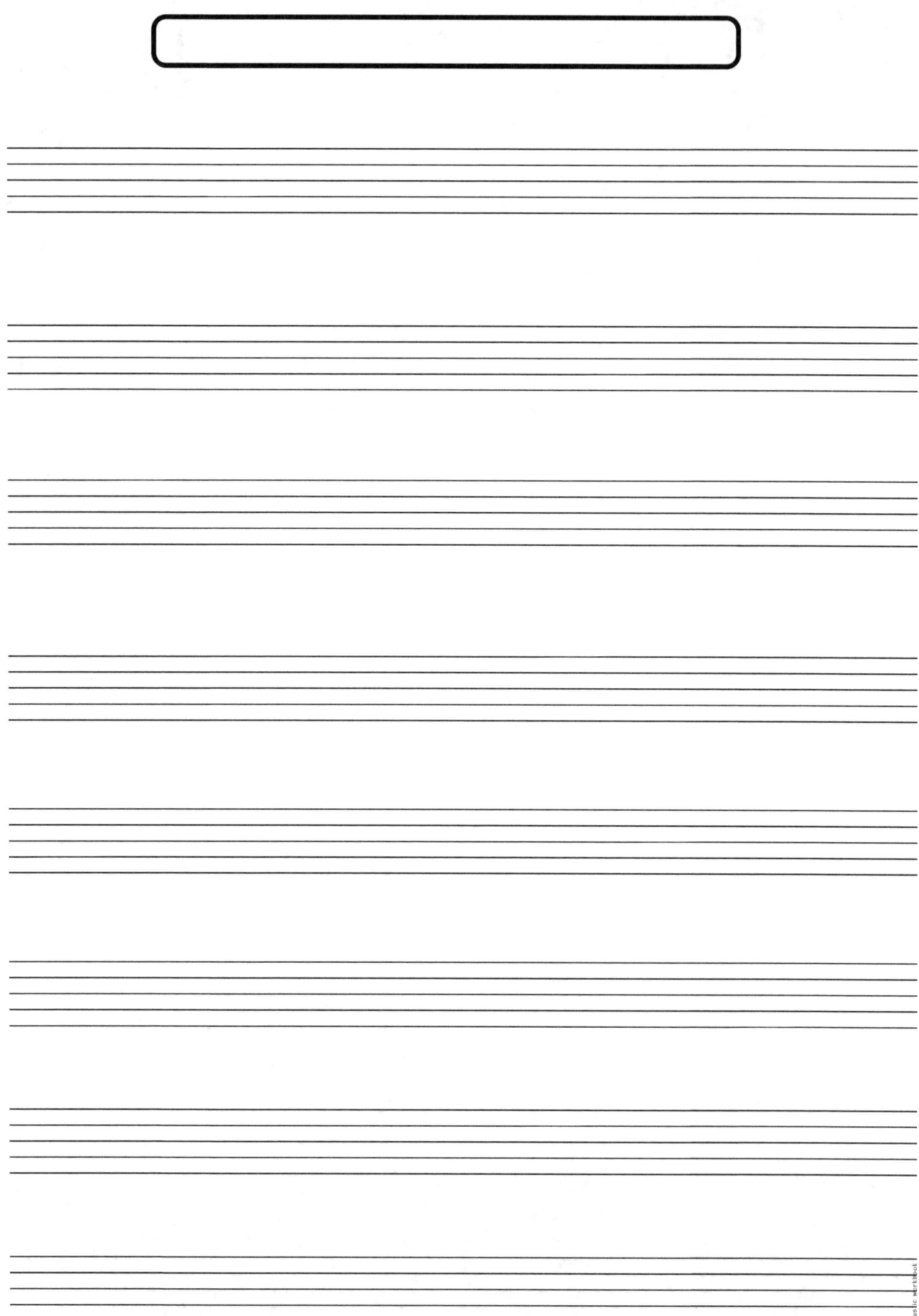

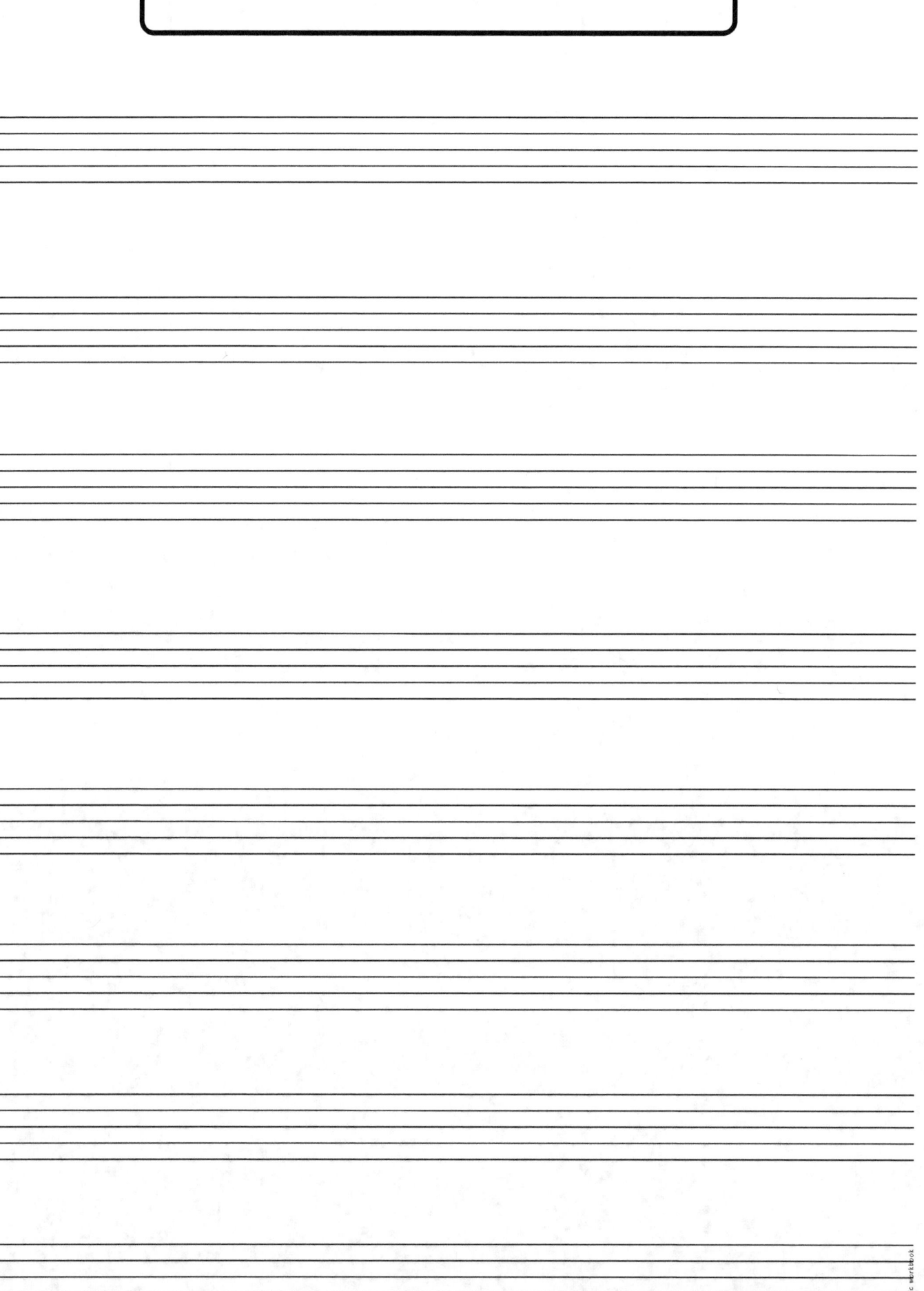

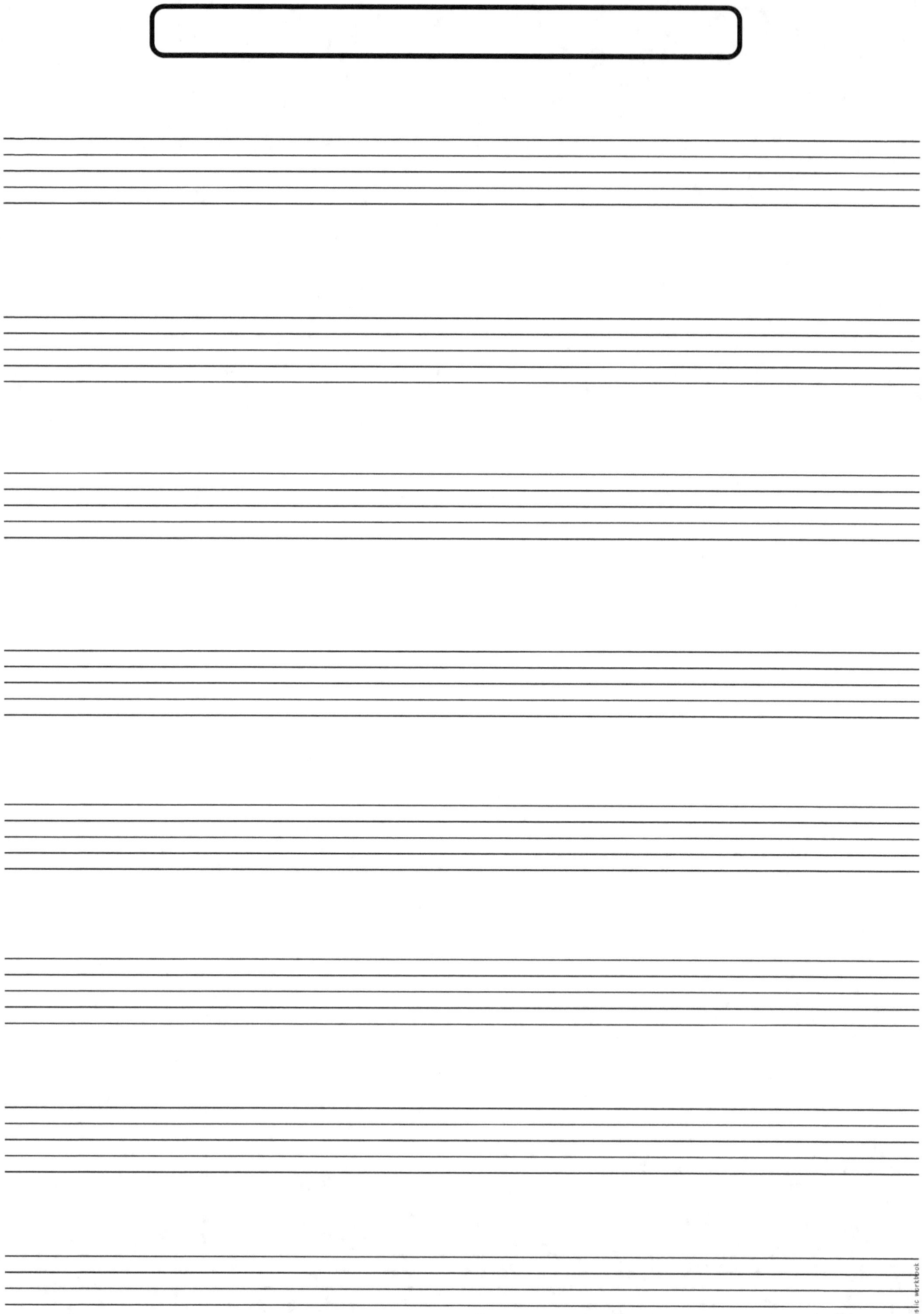

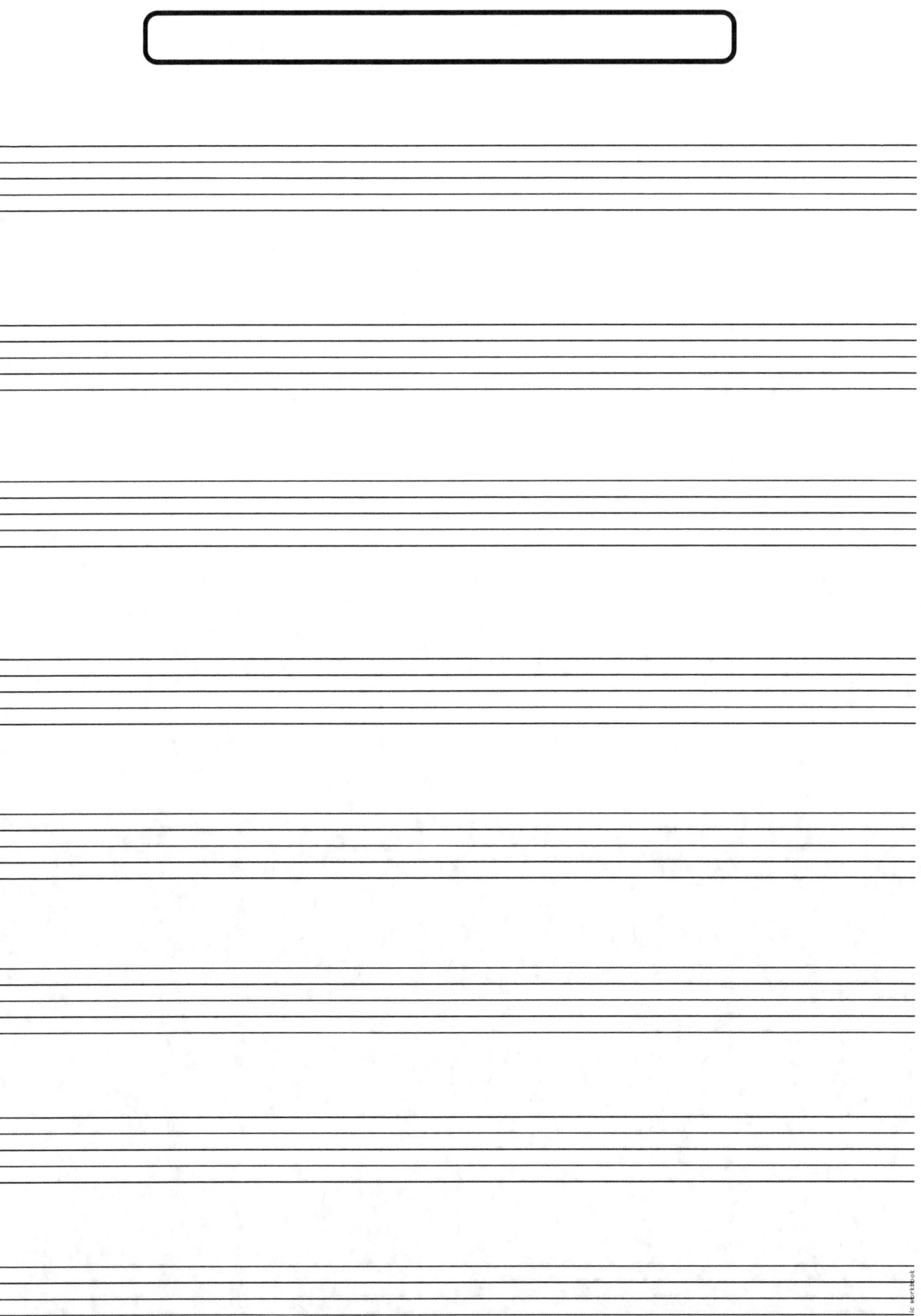

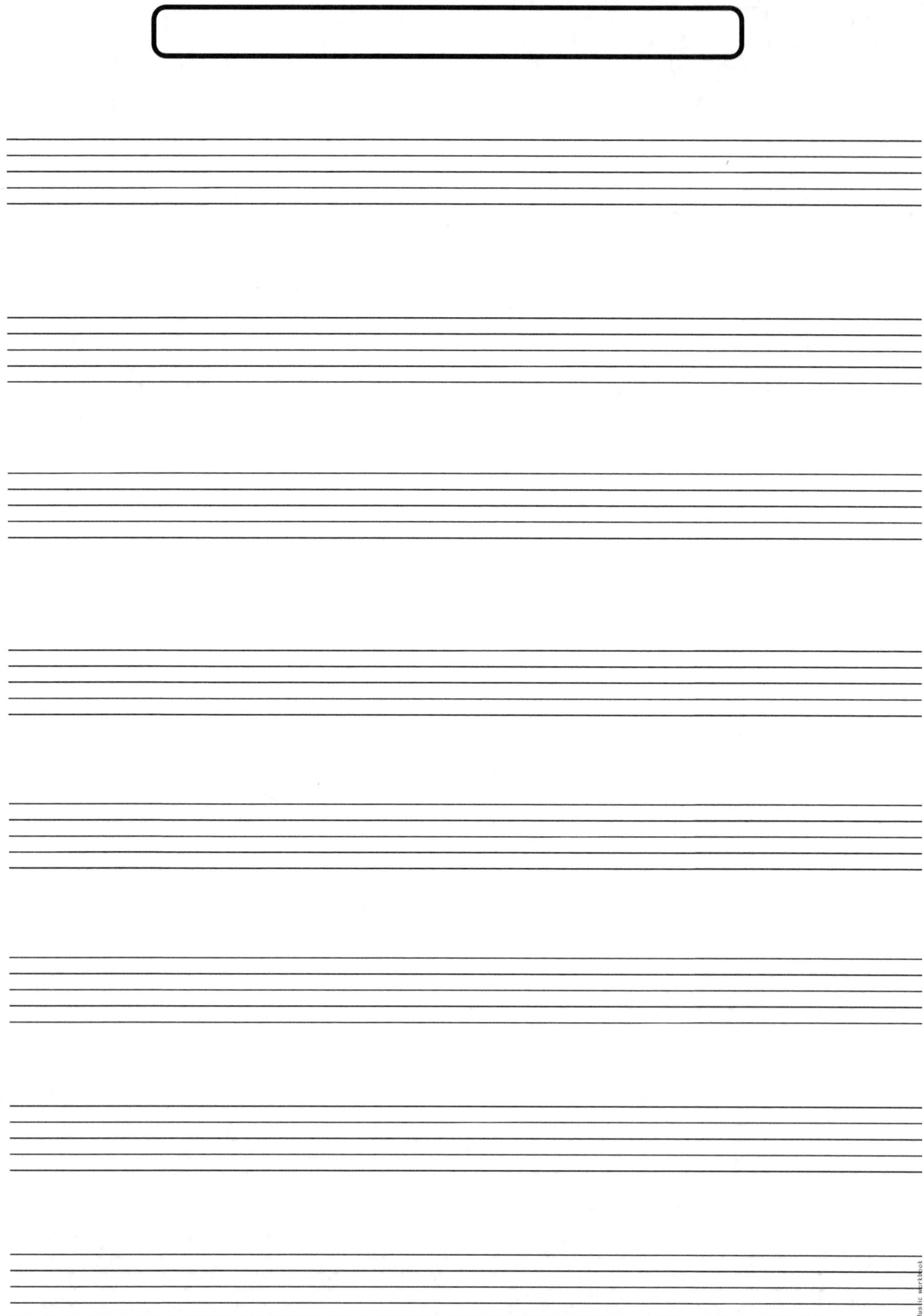

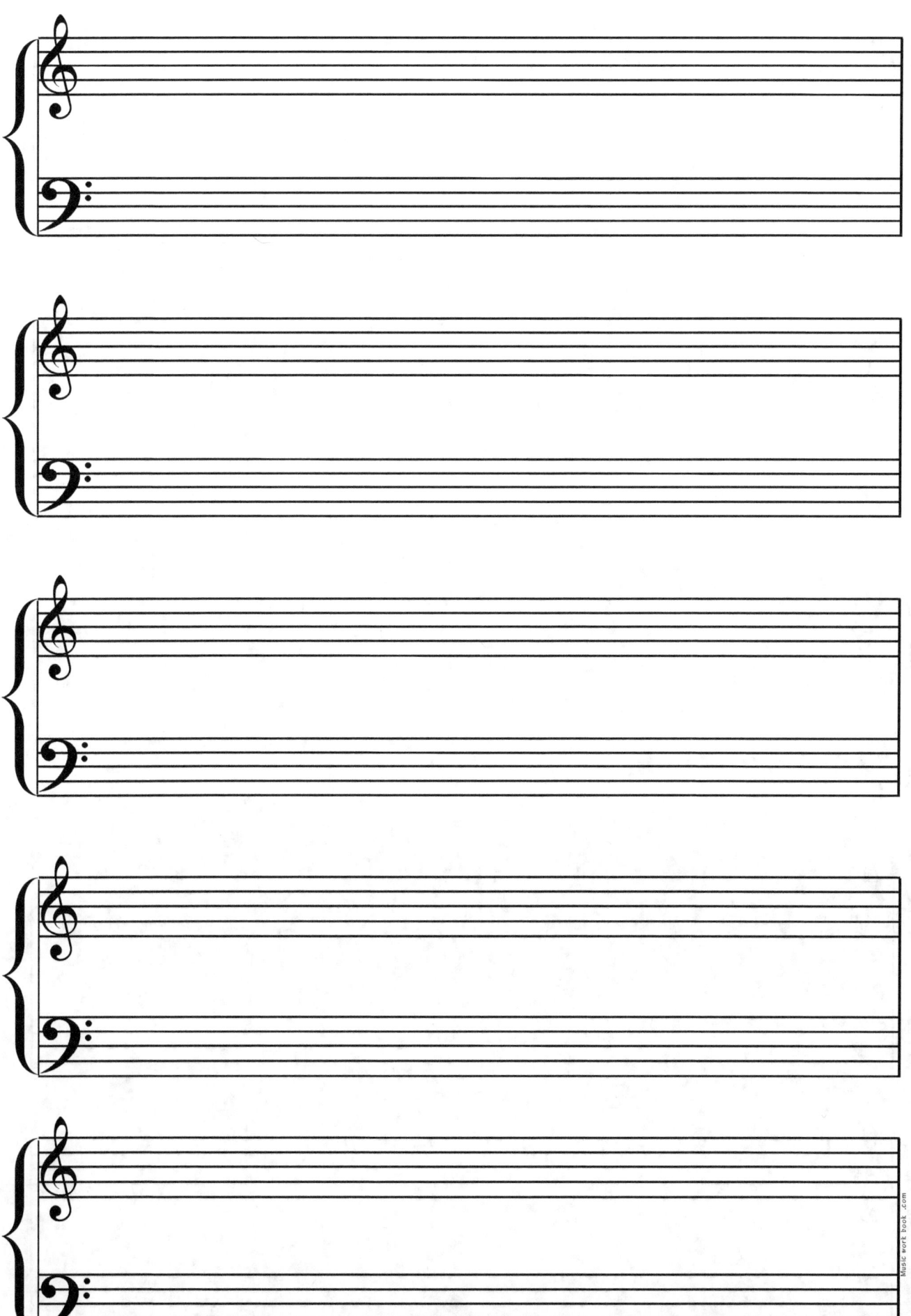

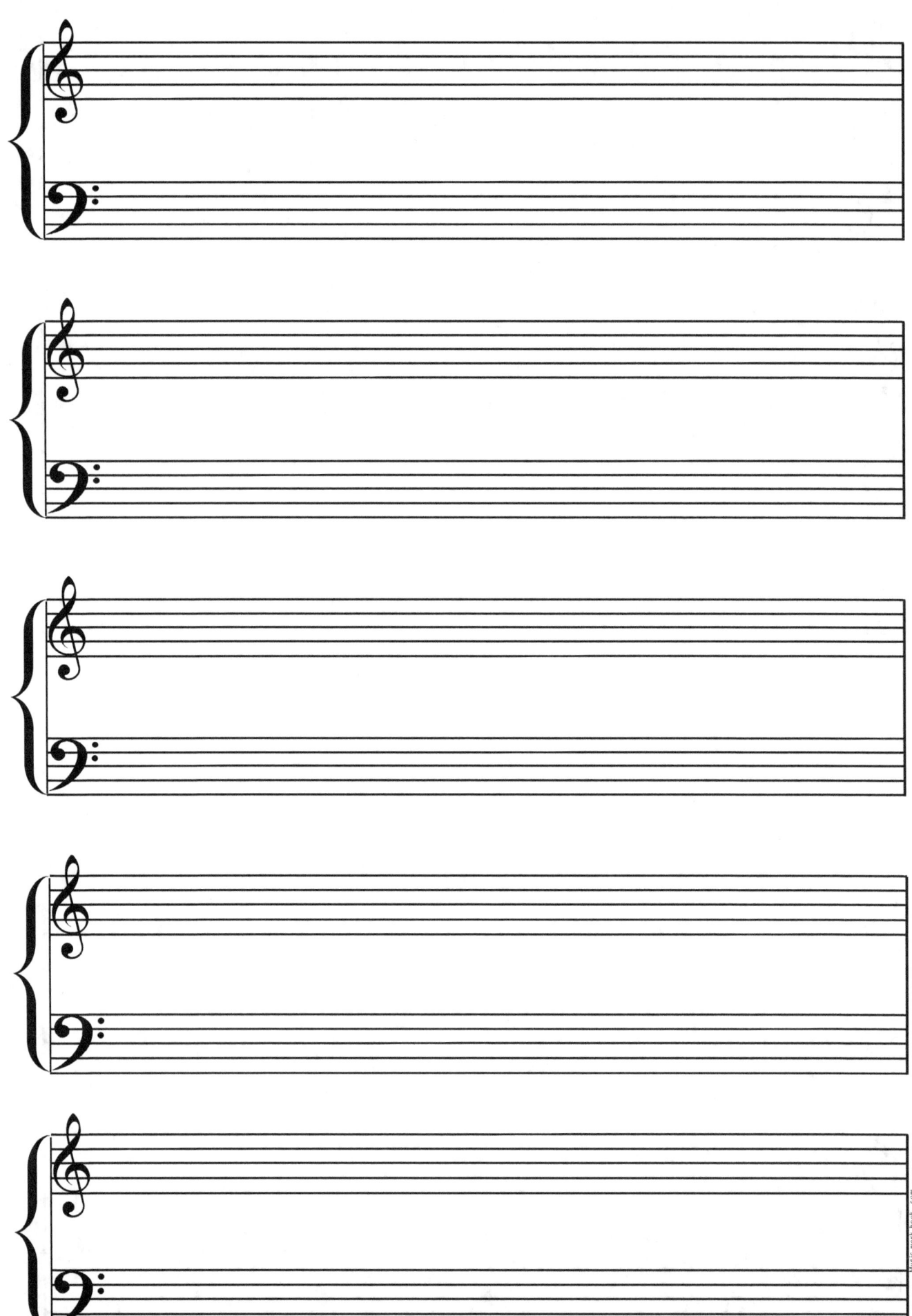

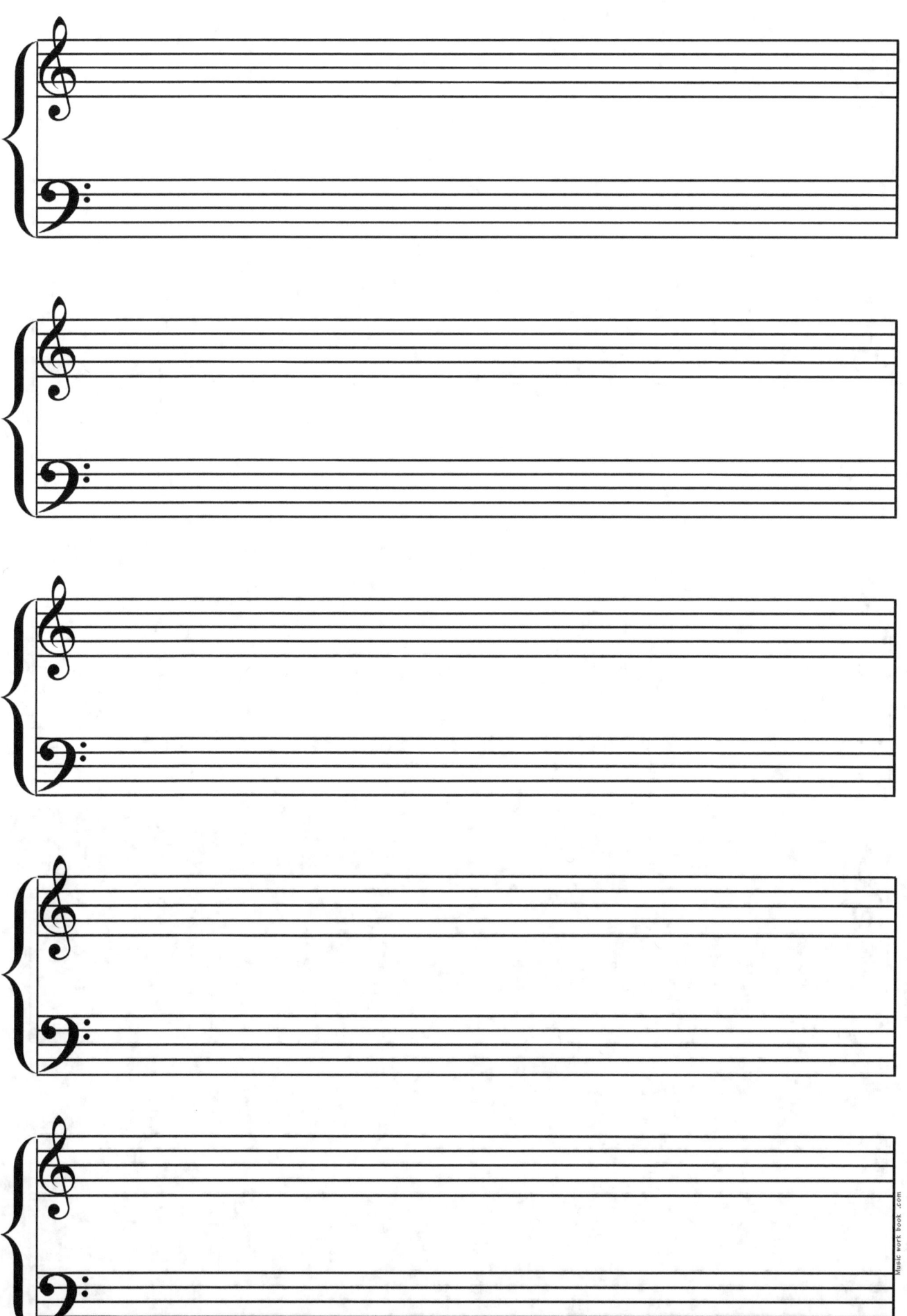

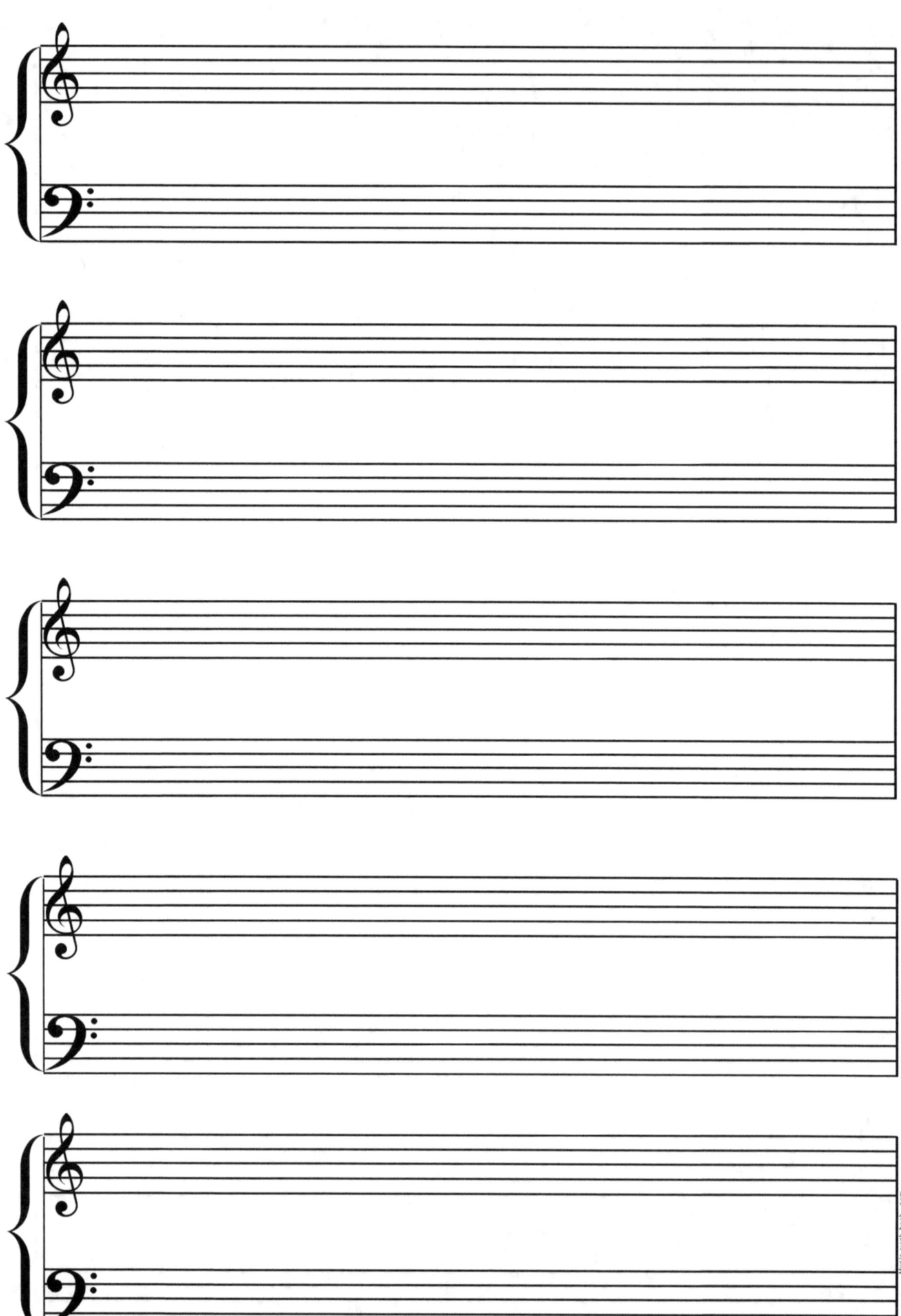

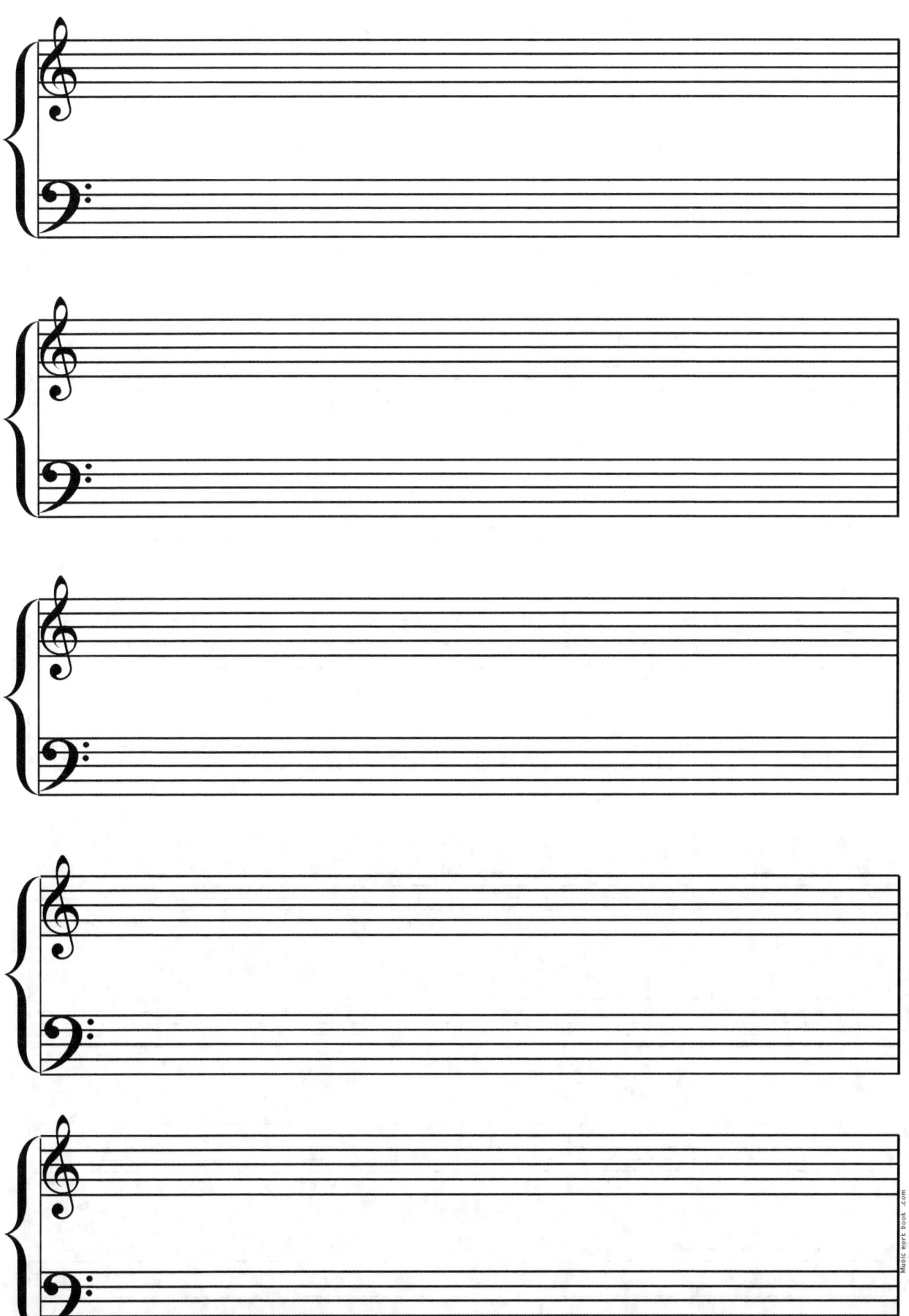

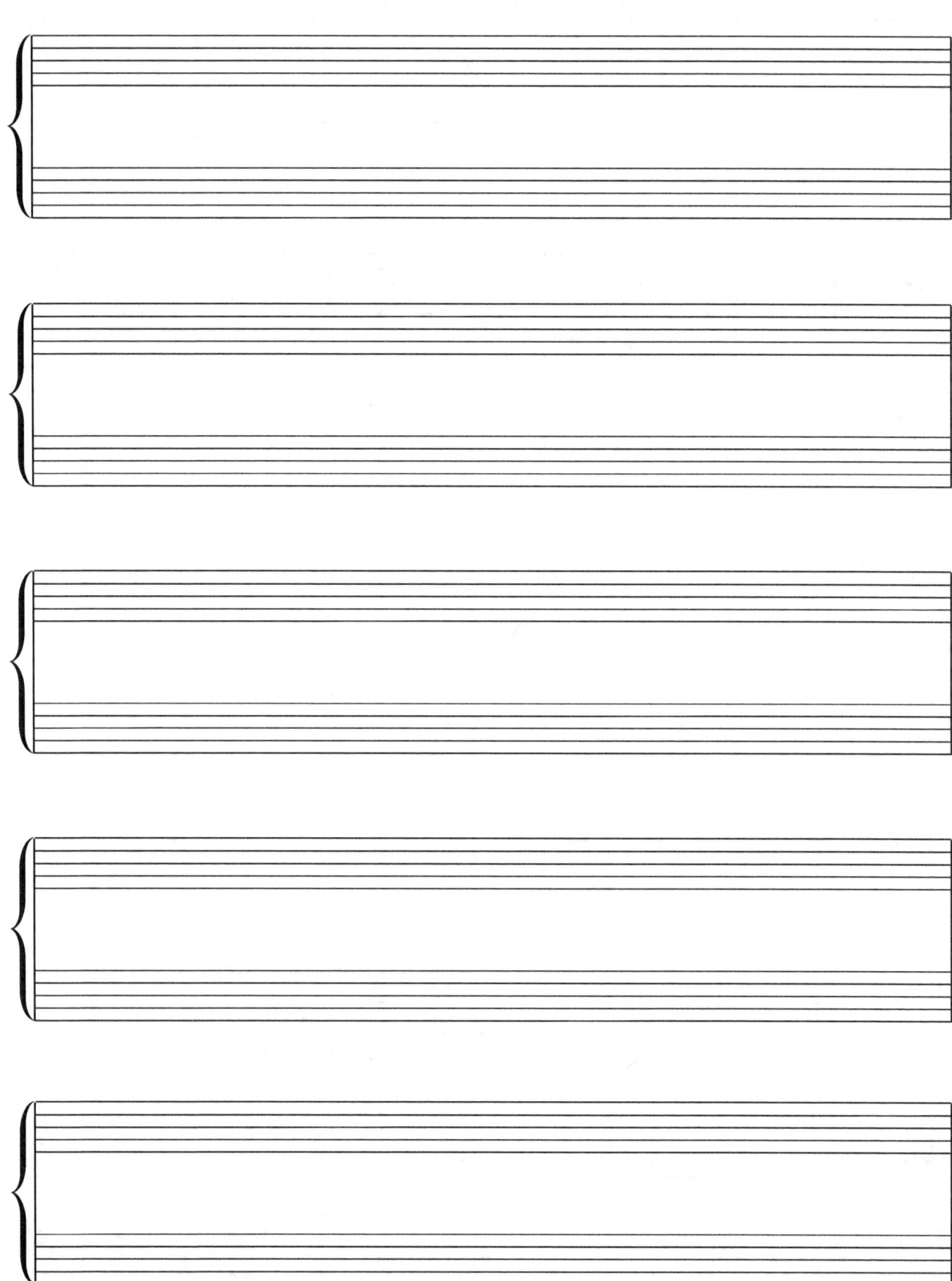

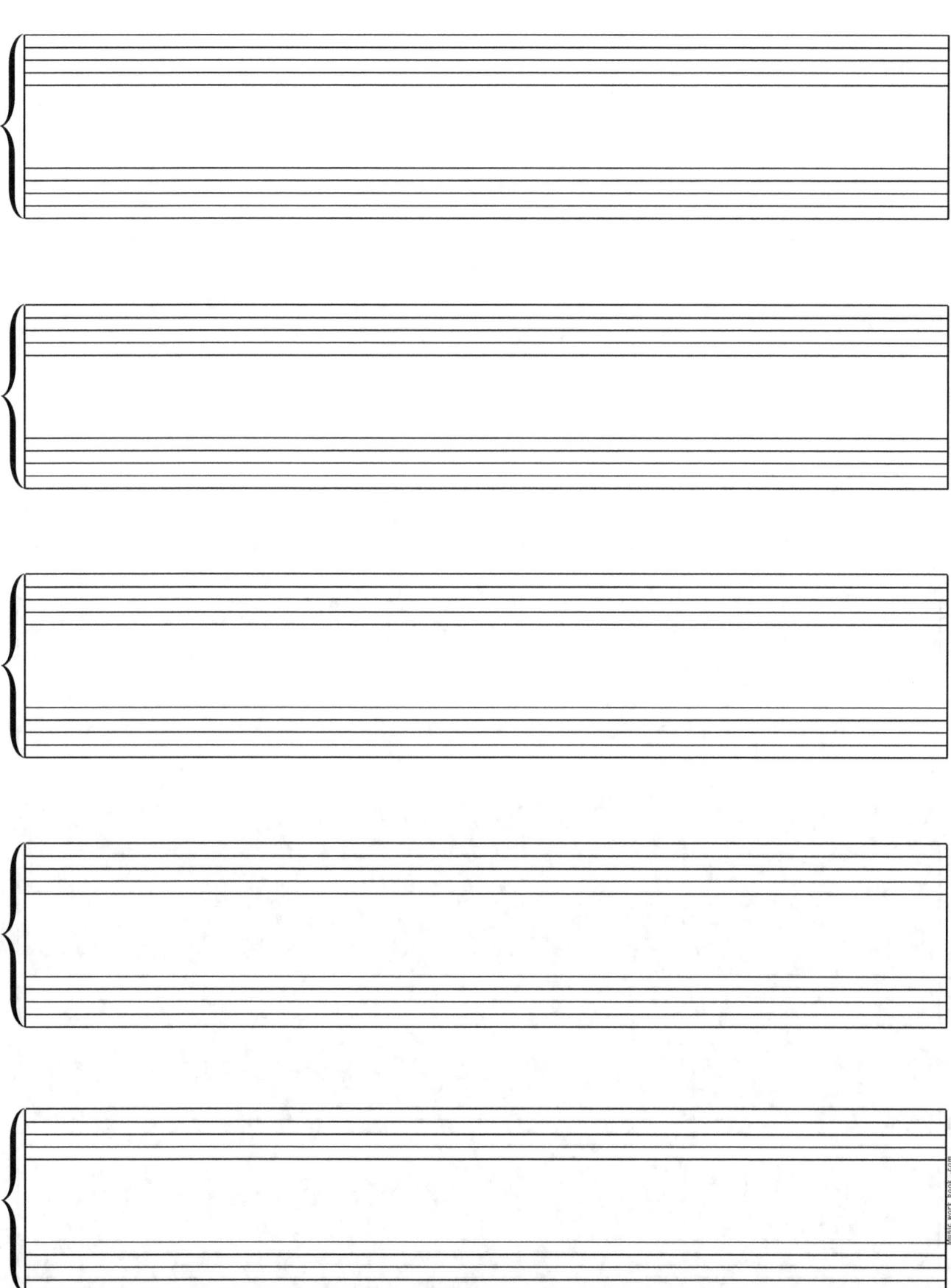

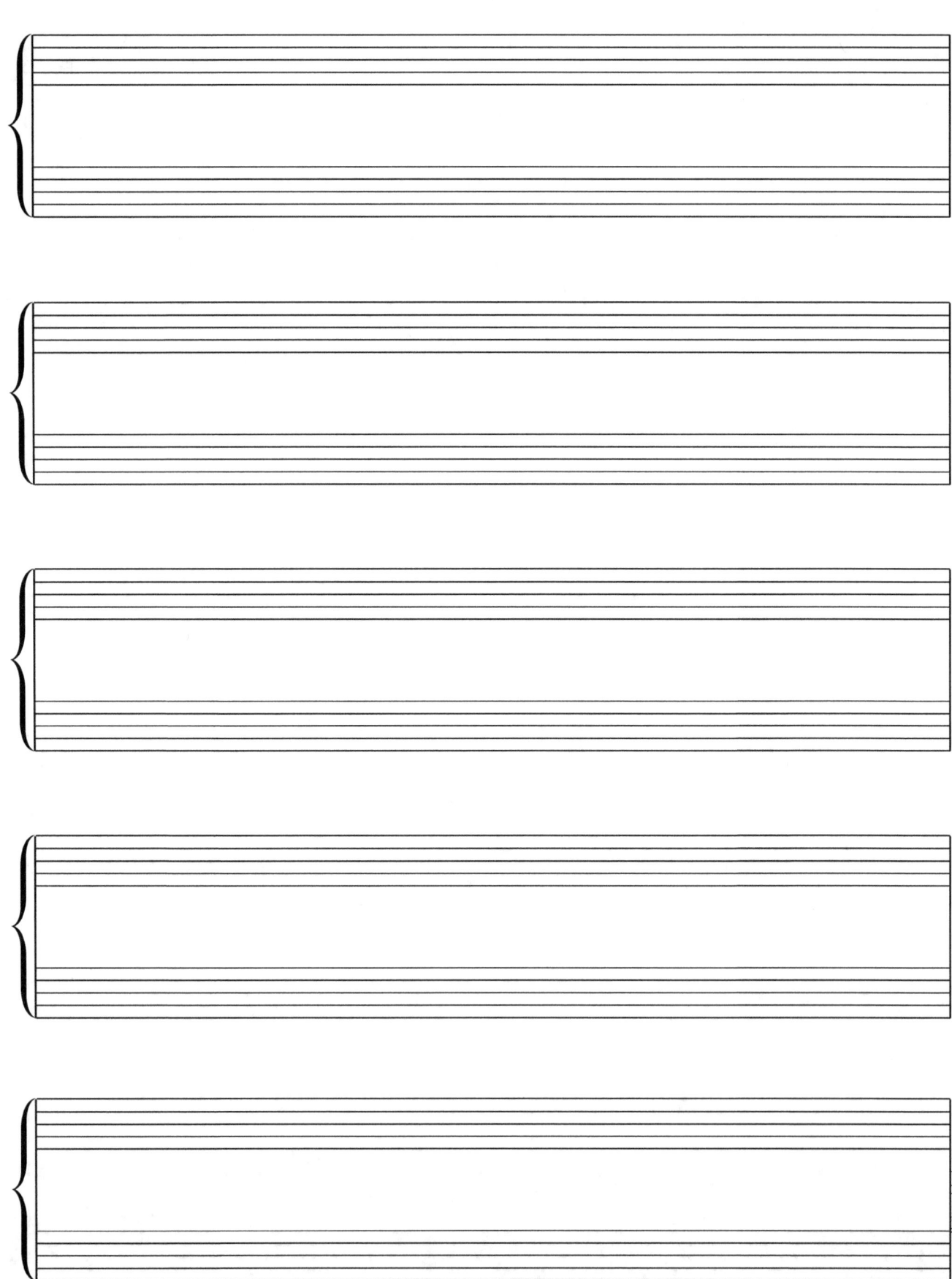

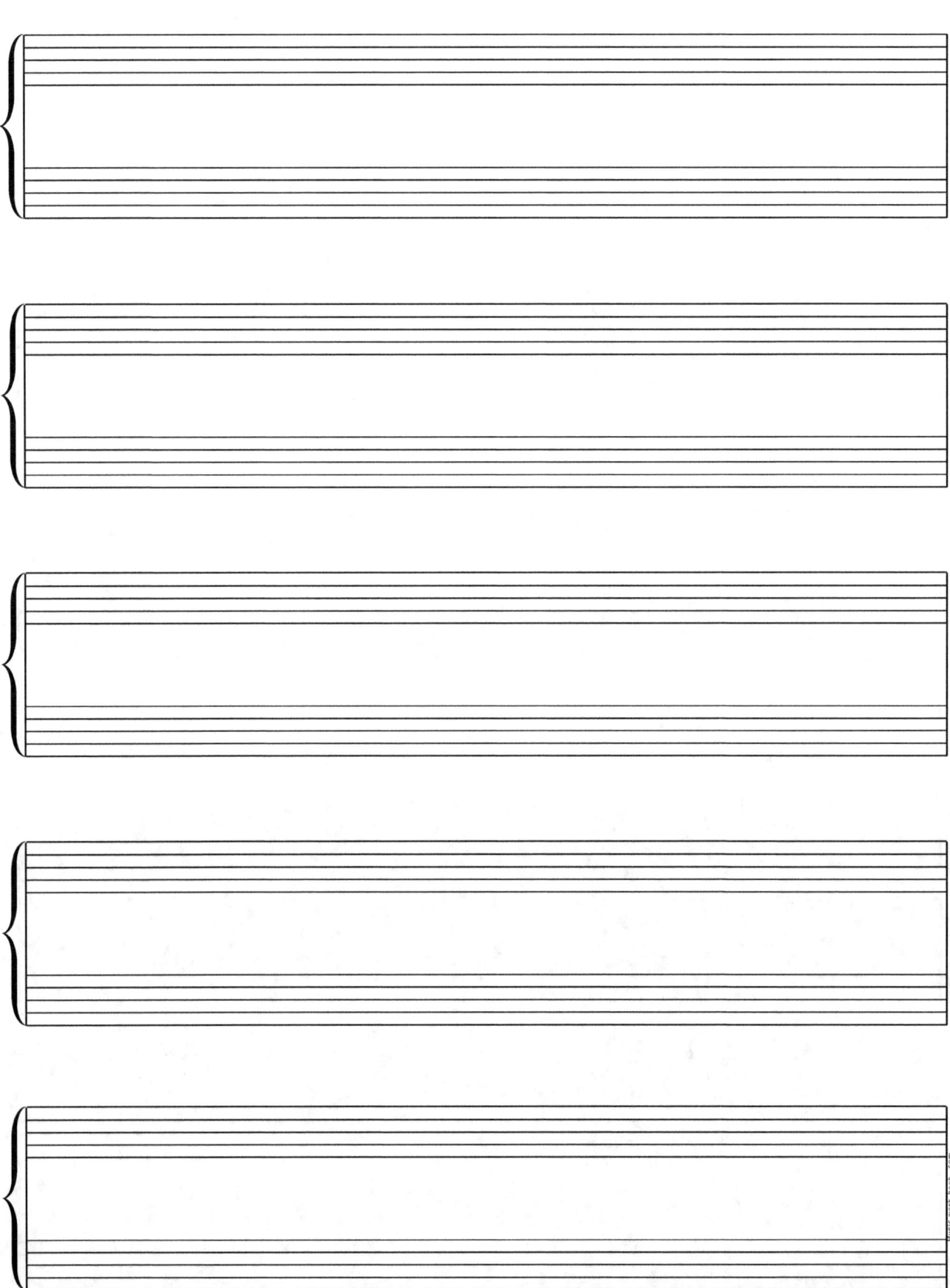

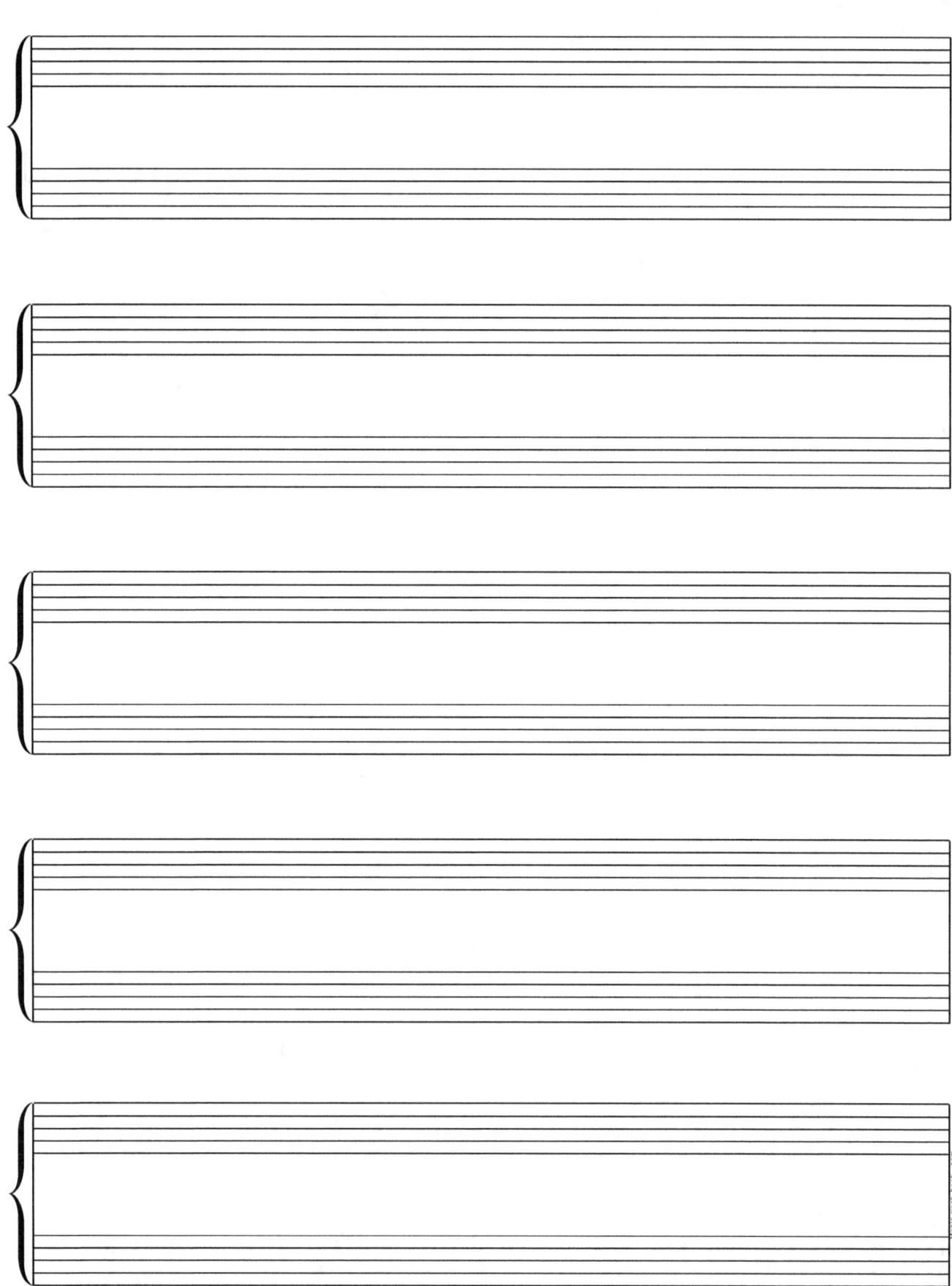

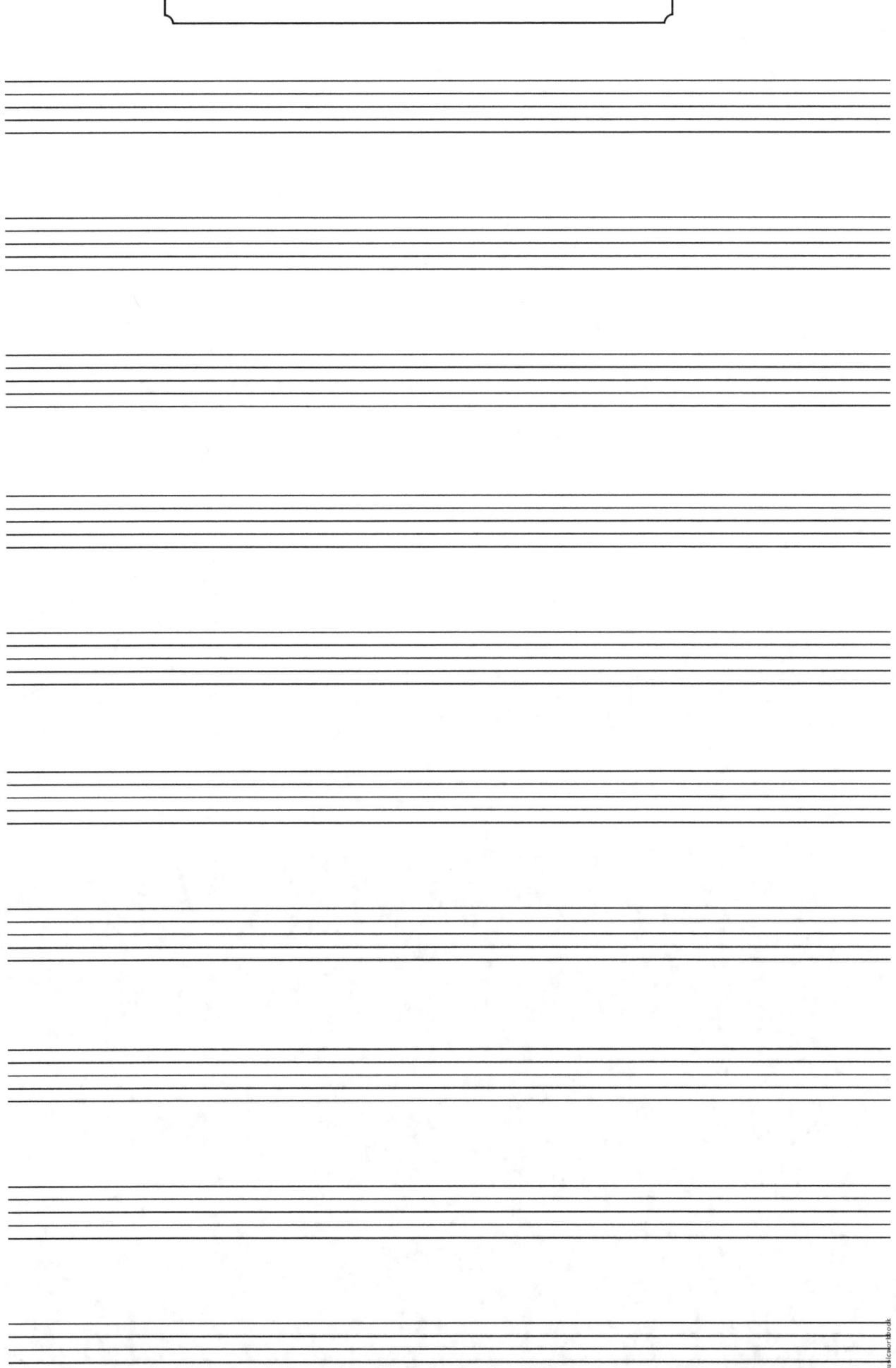

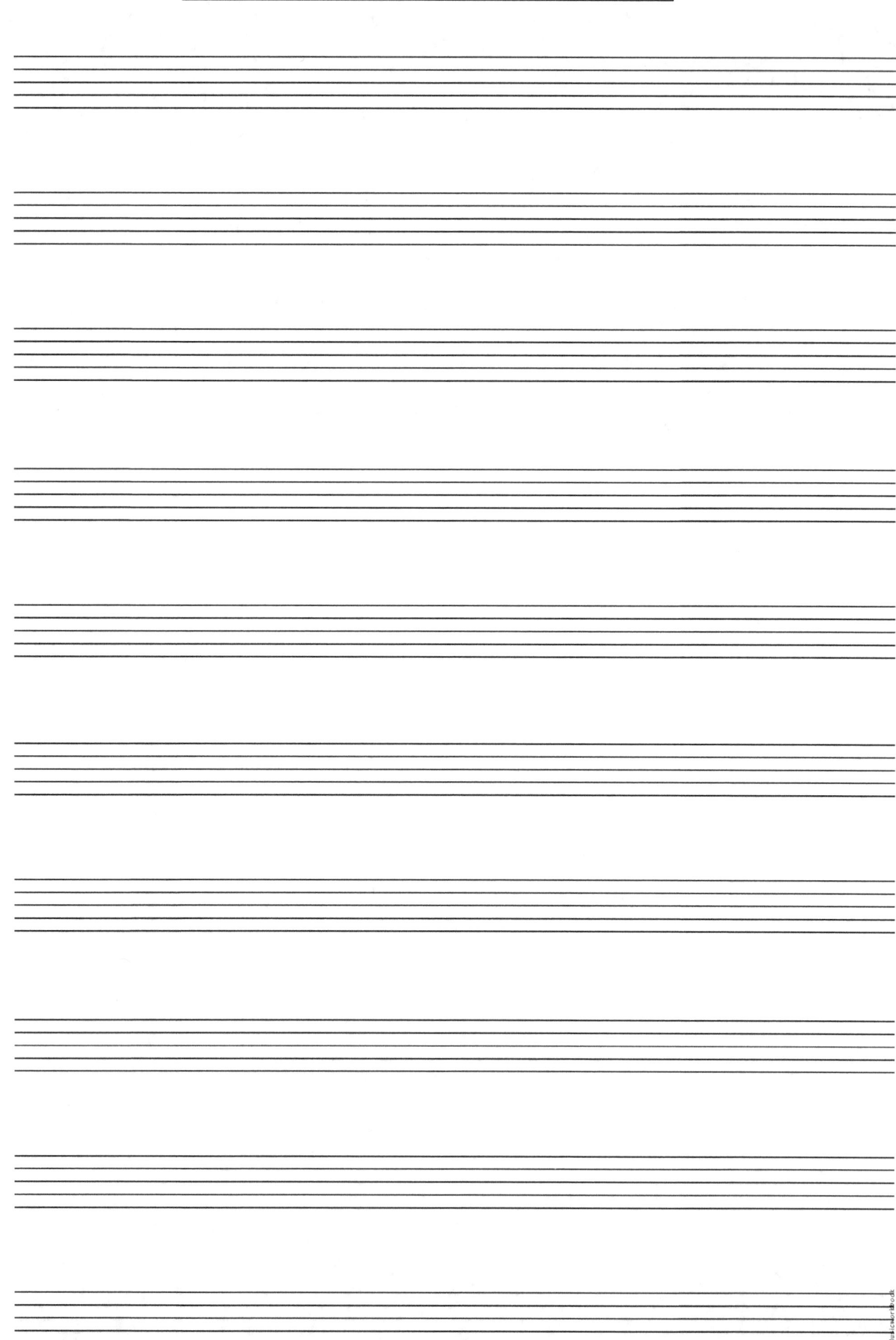

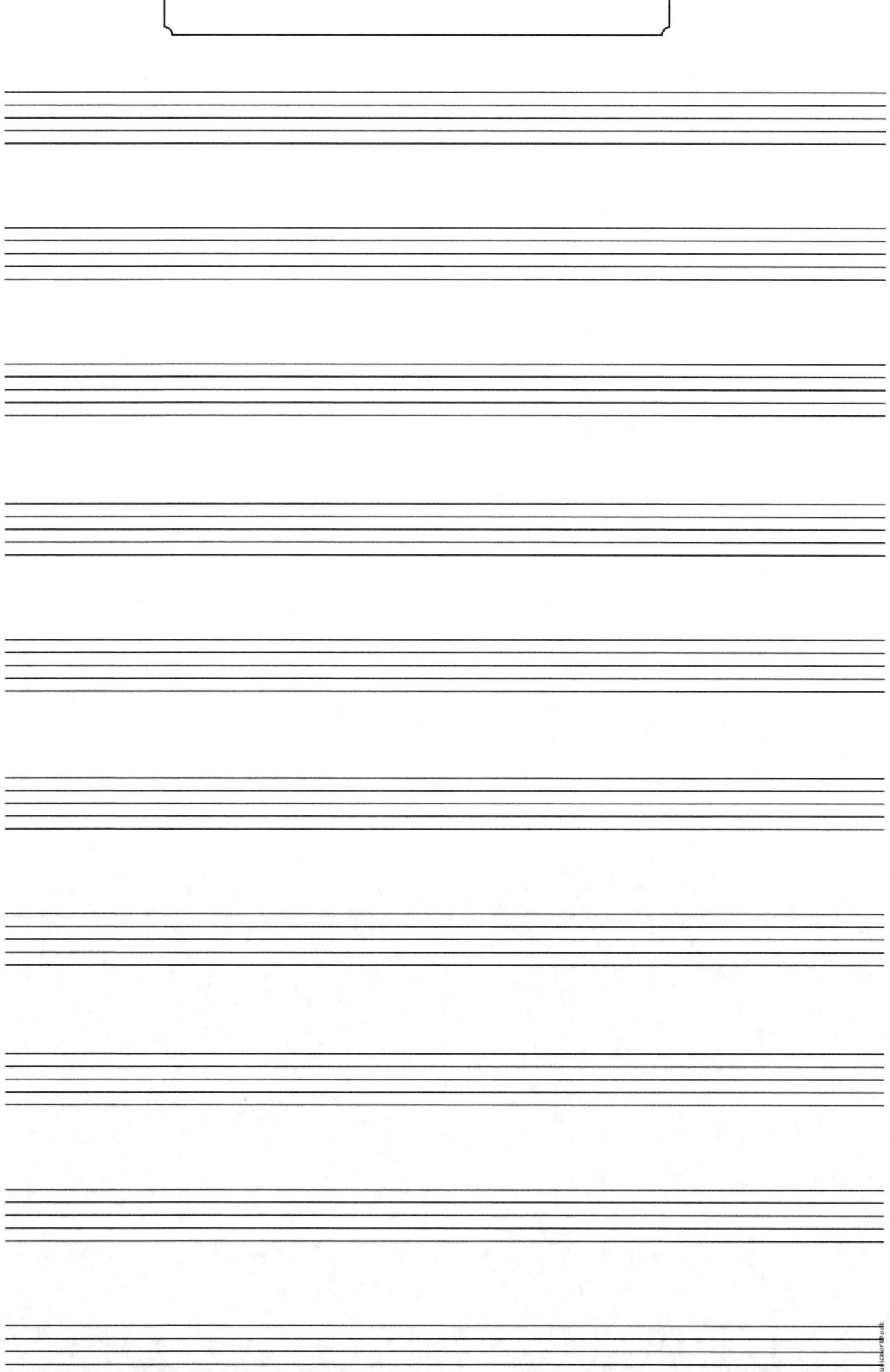

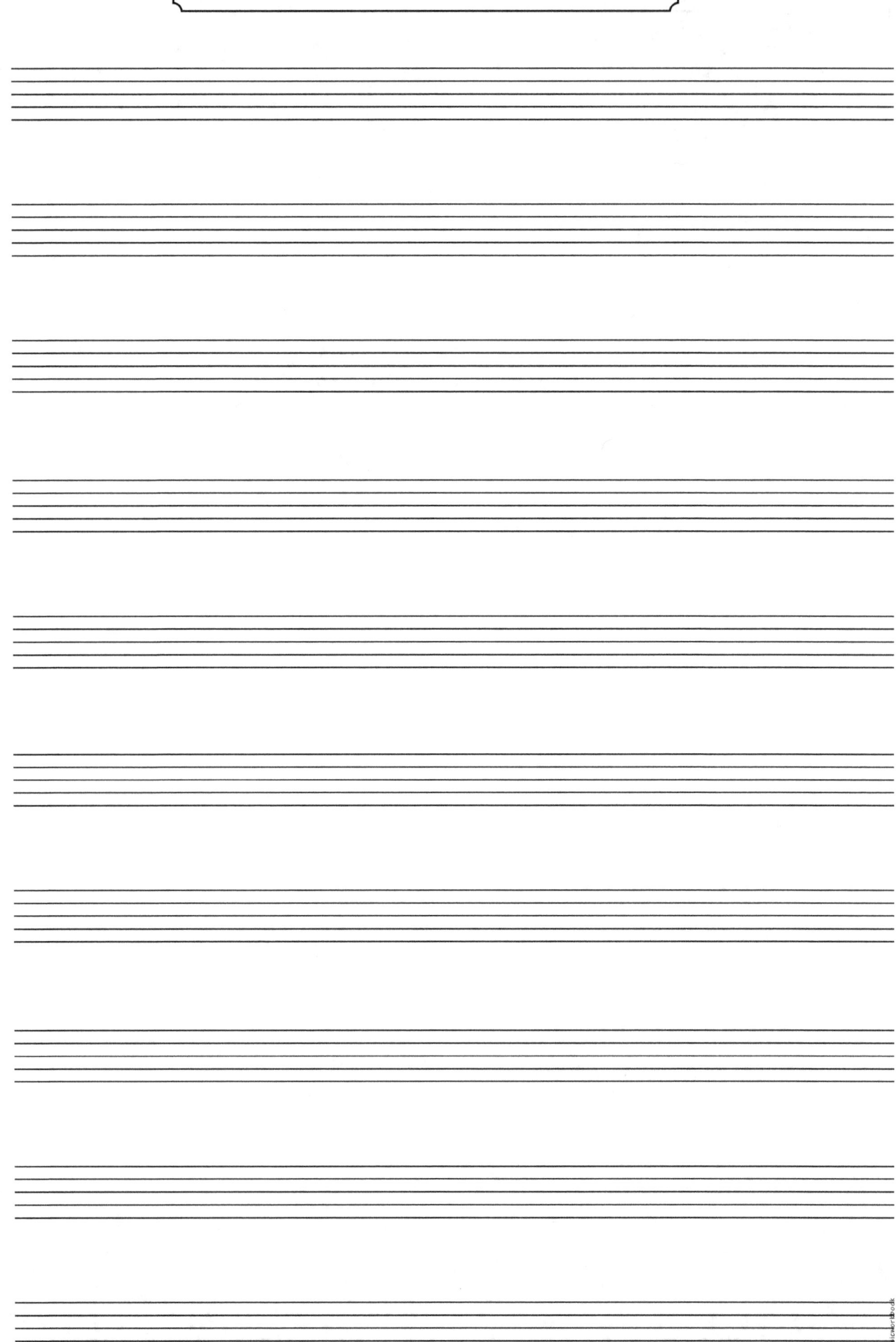

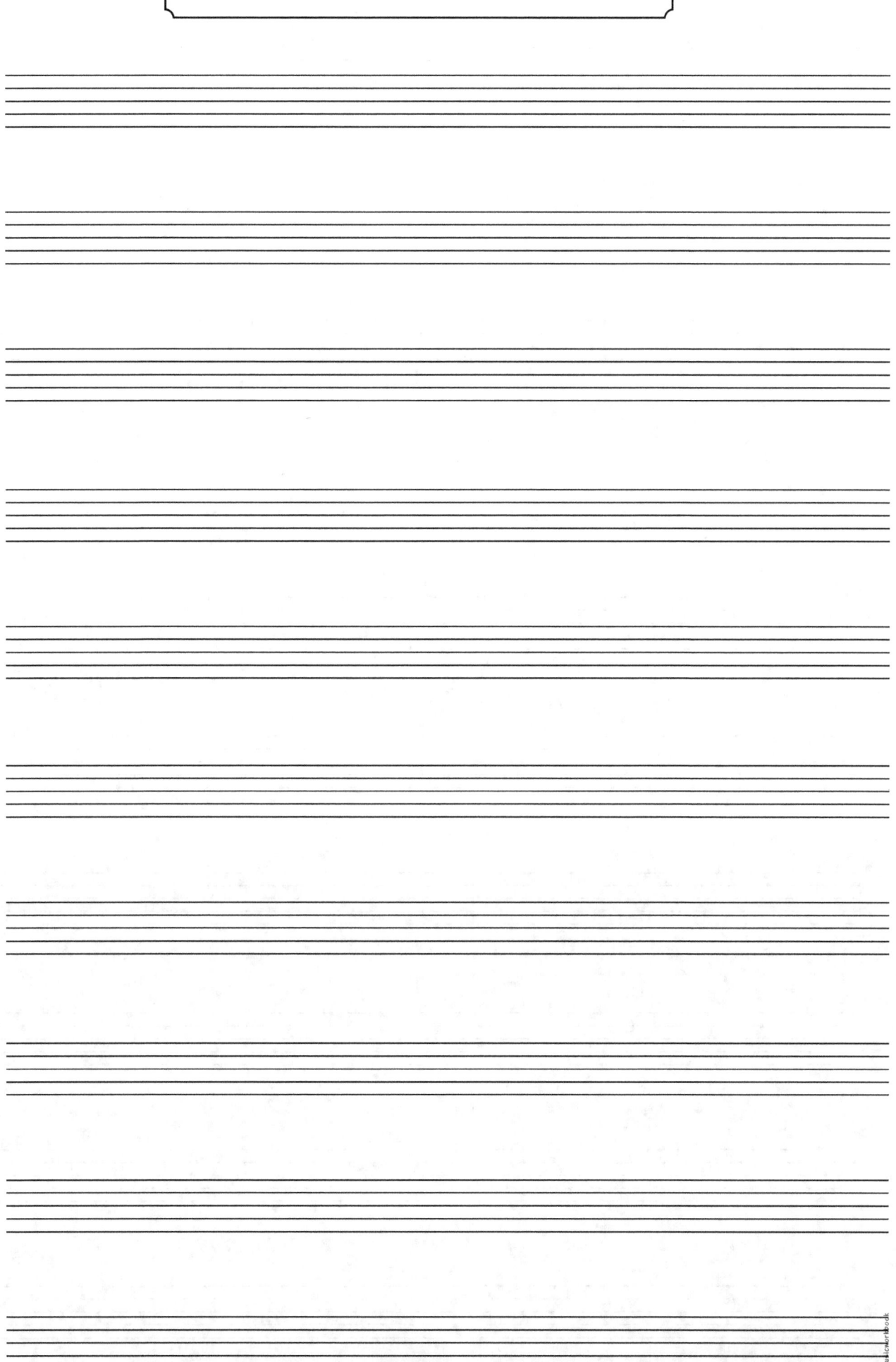

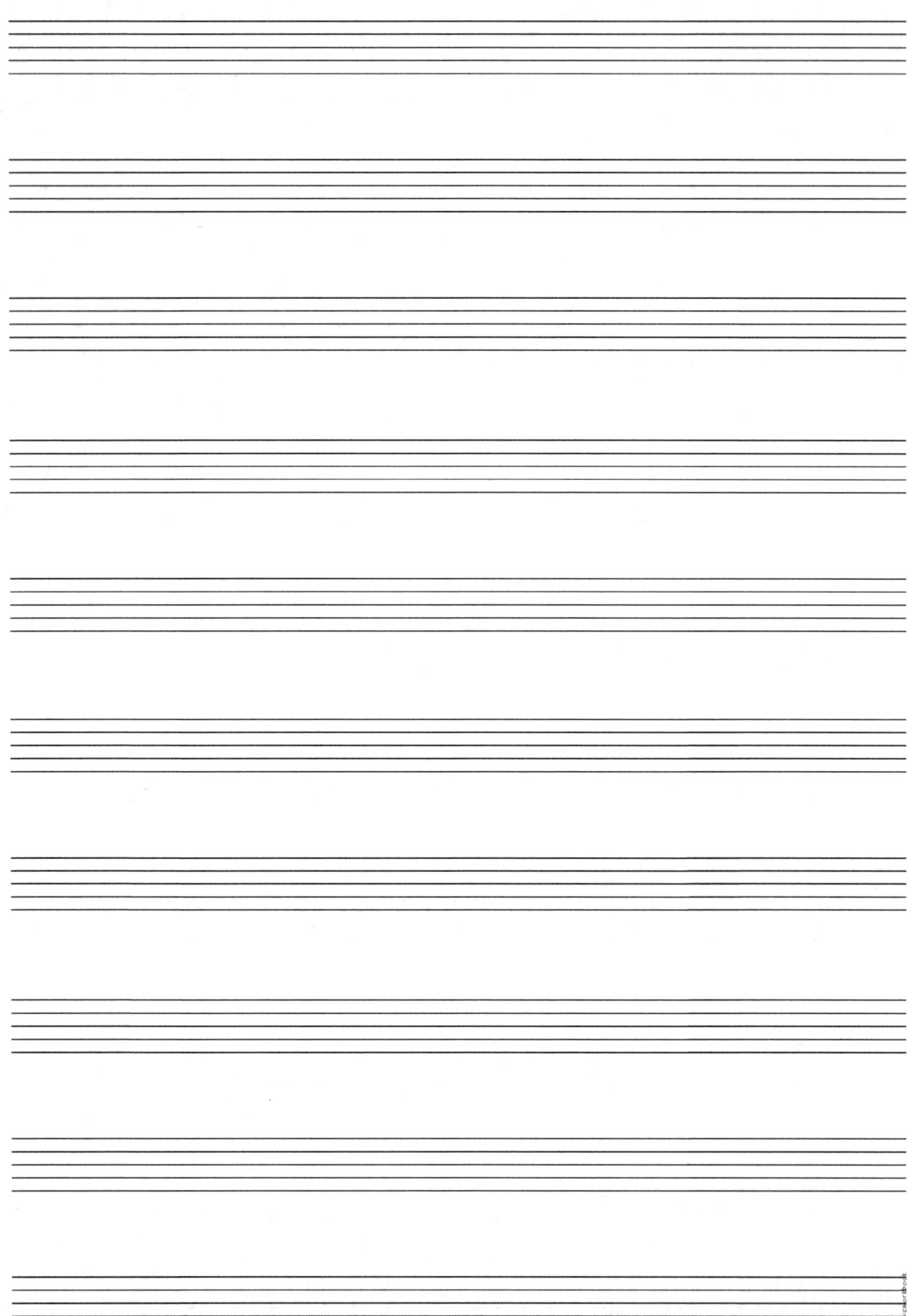

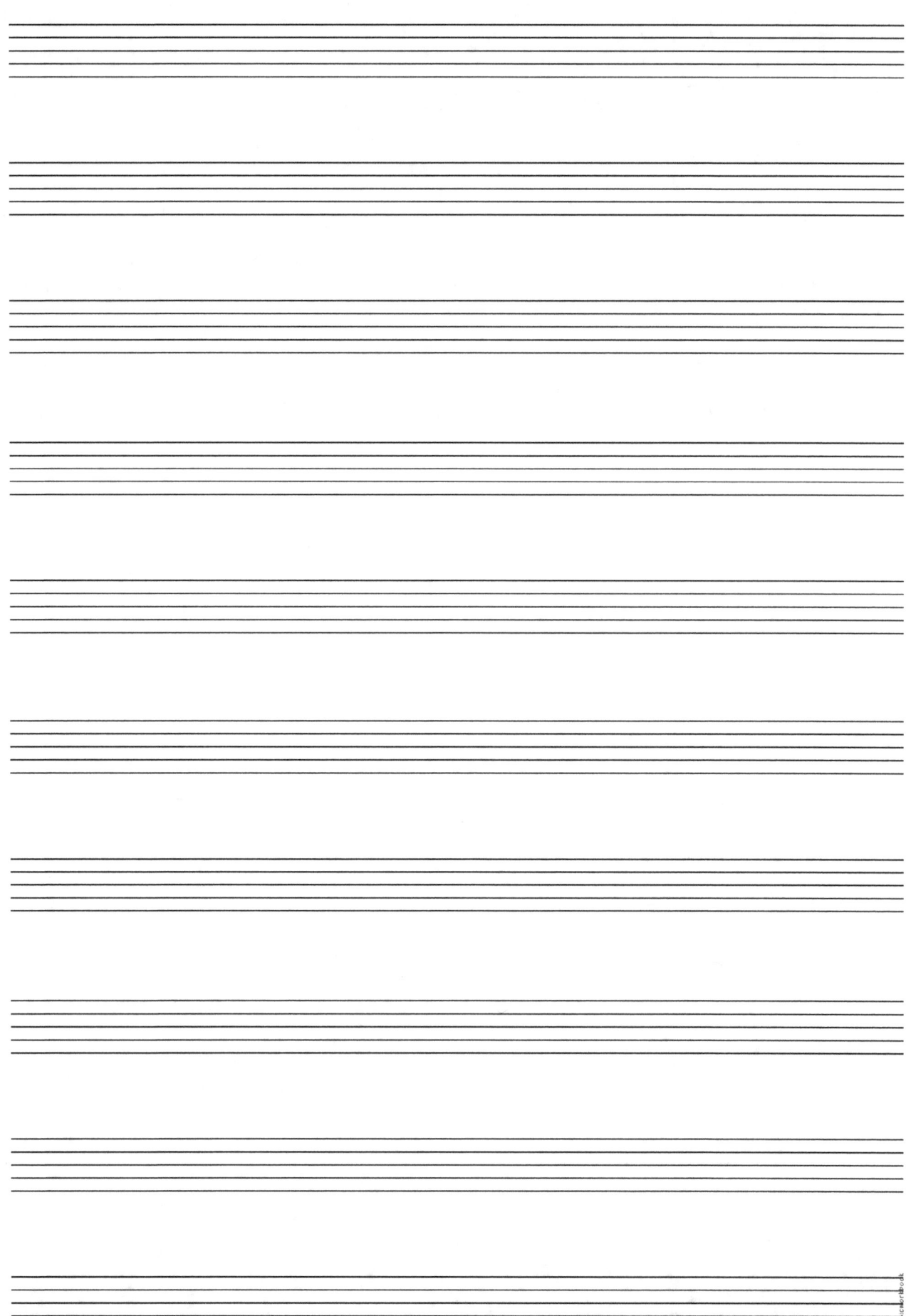

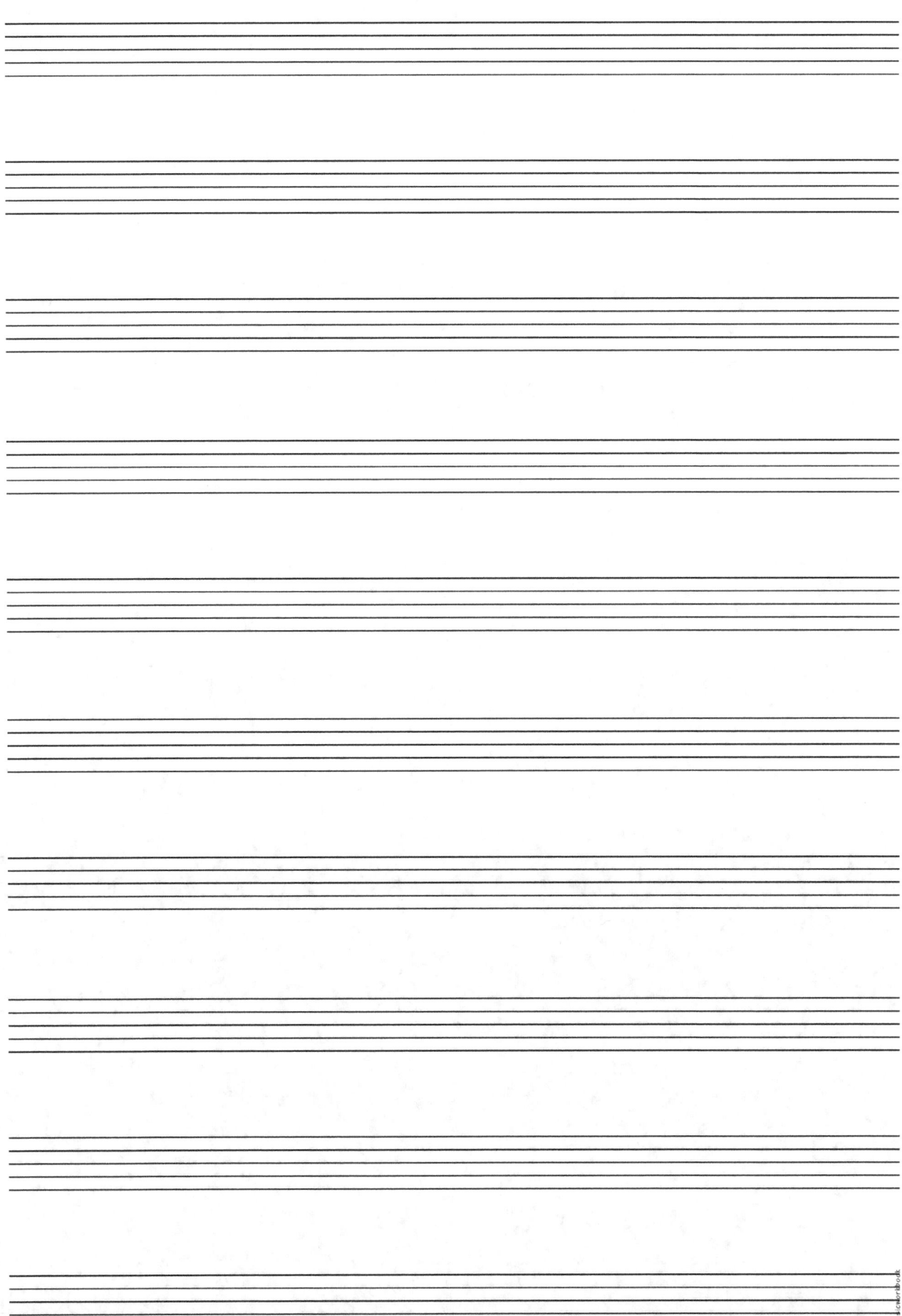

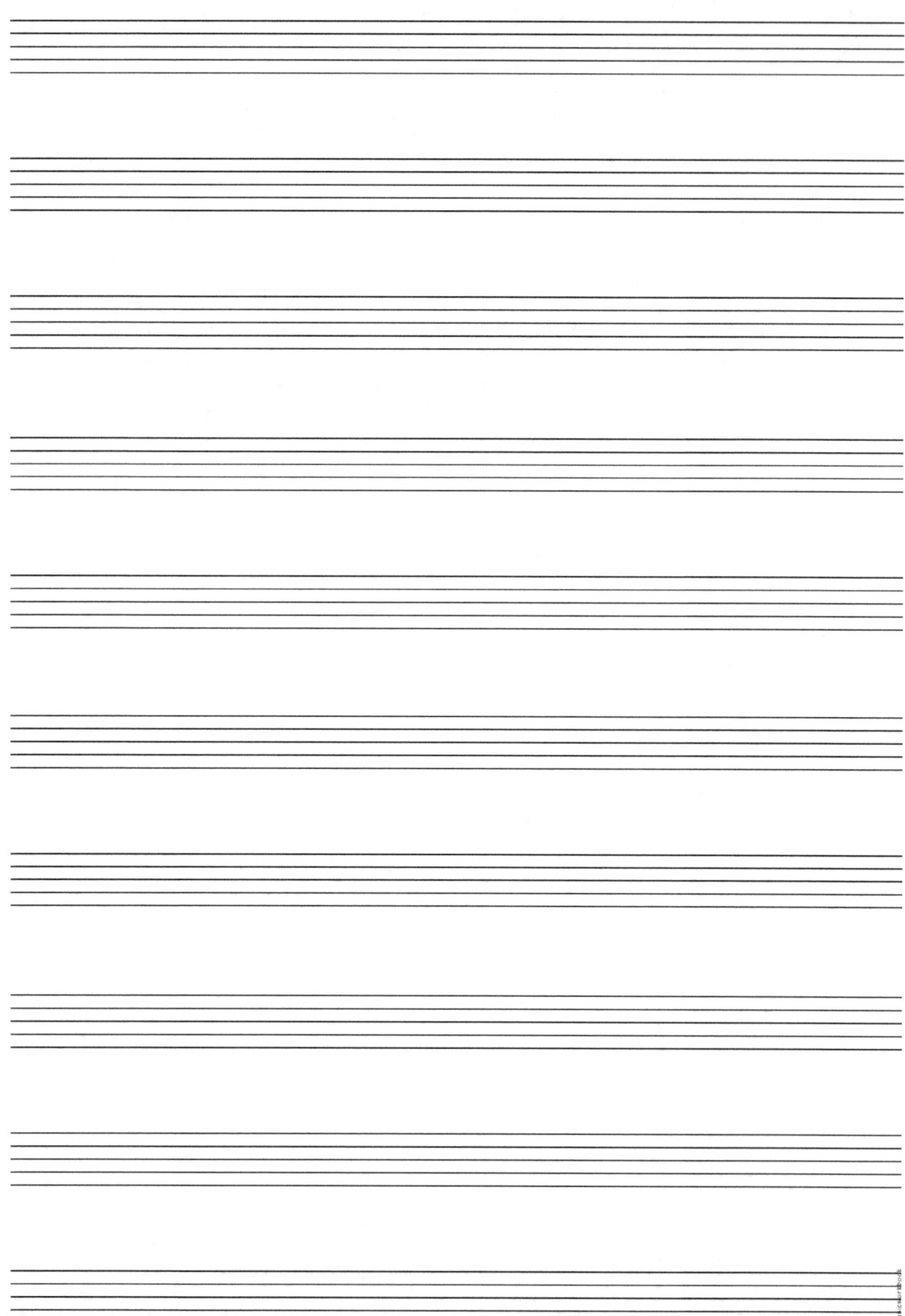

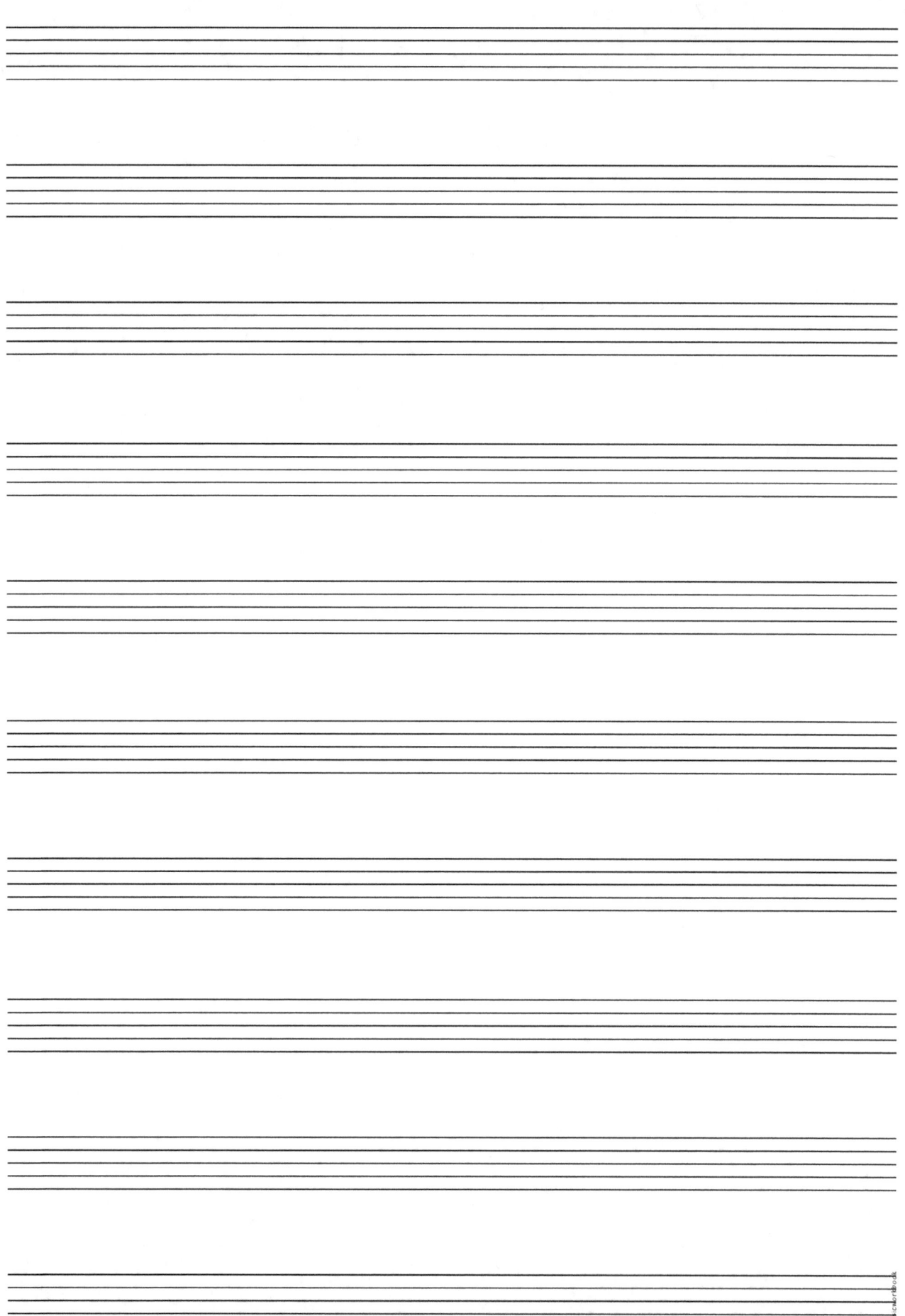

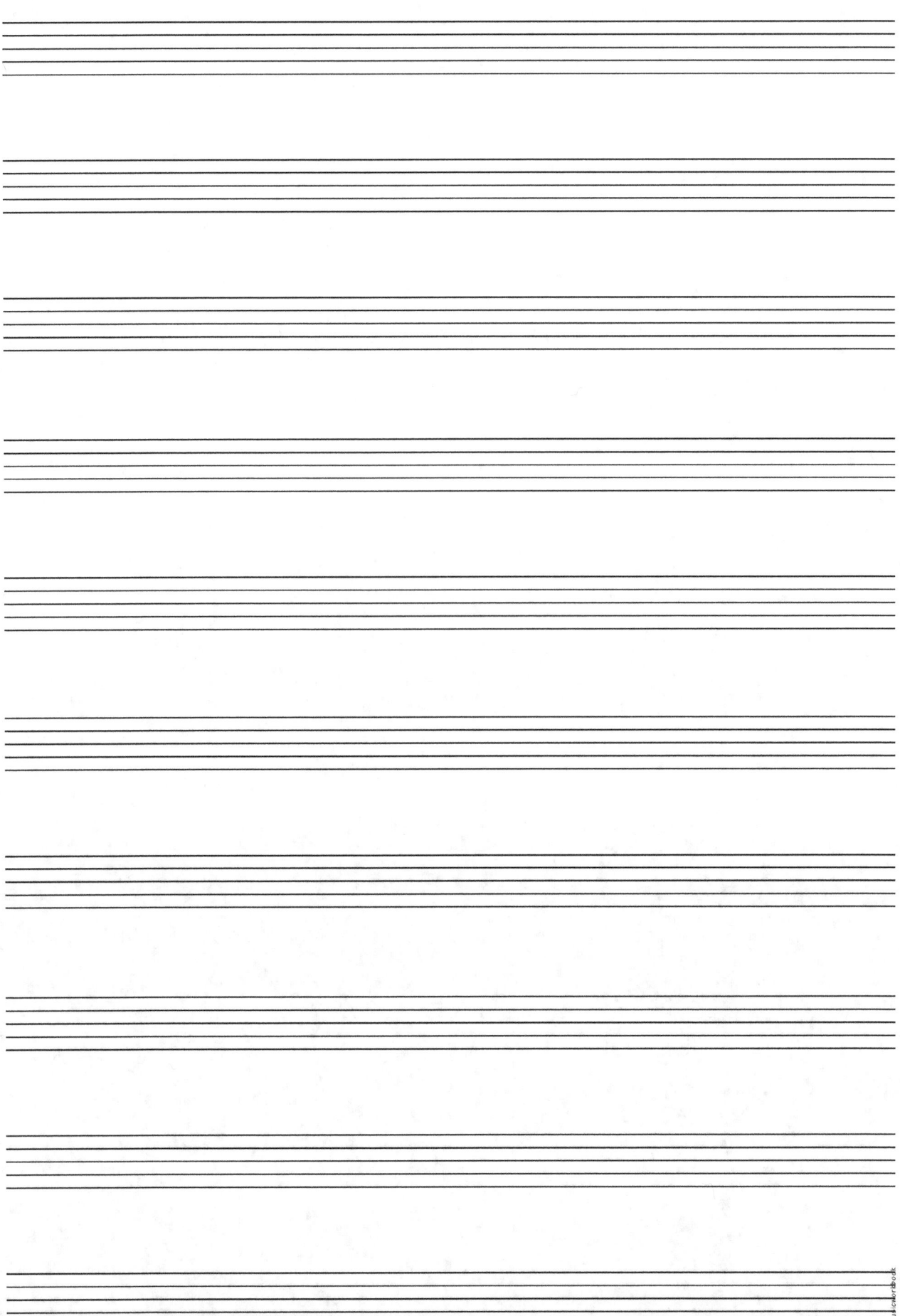

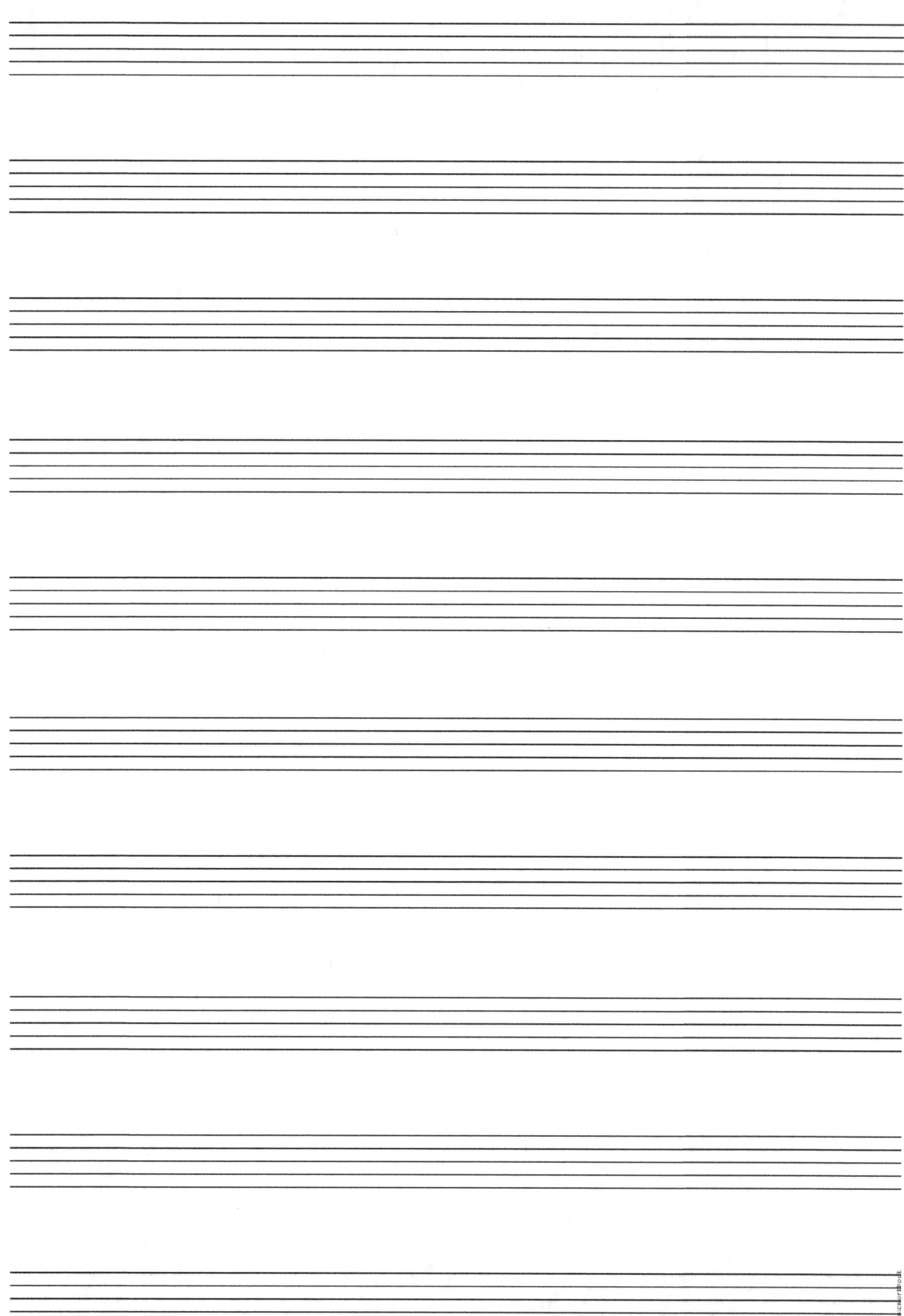

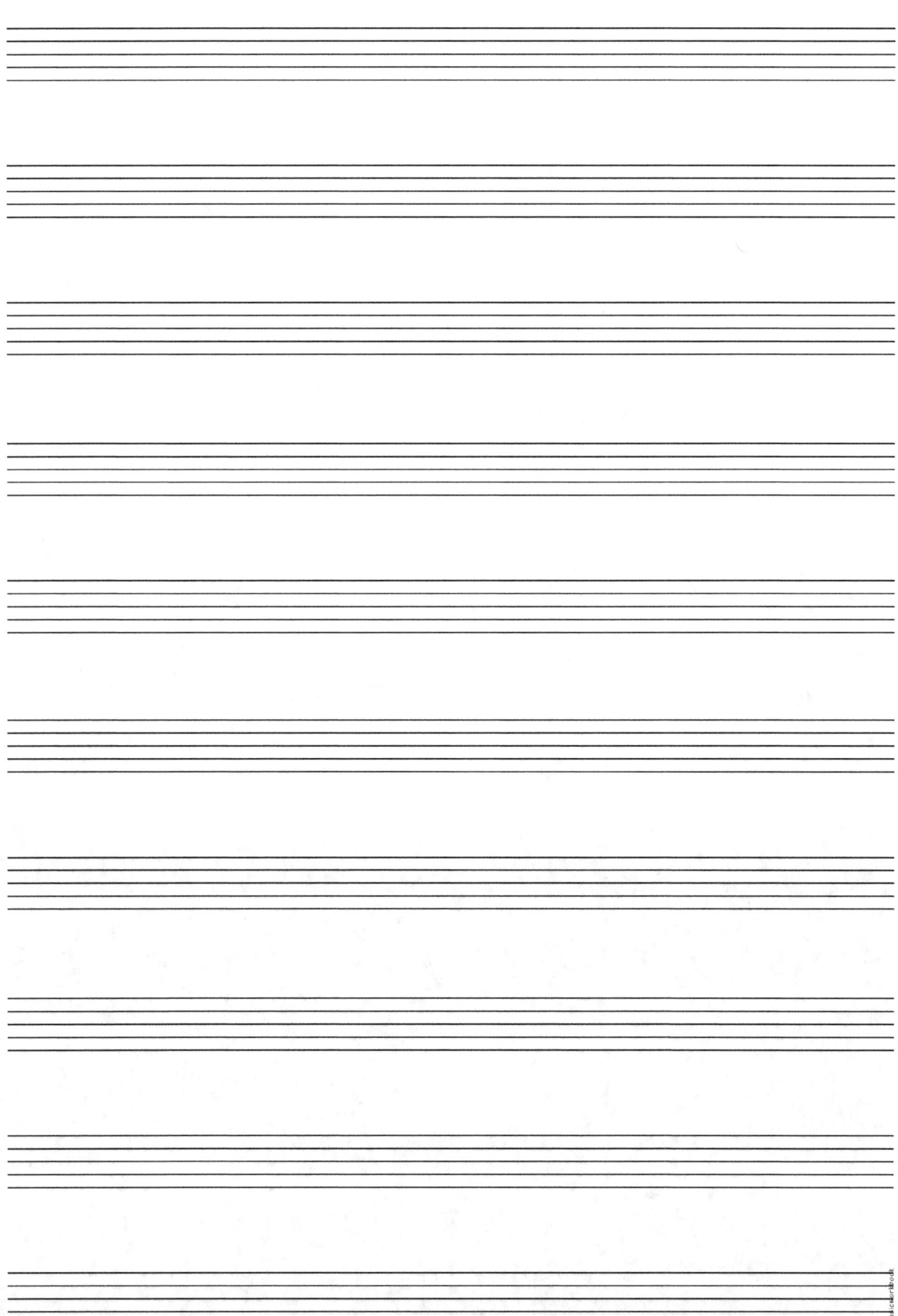

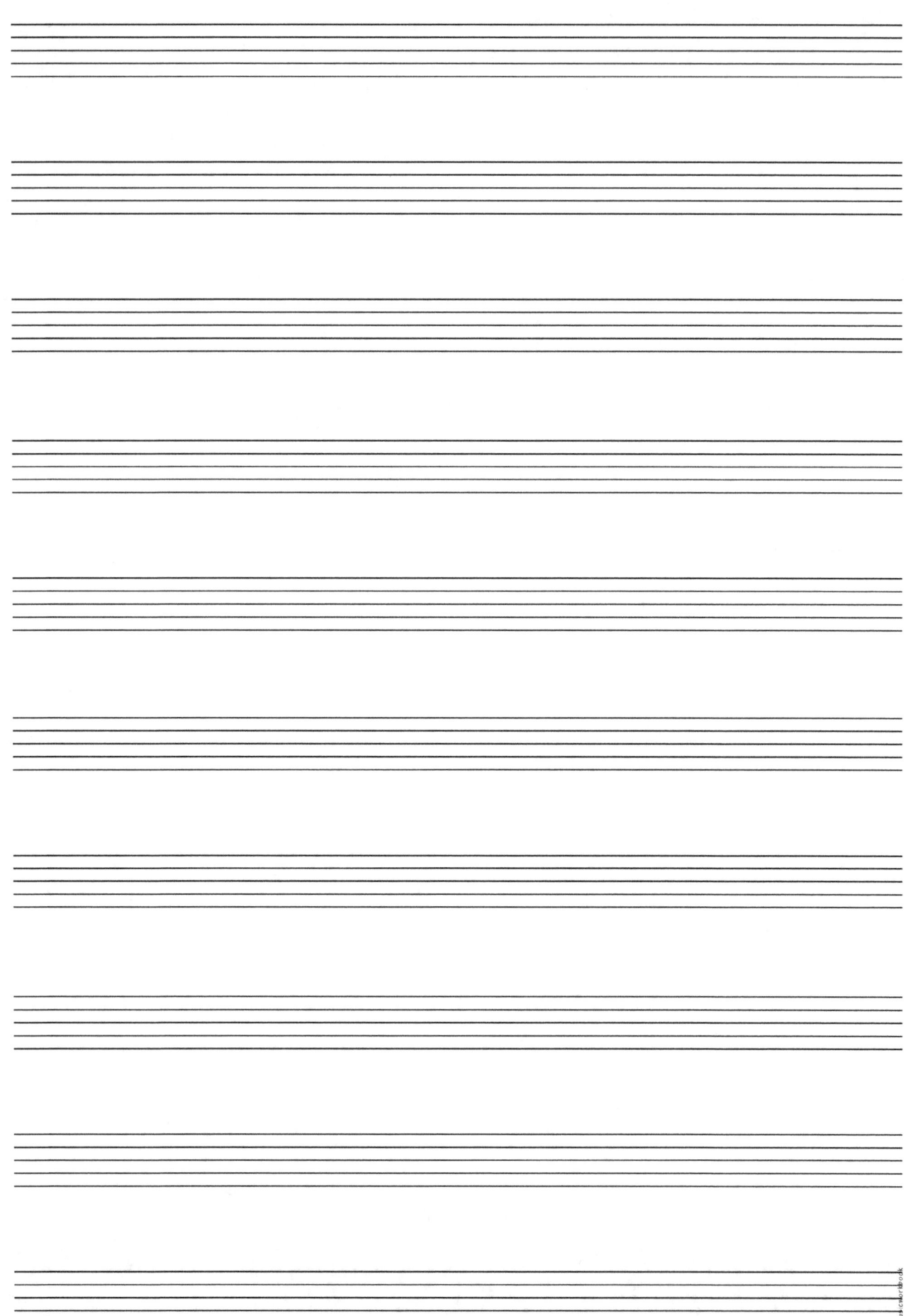

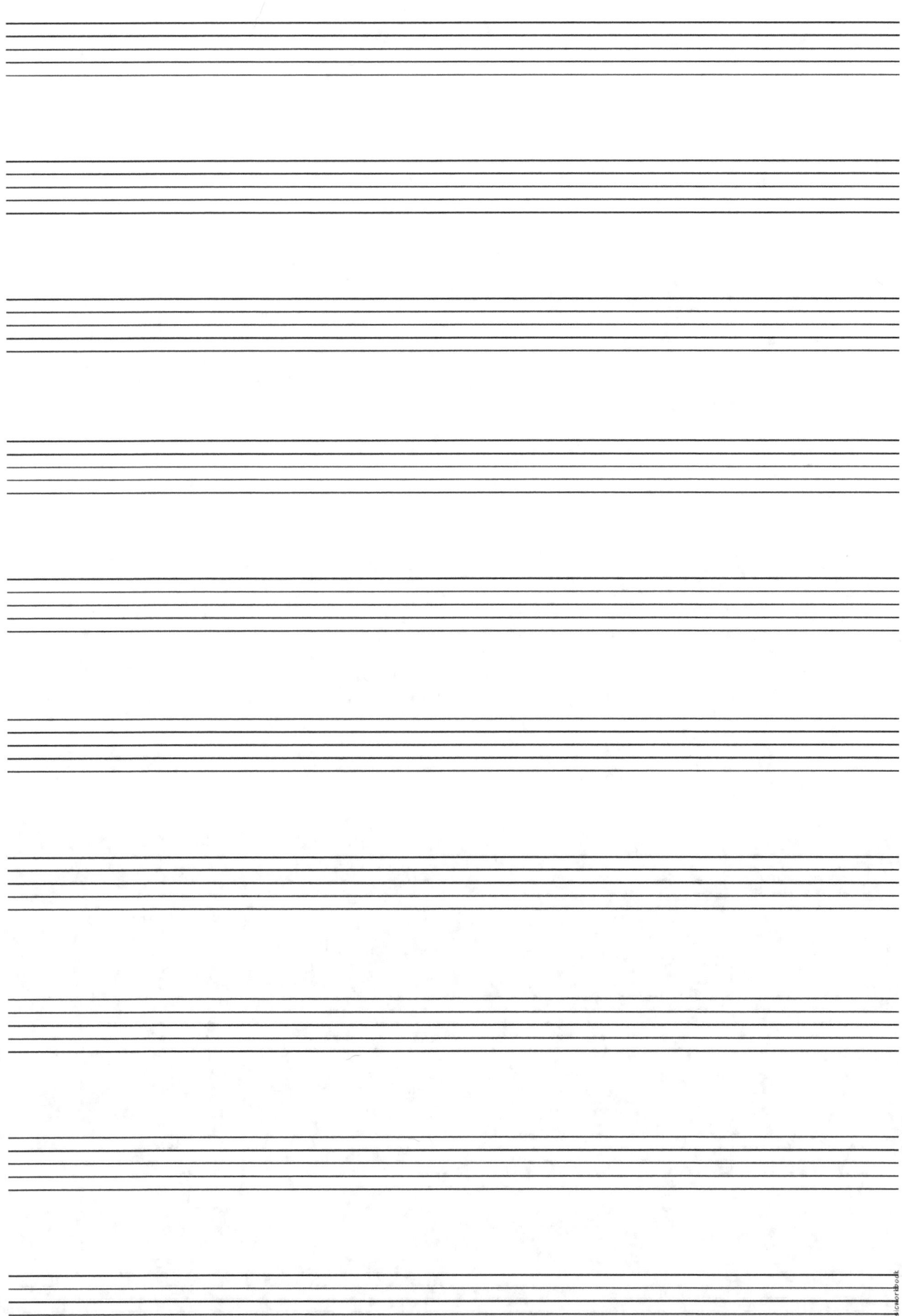

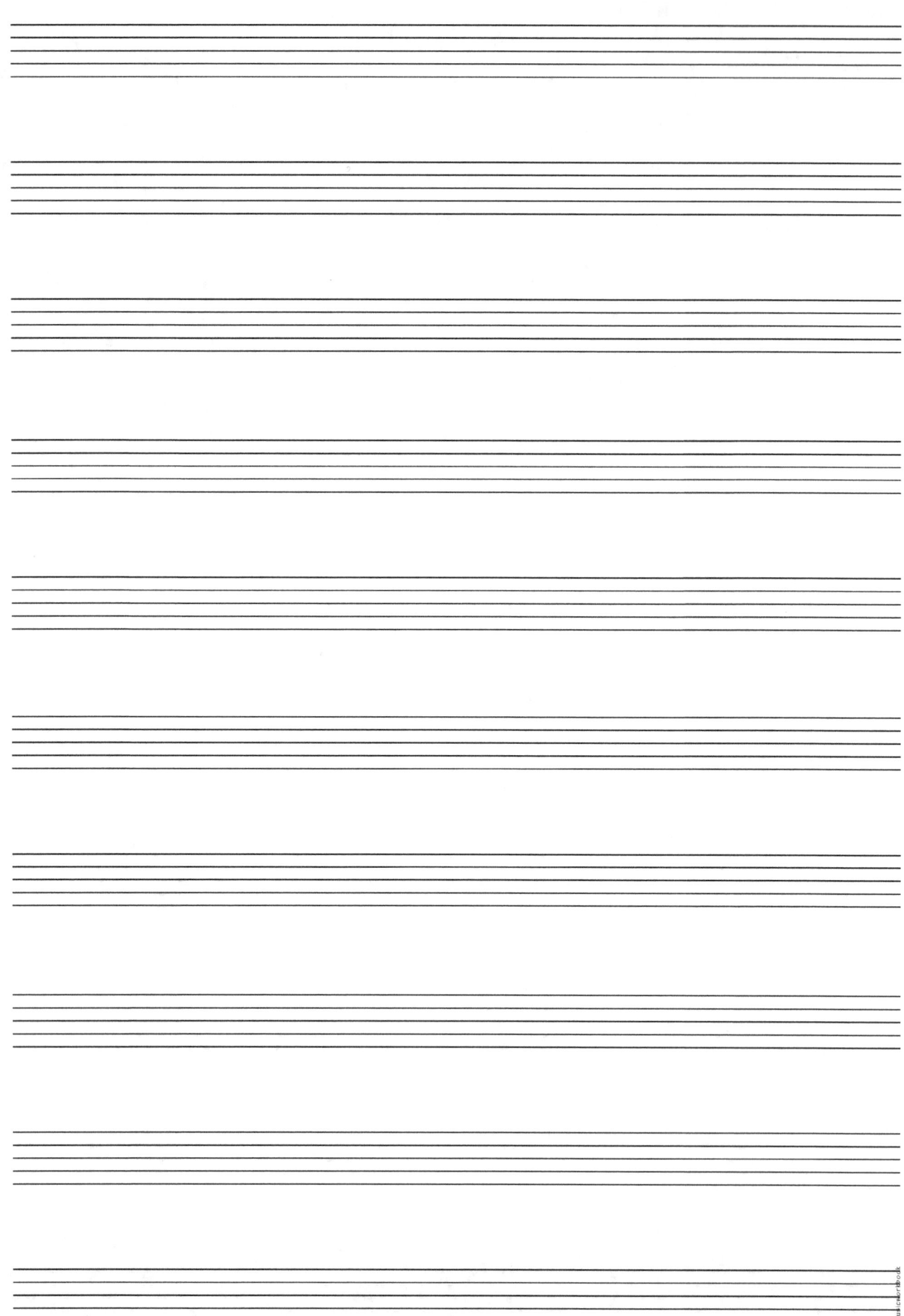

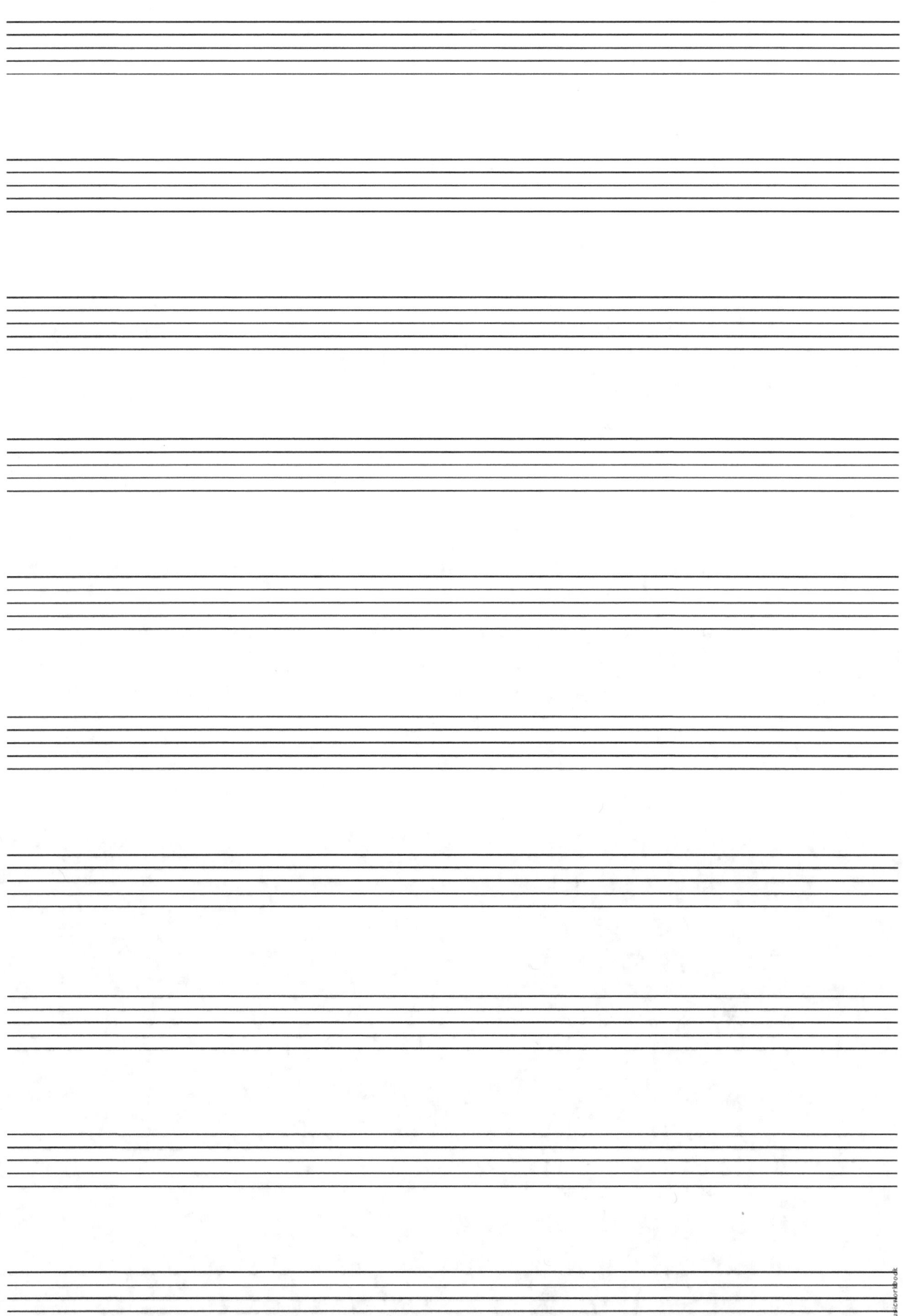

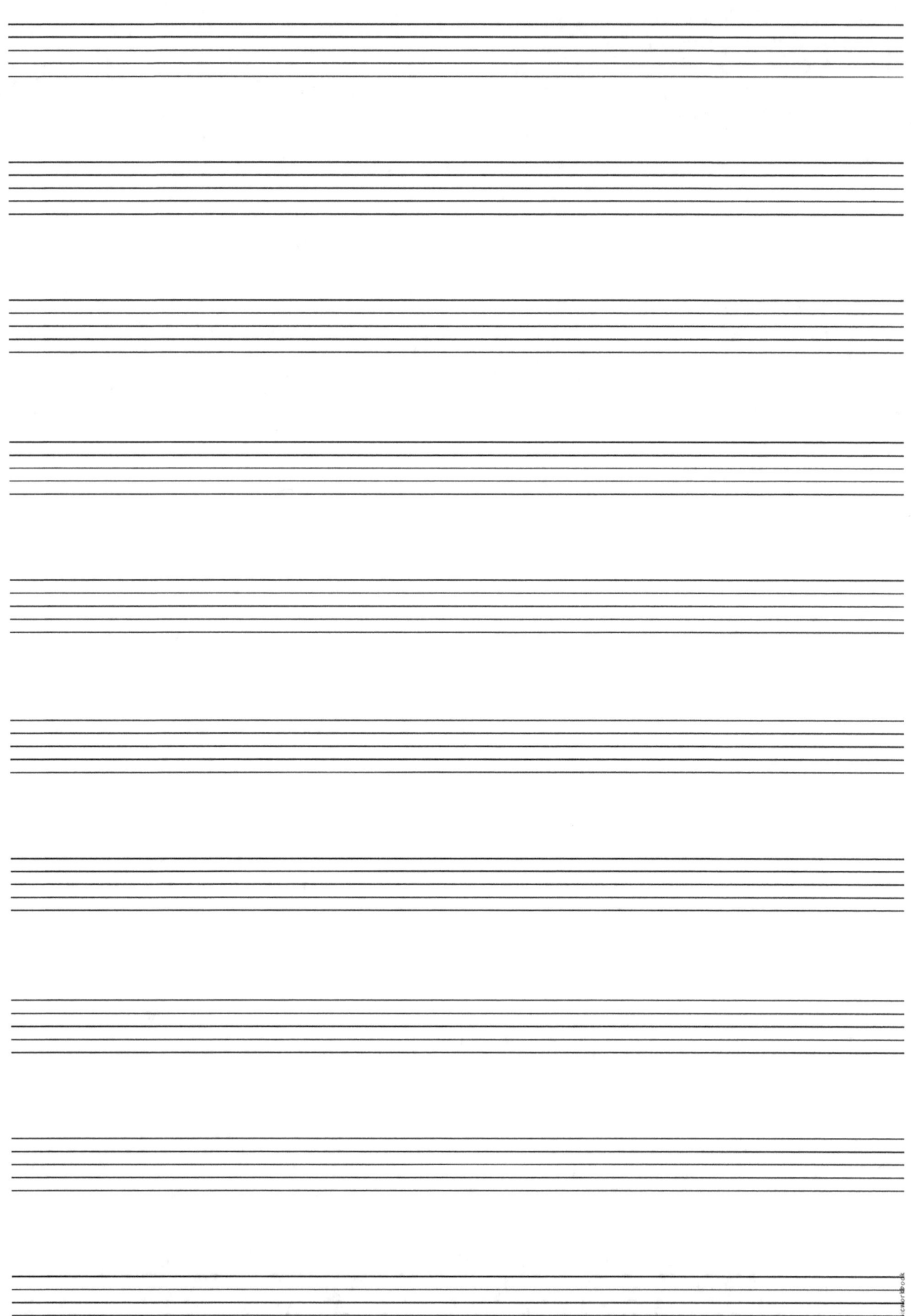

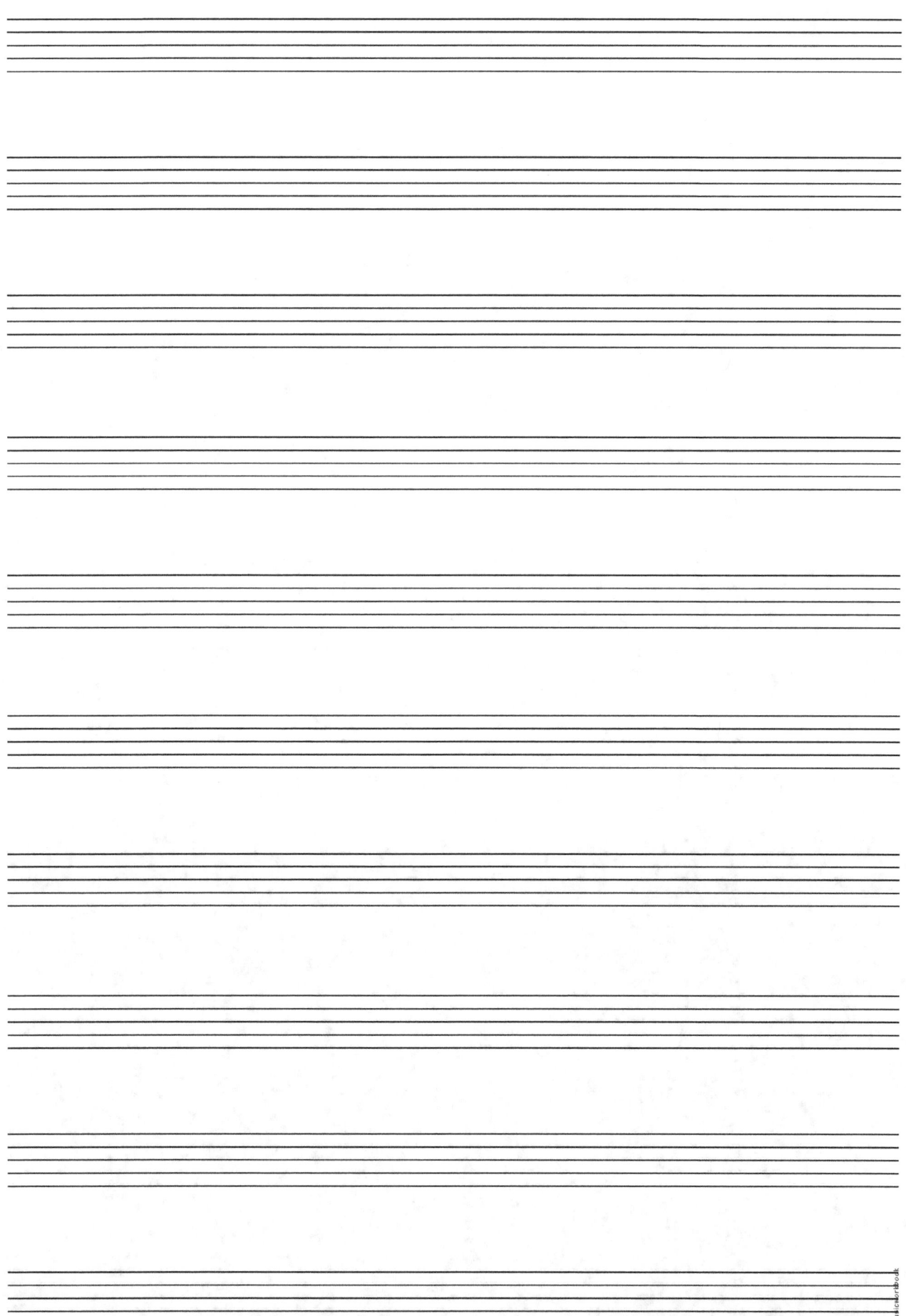

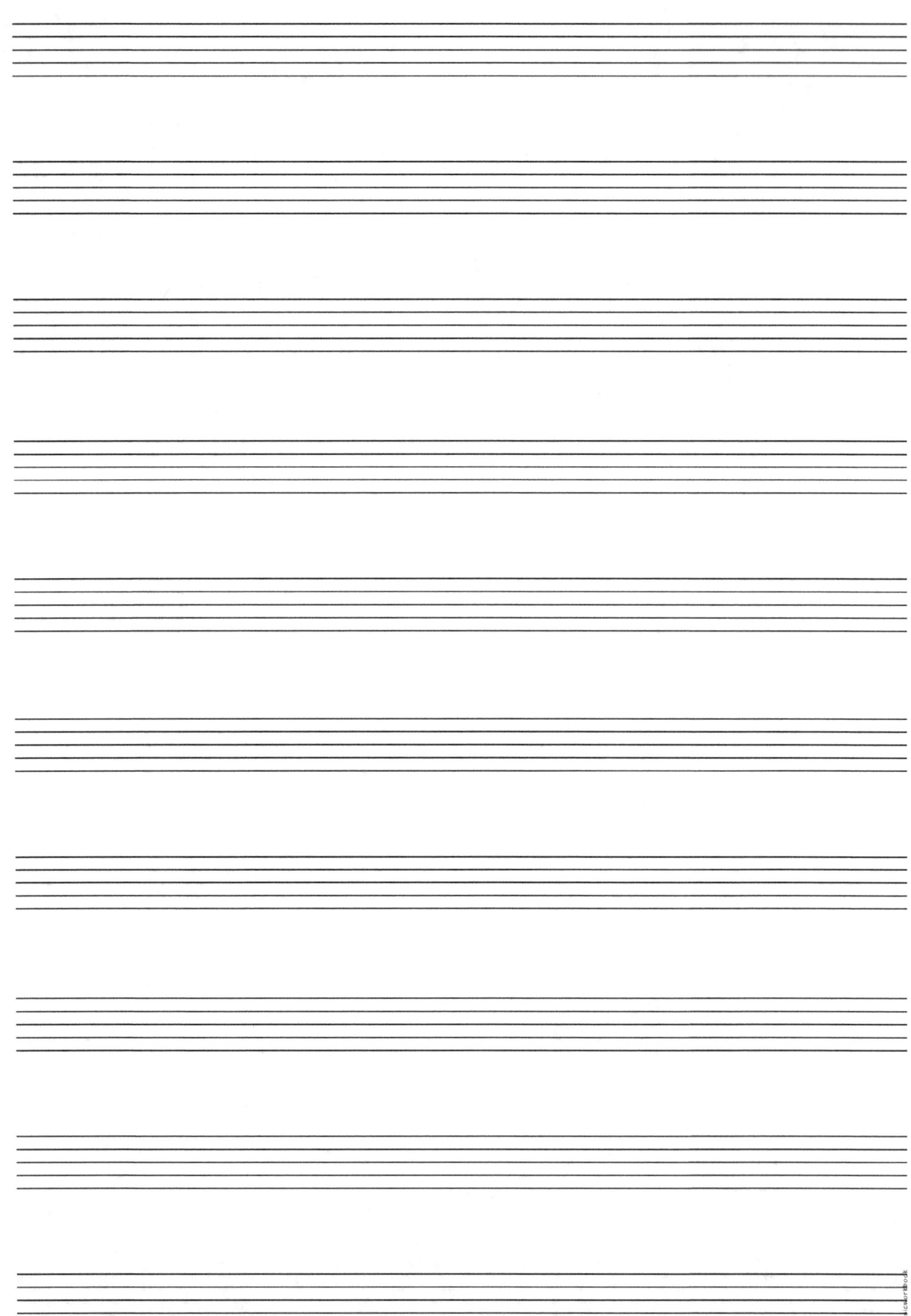

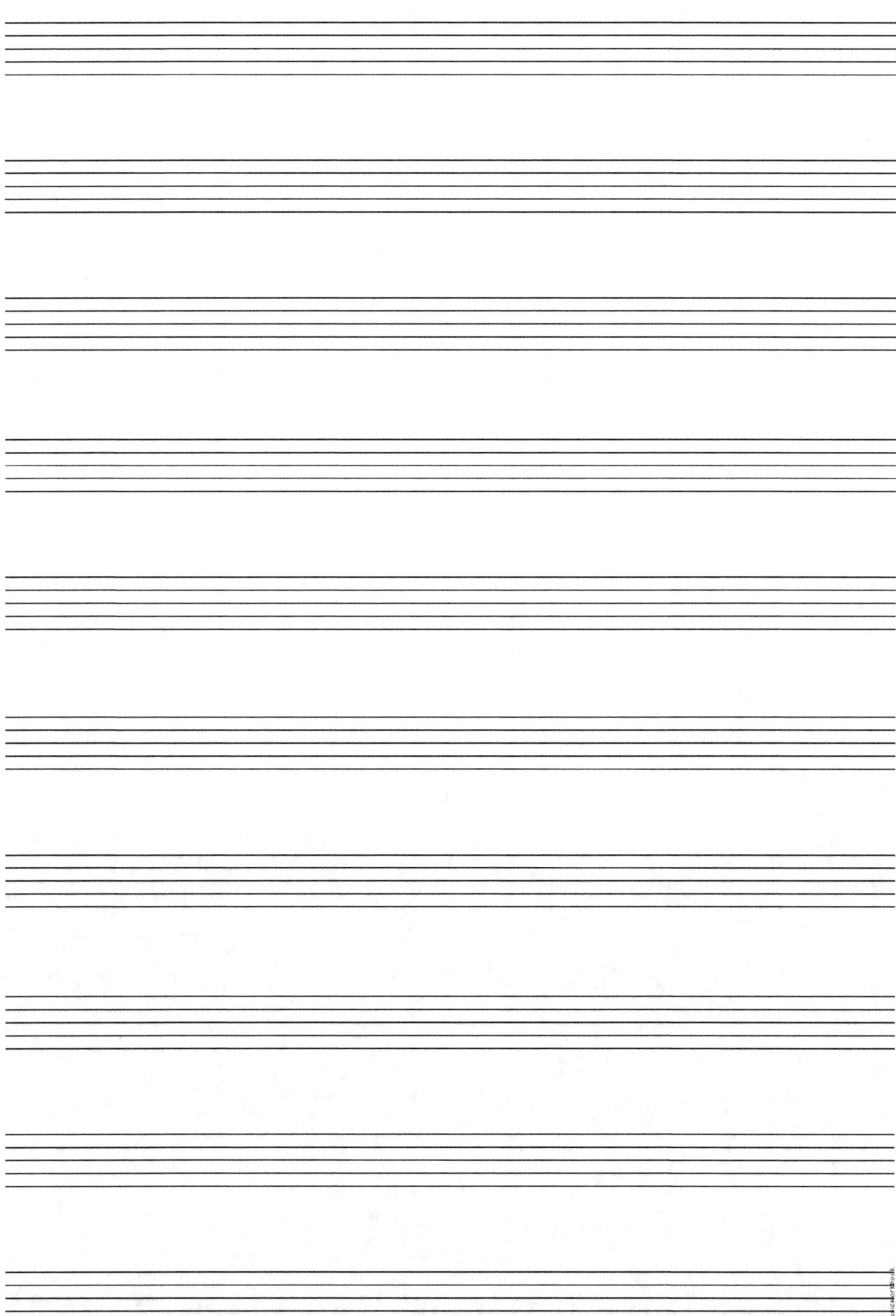

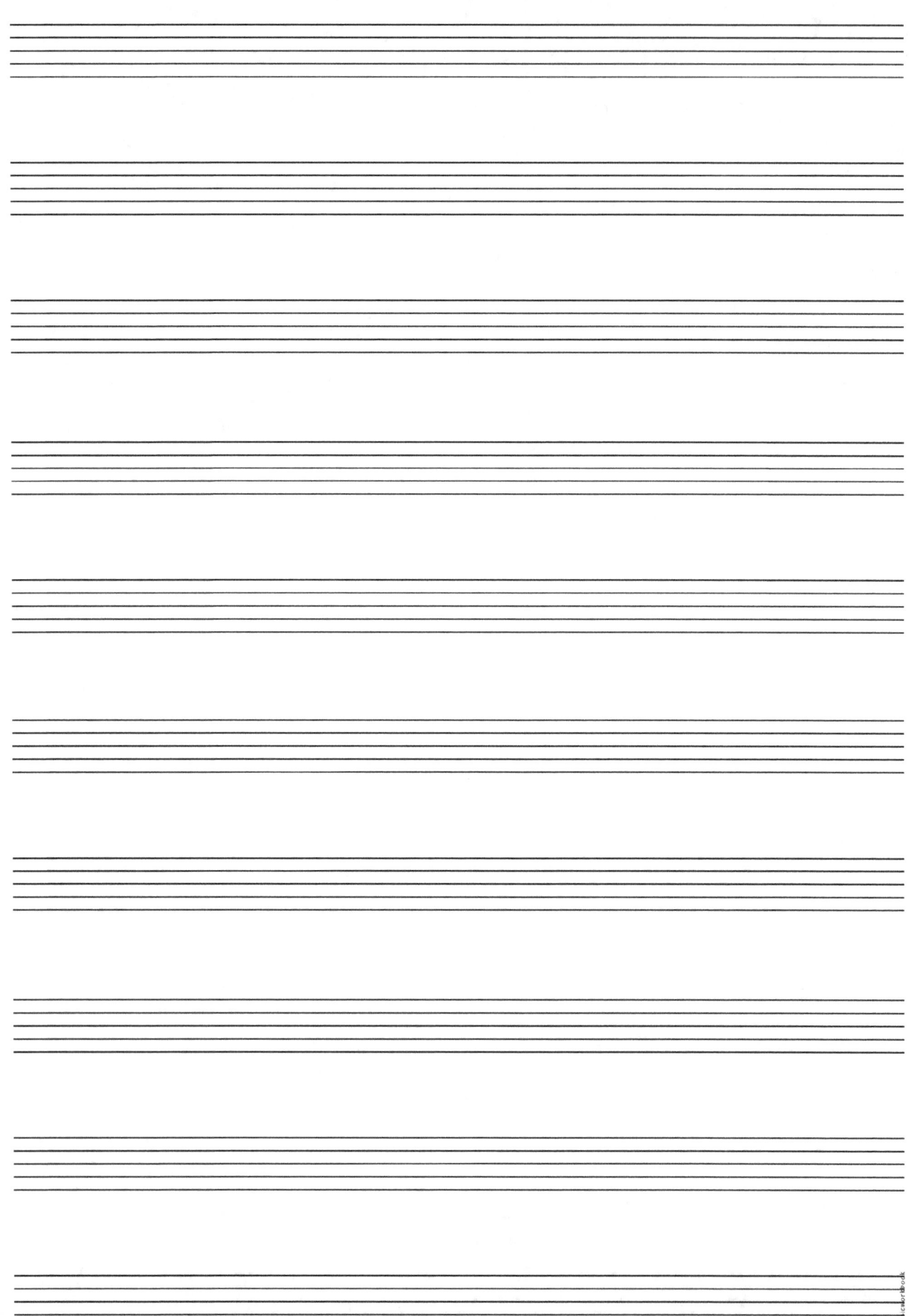

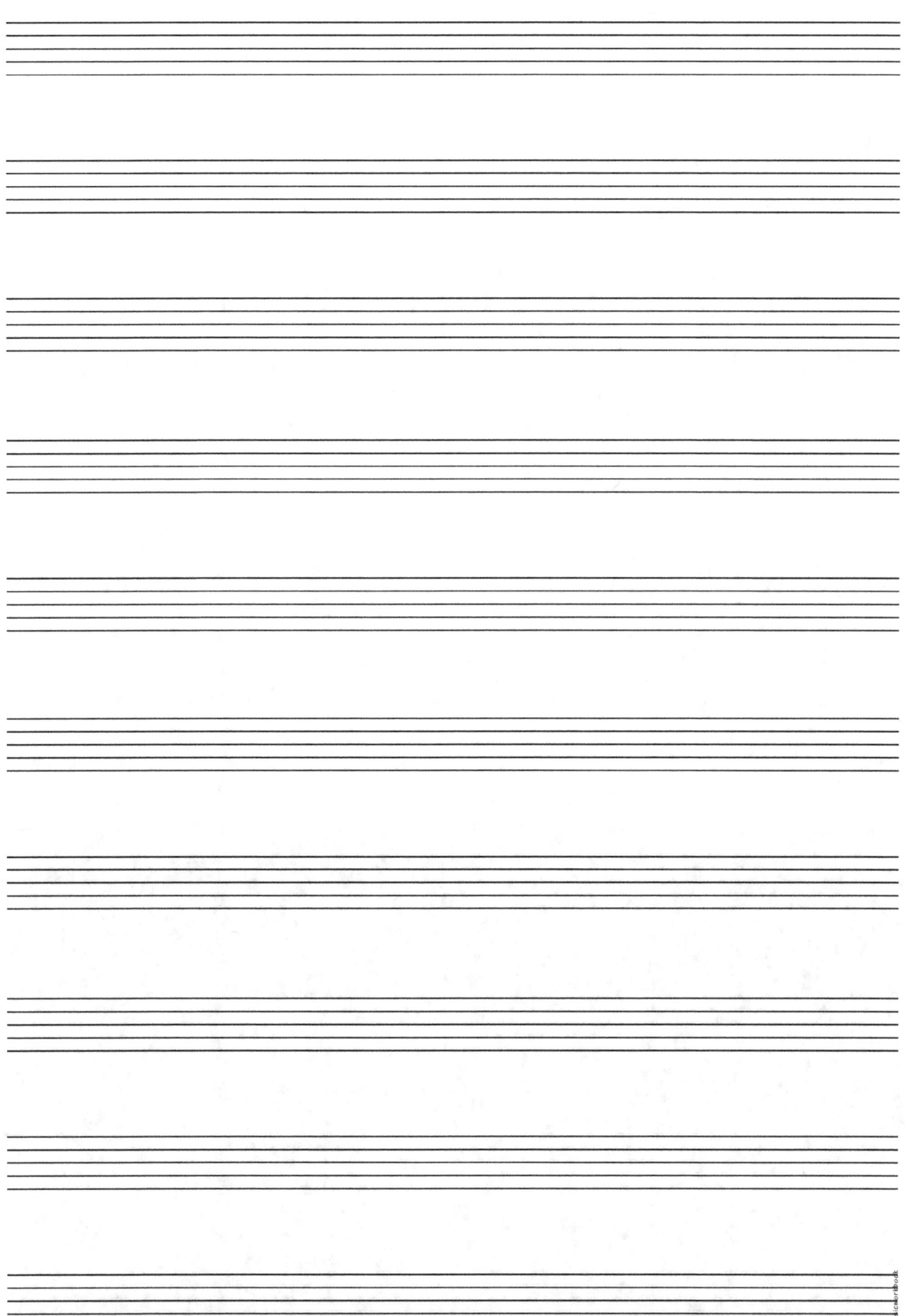

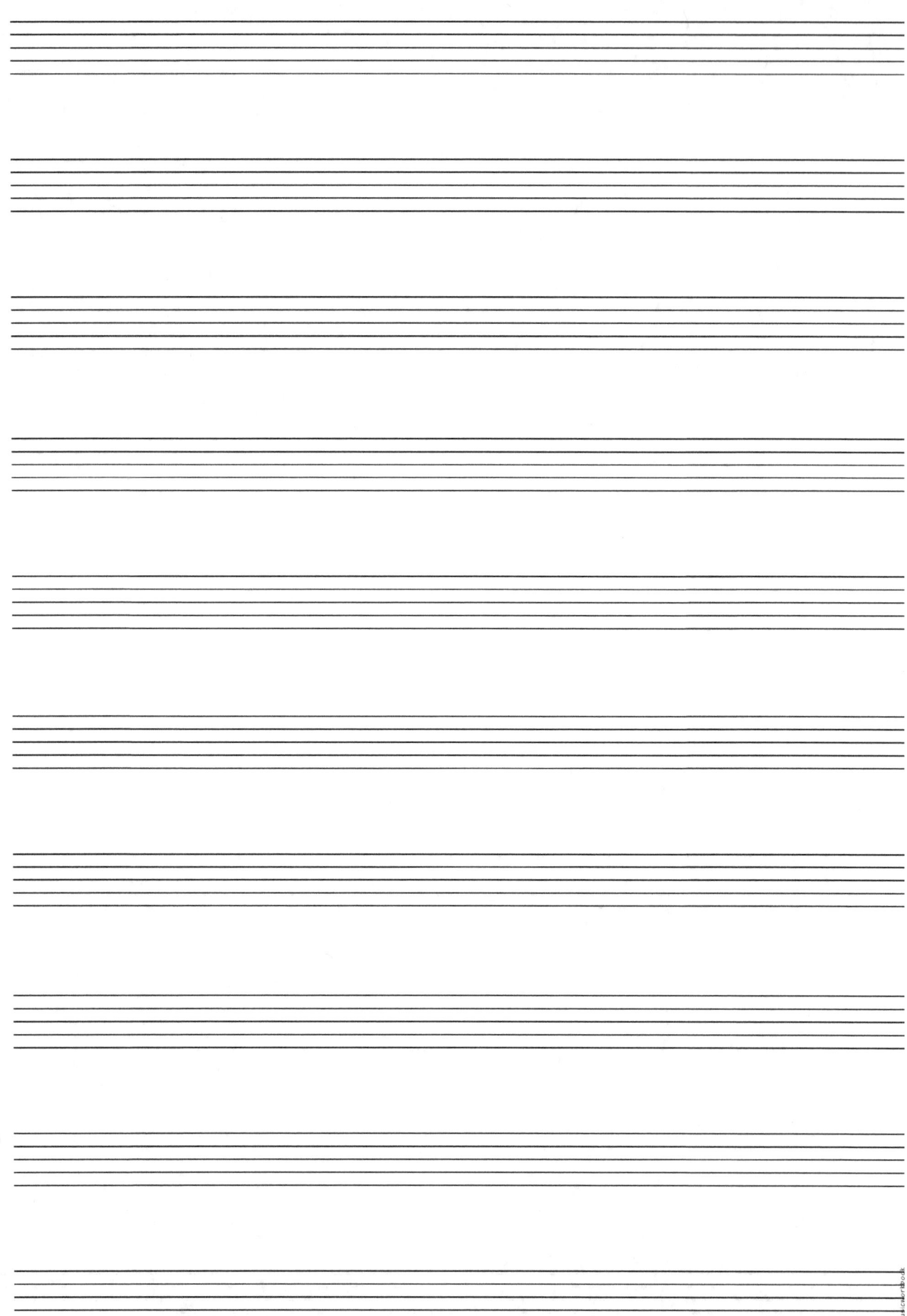

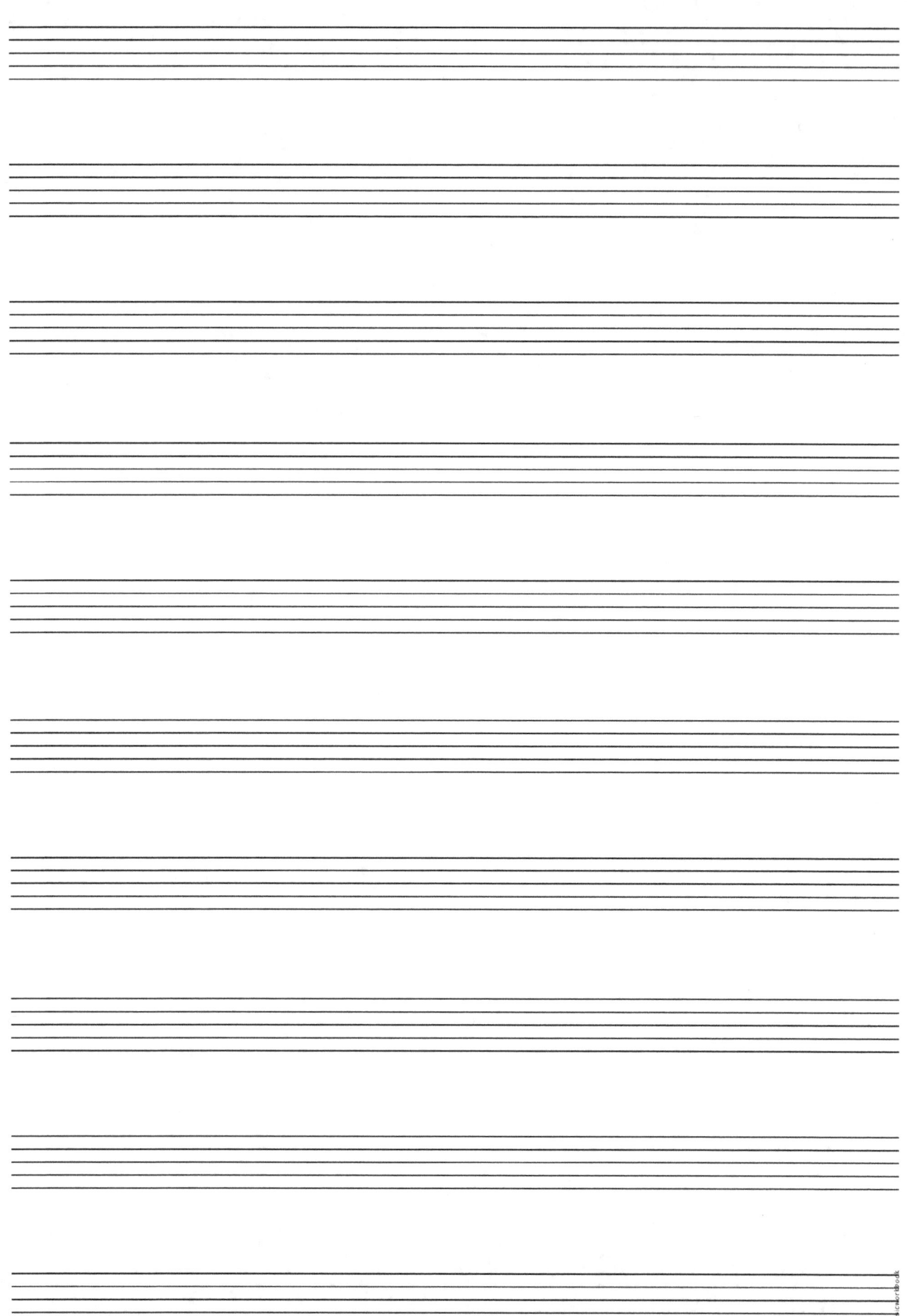

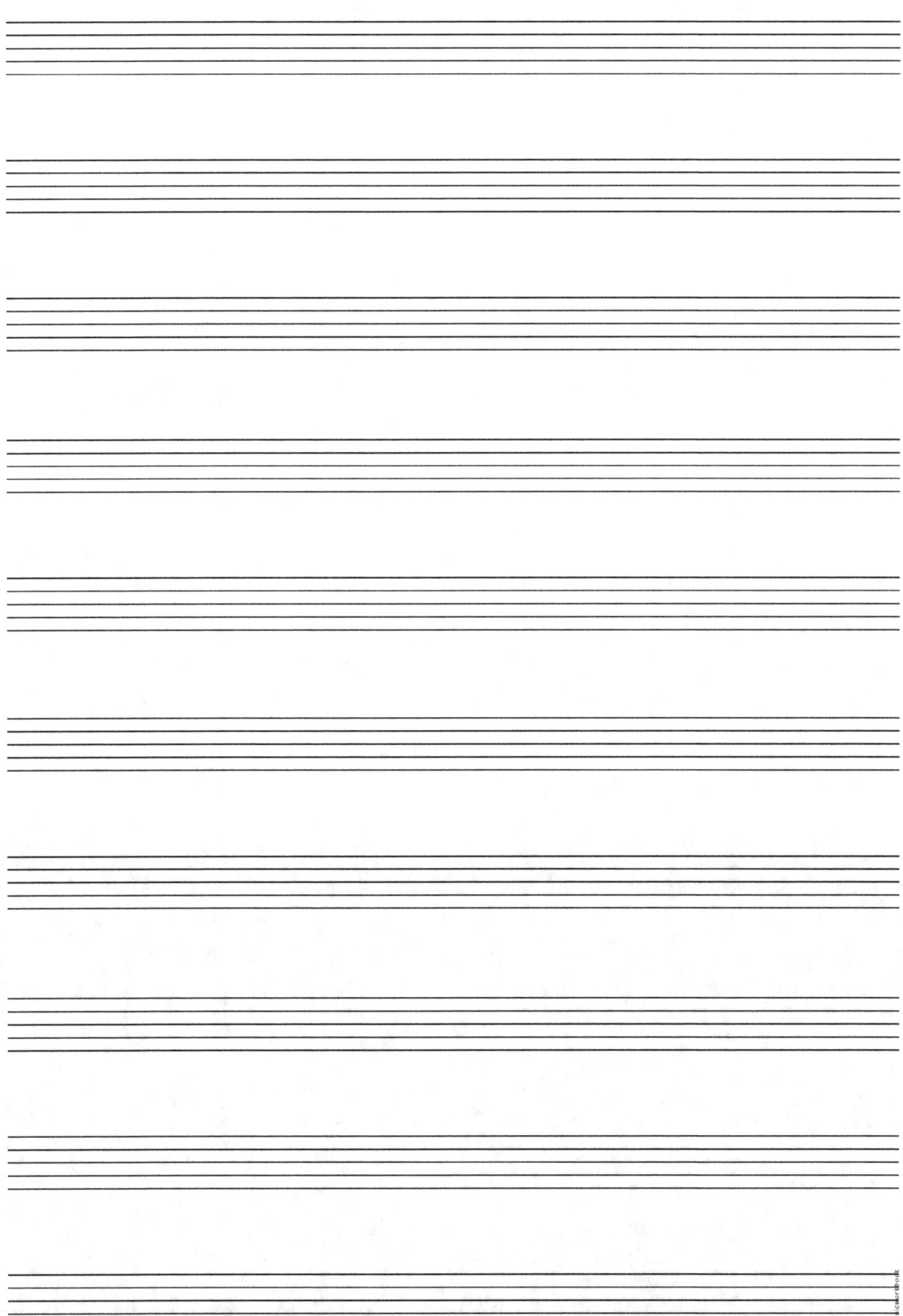

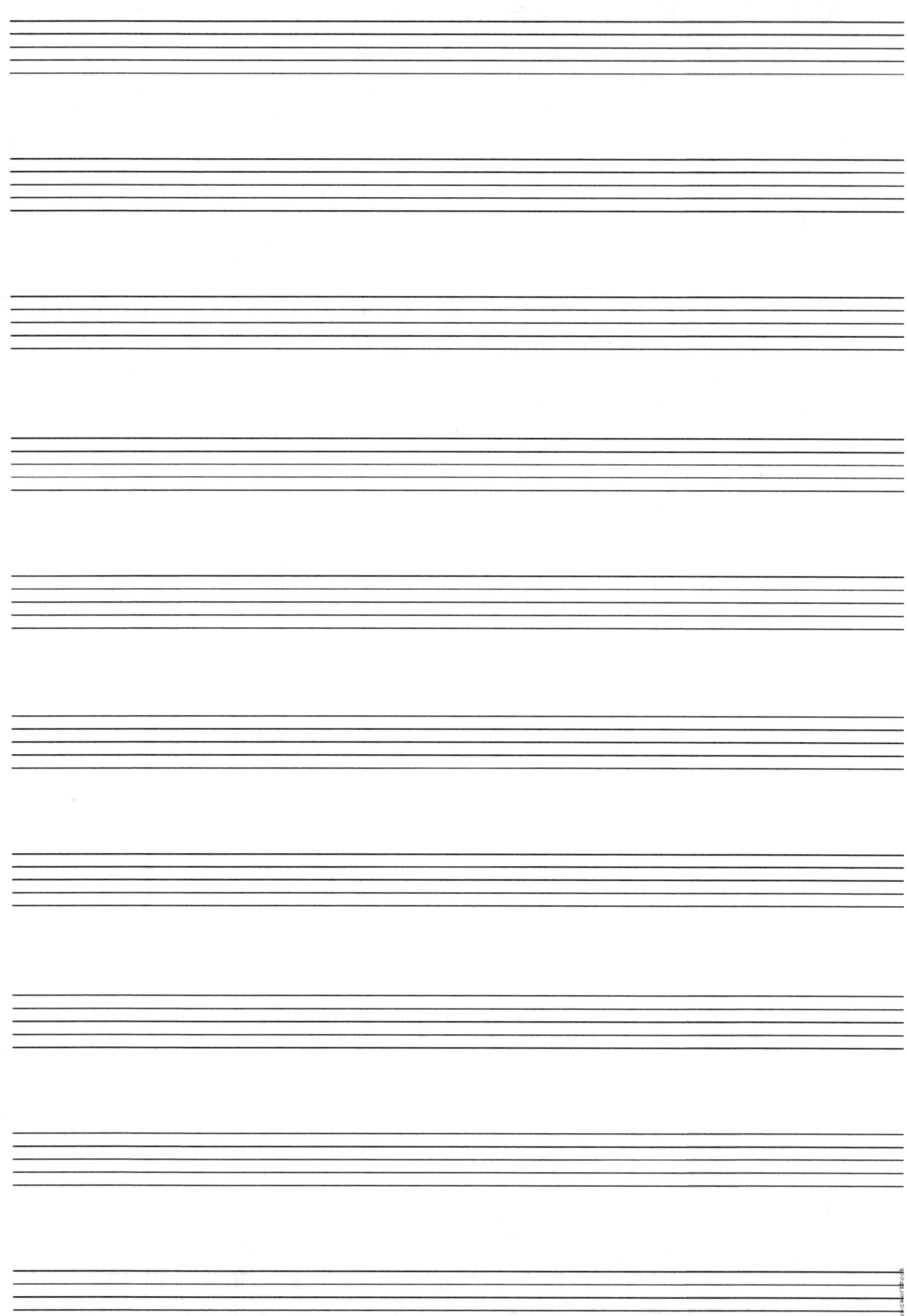

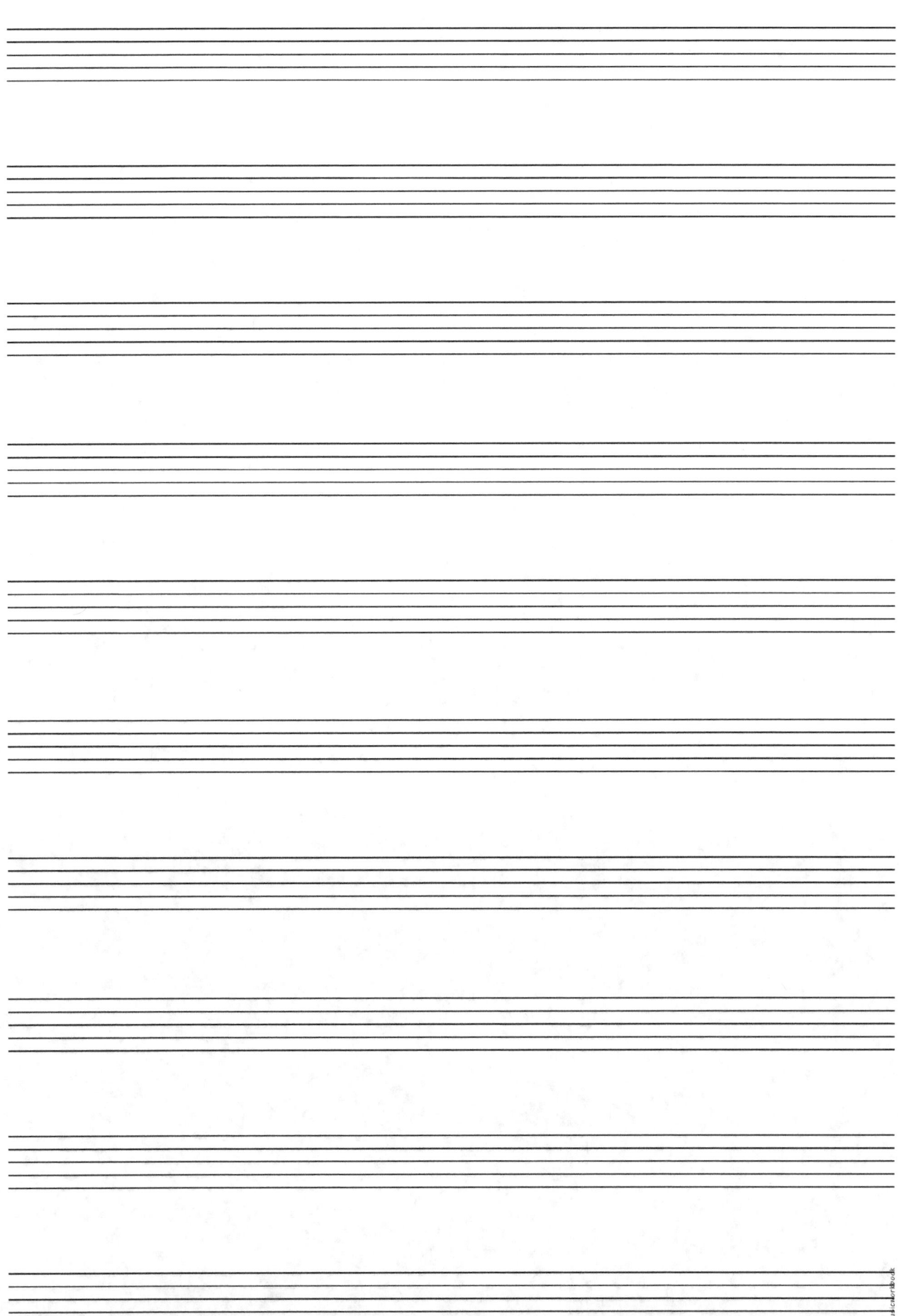

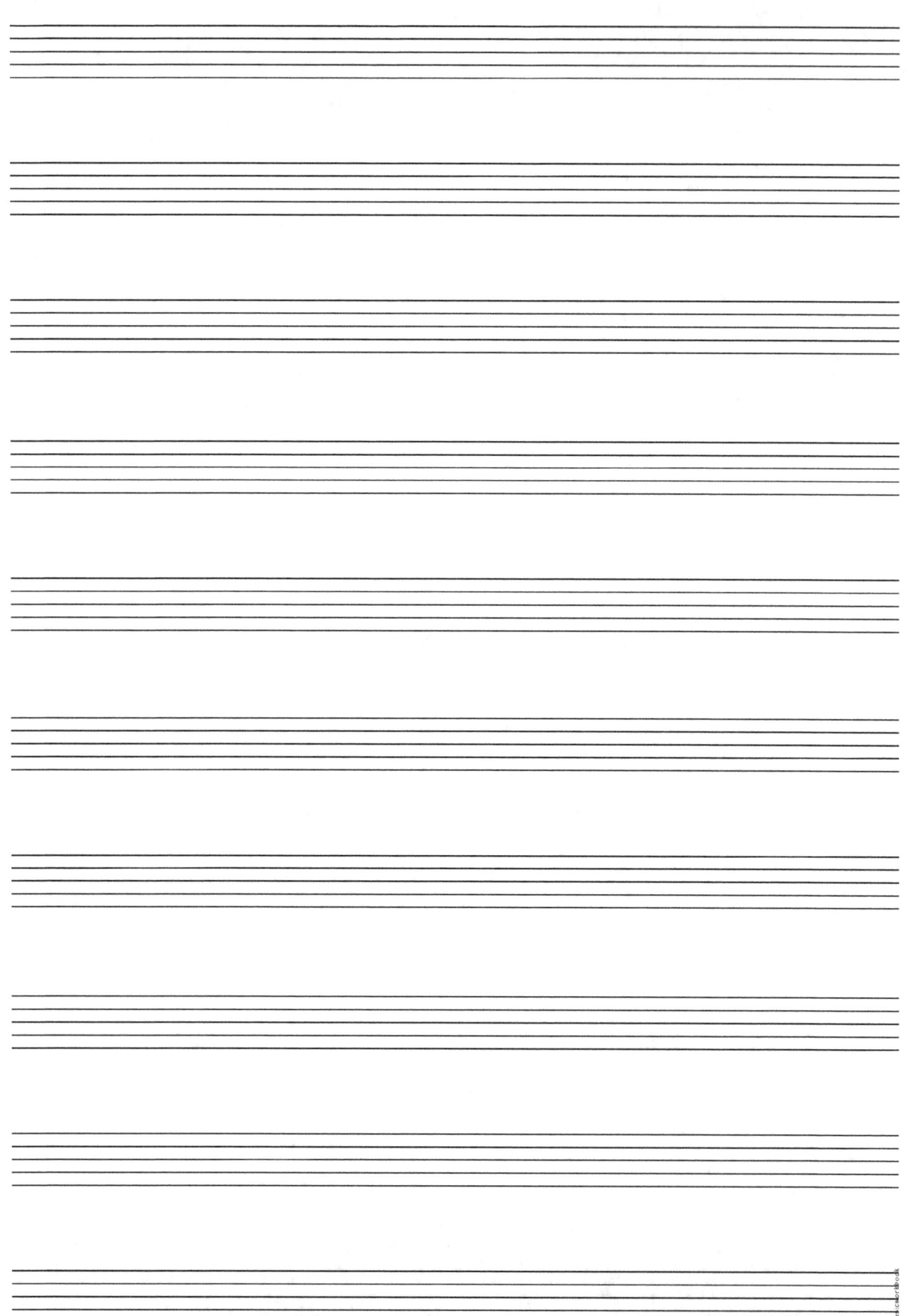

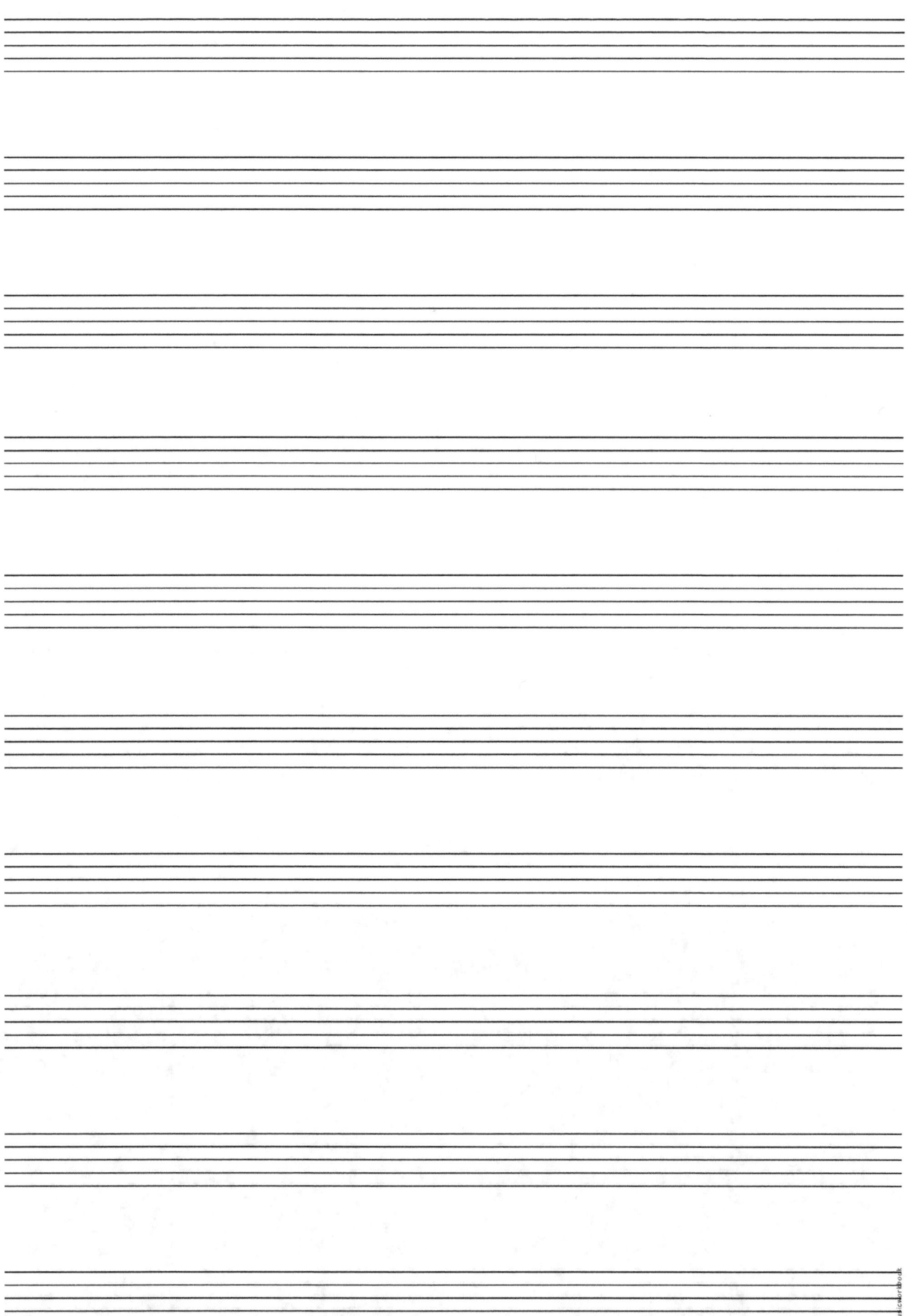

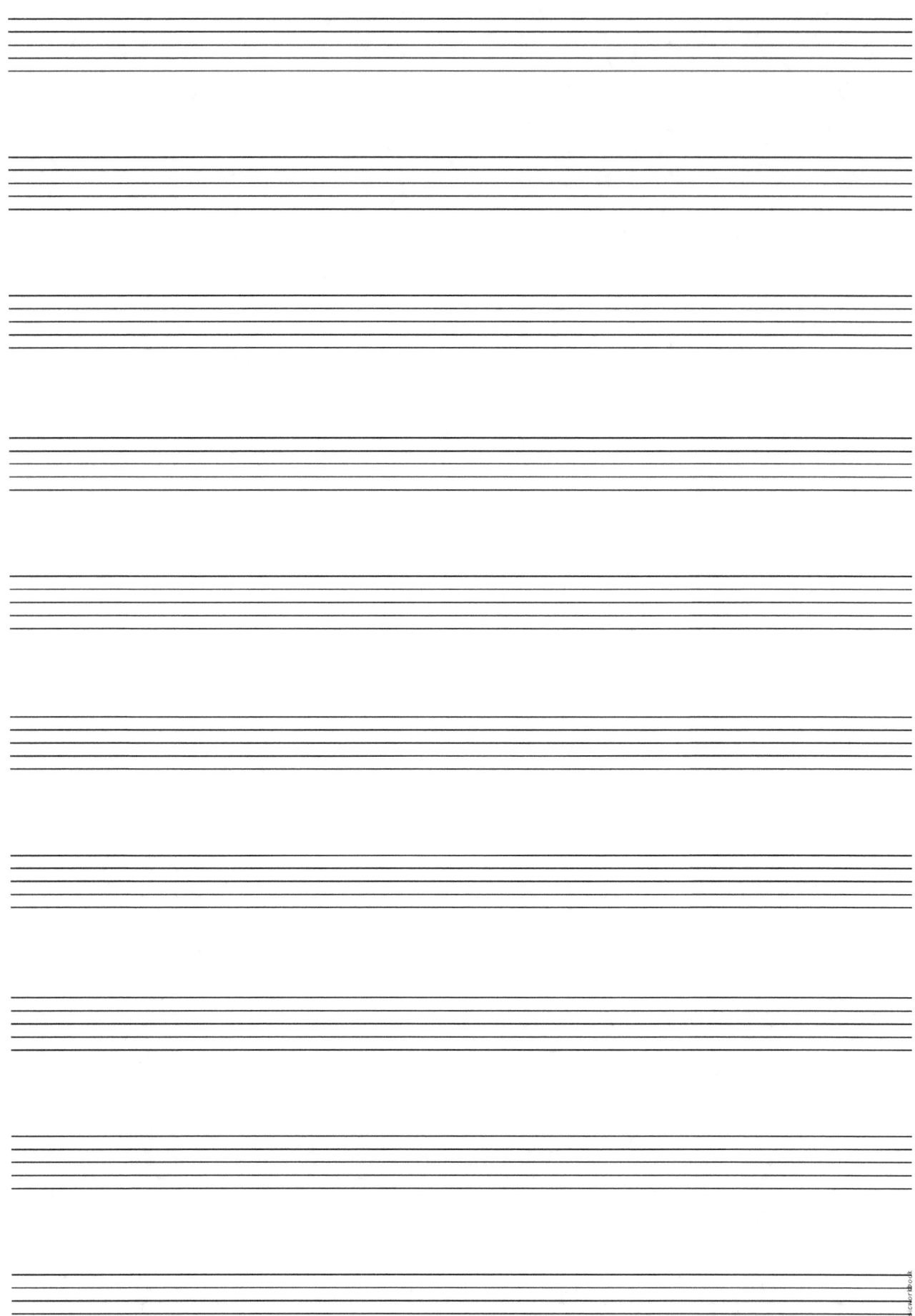

Descant Recorder Fingering Chart

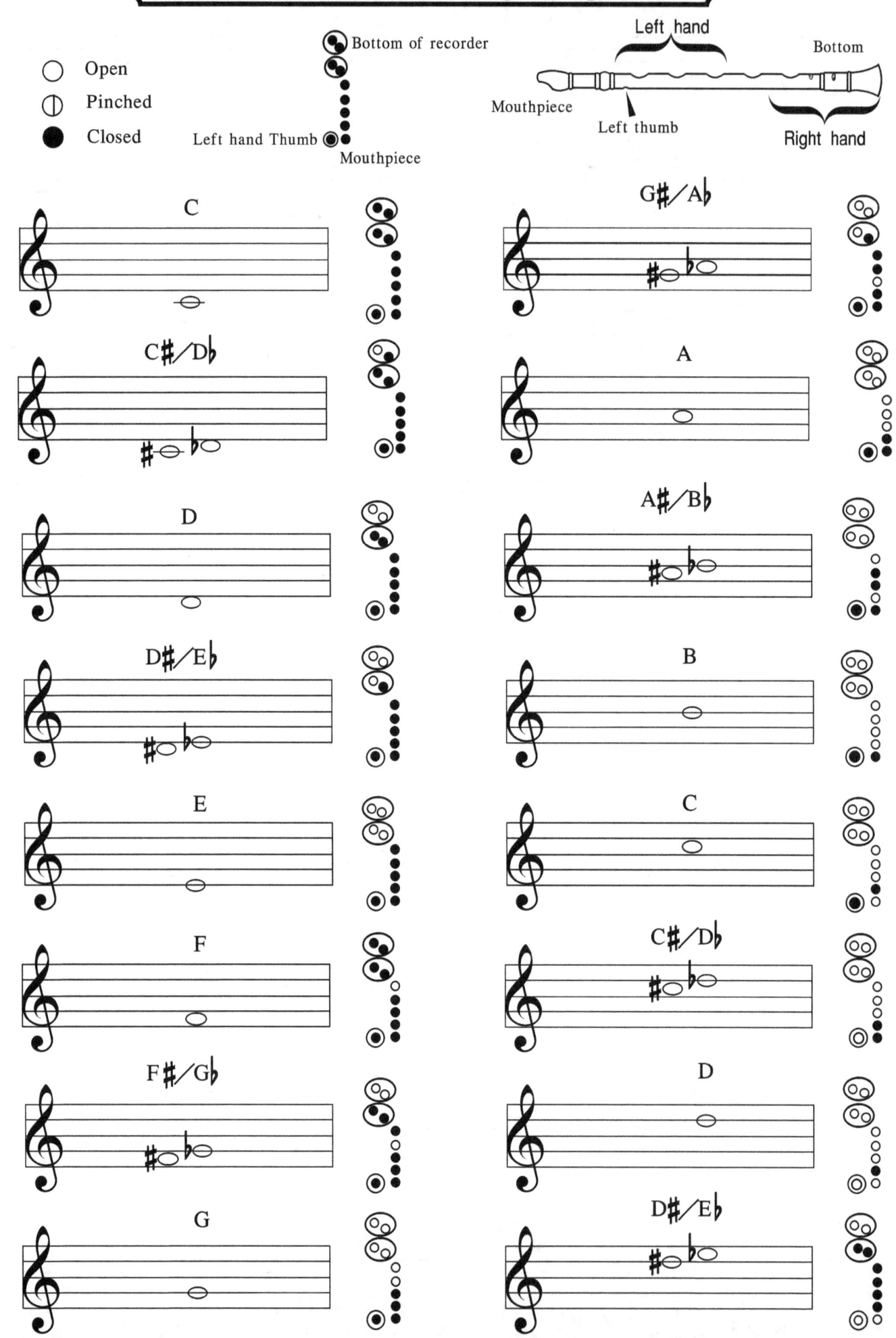

GUITAR CHORDS

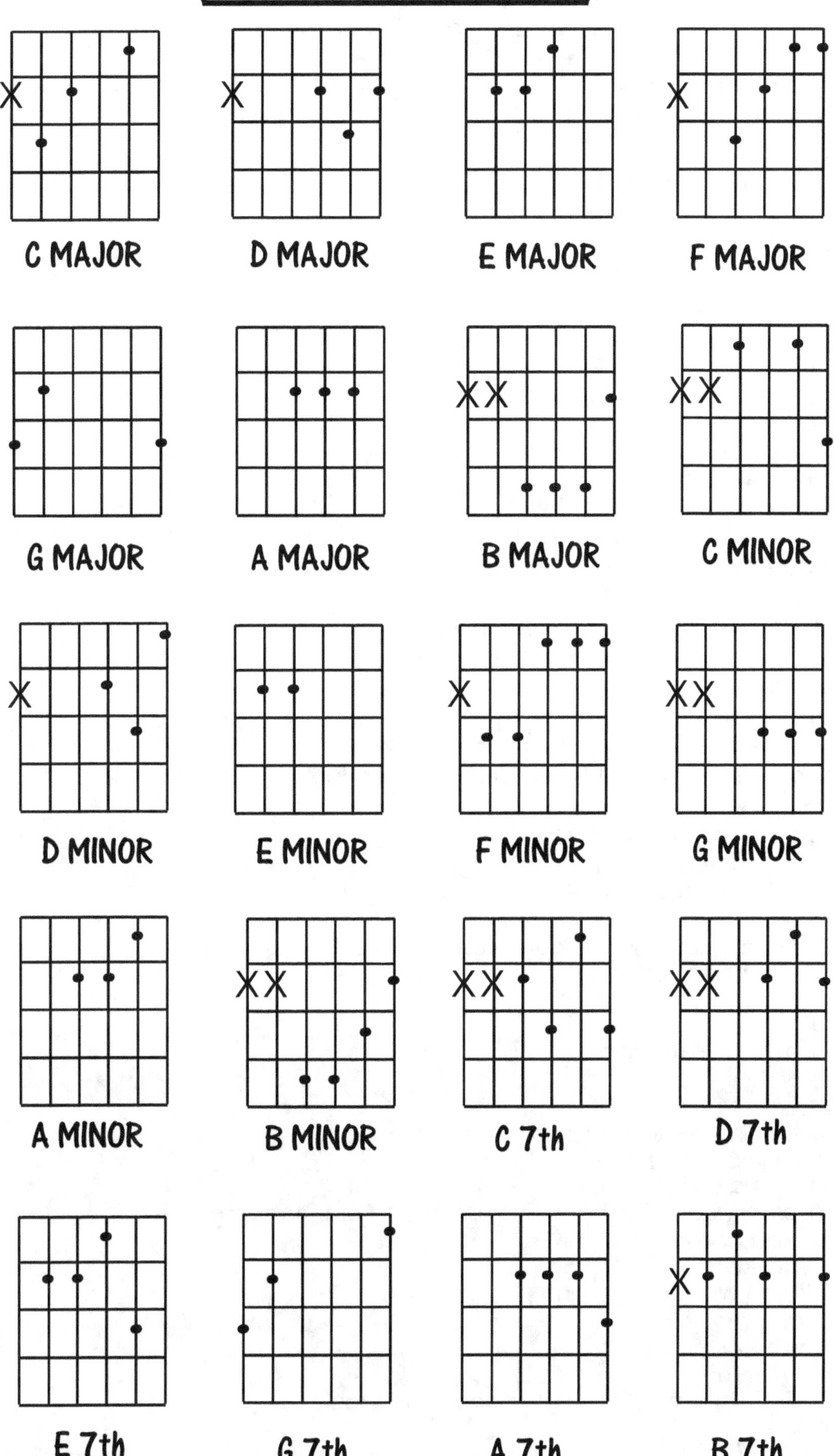

C MAJOR   D MAJOR   E MAJOR   F MAJOR

G MAJOR   A MAJOR   B MAJOR   C MINOR

D MINOR   E MINOR   F MINOR   G MINOR

A MINOR   B MINOR   C 7th   D 7th

E 7th   G 7th   A 7th   B 7th

Remember the strings on the guitar are (from the base): E A D G B E.
X muted string.

Terms in Music - I

The first of 4 pages as a reference list. Most are Italian terms. It is not necessary to learn them all but the exercises on pages 180, 181 cover the more commonly used terms.

à - To, at

A - At, to, in, for, by, in the style of...

Al, Alla - To the, in the manner of

Al fine - To the end

A tempo - Resume the normal speed

Accelerando - Becoming gradually faster

Ad libitum, ad lib. - At liberty: passage may be played freely

Adagietto - Rather slow : (faster than adagio)

Adagio - Slow, leisurely

Affetuoso - Tenderly

Affrettando - Hurrying

Agitato - Agitated

Alla breve - To be played as if it were two minims to the bar

Alla marcia - In the style of a march

Allargando - Broadening (slowing), often with an increase of tone

Allegro - Lively, reasonably fast

Allegretto - Rather lively (but less so than Allegro)

Amabile - Sweet, agreeable, amiable or pleasant

Amore - Love

Amoroso - Loving

Andante - (literally *walking*) At a moderate pace

Andantino - Alternatively faster or slower than Andante

Anima - Spirit, soul

Animando - Becoming more lively

Animato - Animated or lively

Appassionato - With passion

Assai - Very...

Arco - (For string players): Resume the use of the bow after pizzicato

Attacca - Go on immediately

Avec - With

Ben - Well

Ben marcato - Well marked

Brillante - Brilliant

Brio - Vigour

Calando - Fading away (getting softer and slower)

Cantabile - In a singing style

Cantando - In a singing style

Capo - (literally *head*) The beginning (da capo-from the beginning)

Col,coll'(colla,collo) - With the

Colla Destra - With the right hand

Colla Sinistra - With the left hand

Come prima - As before

Come sopra - As above

Come - As, Similar

Com(m)odo, Com(m)oda - Convenient, comfortable

Con - With

Con anima - With life

Con brio - With fire, spirit, vivacity

Con espressione - With expression

Con moto - With movement

Terms in Music - II

Con sordini - With the mutes

Corda - A string

Crescendo (Cresc.) - Becoming gradually louder

Da - From

Da capo (D.C.) - From the beginning

Dal segno (D.S.) - From the sign

Deciso - With determination

Decrescendo (Decresc.) - Becoming gradually softer

Delicato - Delicate

Diminuendo (Dim.) - Becoming gradually softer

Dolce - Sweetly

Energico - Energetic

Espressivo (Espr., Espress.) - With expression, with feeling

Facile - Easy

Fine - The end

Forte (f) - Loud

Fortepiano (fp) - Loud, then soft

Fortissimo (ff or fff) - Very loud

Forza - Force

Furioso - With fury, passion

Forzando (fz) - Forcing; a sudden accent

Fuoco Fire

Giocoso (Giojoso) - Merry

Giusto - Exact, Strict

Glissando - A rapid scale played with the finger

Grave - Very slow, solemn

Grazioso - Gracefully

Lacrimoso, Lacrimosa - Sad

Langsam - Slow

Largamente - Broadly

Larghetto - Less slow than largo

Largo - Slow & stately

Legato - Smoothly

Lentando - Gradually becoming slower

Leggiero - Lightly, Nimbly

Lento, Lent - Slowly

L'istesso - The same

Lunga pausa - Long pause

Ma, mais - But

Maestoso - Majestic

Maggiore - Major

Main droite (Fr.) (Mano destra, M.D.) - The right hand

Main gauche (Fr.) (Mano sinistra, M.G. or M.S.) - The left hand

Marcato (Marc) - Marked, accented

Marziale - In a military style

(Fr. - French)

Terms in Music - III

Meno - Less

Meno mosso - Less movement, slower at once

Mesto - Sad

Mezzo forte (mf) - Moderately loud   *Literally Mezzo - Half*

Mezzo piano (mp) - Moderately soft

Misterioso - Mysteriously

Modere - At a moderate speed

Moderato - Moderately

Moins - Less

Molto - Much.   **Di molto** - very much

Mosso, Moto - Movement

Morendo - Dying away

Nobilmente - Nobly

Non - Not

Non tando - Not so much

Ossia - Or. *The word indicates an alternative version of a passage*

Ostinato - Persistent: a persistently repeated rhythm or melodic figure

Ped - *Depress the right (sustaining) pedal of the piano until the sign* ✻ *is encountered.*
e.g. **𝕻𝖊𝖉**   ✻   or   *𝒫ℇ𝒹* ⎣_____⎦

Perdendosi - Dying away

Pesante - Heavy, ponderous

Piacevole - Pleasing, agreeable

Piano (p) - Soft

Pianissimo (pp or ppp) - Very softly

Plus - More

Più - More

Pizzicato - Plucked (Stringed instruments)

Poco - Little

Poco a poco - Little by little

Possibile - As fast as possible

Presser - Hurry

Prestissimo - As fast as possible

Presto - Very quick

Prima (Primo) - First

Quasi - As if, resembling

Rallentando (Rall) - Becoming gradually slower

Ralentir - Slow down

Retenu - Held back

Risoluto - Resolute, bold

Ritardando (Ritard) - Gradually slower

Ritenuto (Rit.) - Held back

Ritmico - Rhythmically

Rubato (Tempo Rubato) - With some freedom of time

Ruhig - Peaceful

Terms in Music - IV

Sans - Without
Scherzando - Playful
Scherzo - A joke
Seconda (Secondo) - Second
Segno - A sign; dal Segno (D.S.) - From the sign
Semplice - Simple, Plain
Sempre - Always
Senza - Without
Sforzando (Sforzato or *sf* or *sfz*) - With a sudden accent
Simile - In a like manner
Sordini - Mutes
con Sordini - With mutes. *A direction for string or brass players.*
Sonoro - Resonant, with rich tone
Sopra - Above
Senza Sordini - *Depress the "sustaining pedal" (dampers allowing the strings to vibrate freely)*
Sostenuto - Sustained
Sotto - Below
Spiritoso - Spirited
Staccato (Stacc.) - Short, Detached
Stringendo - Gradually faster
Subito - Suddenly
Tanto - So much
Tempo - The speed of the music
Tempo commodo - At a convenient speed
Tempo di Gavotta - In the time (& style) of a Gavotte
Tempo primo (Tempo 1) - Resume the original speed
Tenuto (Ten.) - Held
Tranquillo - Calm, tranquil
Tre corde - *(literally three strings) Release the left (soft) pedal of the pianoforte*
Tres - Very
Triste, Tristamente - Sad, Sorrowful
Troppo - Too much
Un, Une - One
Una corda - *(One string) Depress the left pedal of the pianoforte*
Veloce - Swift
Vif - Lively
Vite - Quick
Vivace - Lively, brisk
Vivo - Lively, quick
Voce - Voice
Volta - Time

8va ——————⌐ Play piece an octave higher

8va ——————⌐ Play piece an octave lower

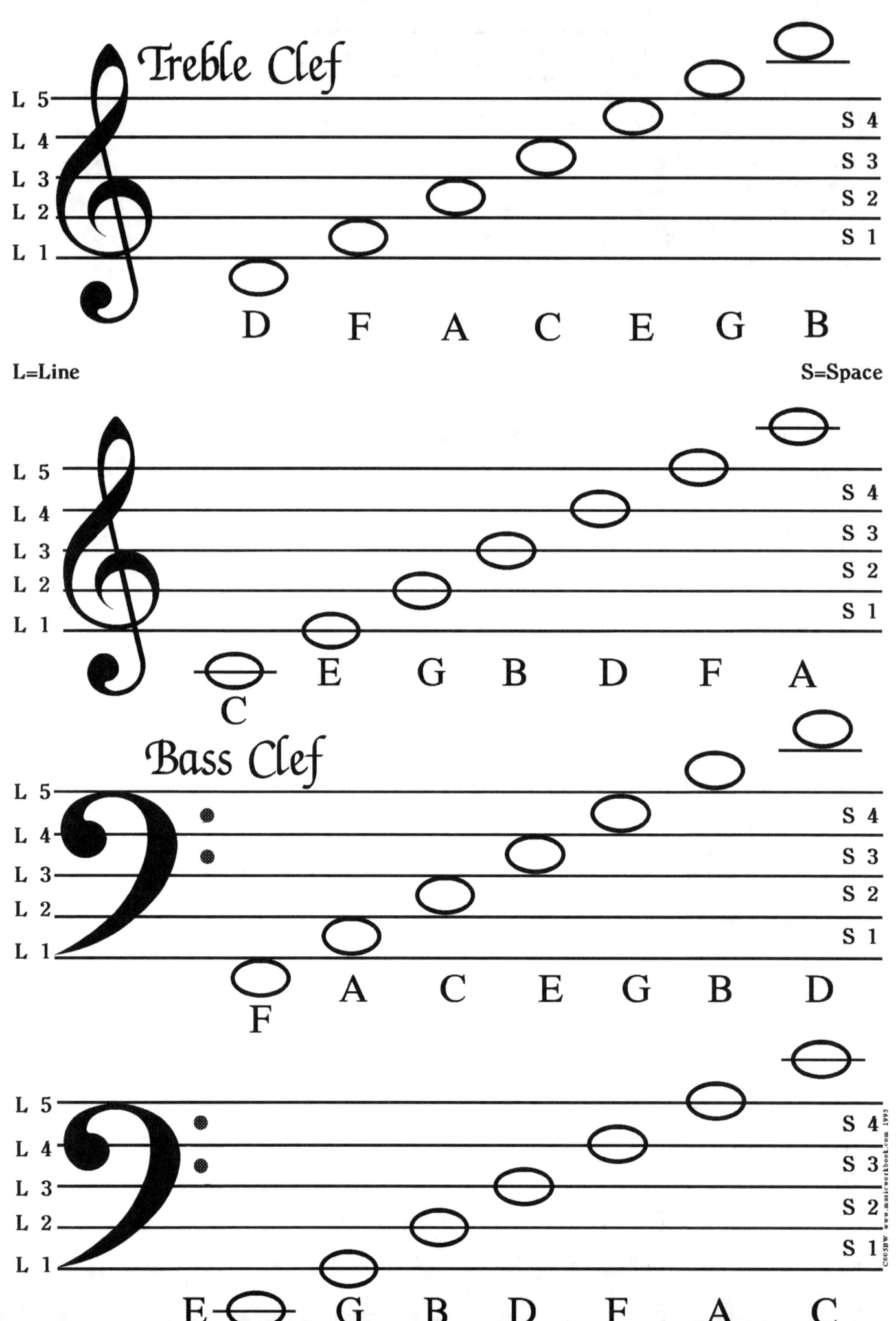

__Claire's MusicWorkBook- Music Theory and Exercises: for piano and all instruments.__

Ever wanted to read and play music and unable to have lessons, or having lessons but want to progress more rapidly? This book was co-written with a young lady with several years' teaching experience - you too can teach yourself to play the keyboard and piano. This book comes with easy DIY exercises and a modern clear layout but without any colour sketches using up valuable space. You can use this book for formal music exams, GCSE or for your own fun - play popular music from sheet music or light classics. Over 50 tunes graded in difficulty are included.

This 2011 edition now includes a Steelpan supplement with a specially written foreword by Liam Teague, Associate Professor of Music at Northern Illinois University. Steelpan layouts have been supplied by the Trinidad and Tobago Bureau of Standards in consultation with Pan Trinbago.

"Claire's Workbook" has evolved over 20 years' teaching experience with students from 4 to 72 years of age, and originally started as single-sheet handouts for use during class. As they developed, they were eventually collated and bound to help students organize their work. Active feedback and suggestions led to continual improvements based upon helping students with widely differing abilities, backgrounds, ages and experience. This book is also recommended for high school level music courses.

This collection now addresses most of the typical theory requirements of the major examining boards of music, covering from introductory to the next successive stages, Grades 1 to 2 or 3 depending on the examining board. The workbook endeavours to introduce theory concepts gradually thus helping the novice to read and understand notation and theory rather than merely satisfying a particular board's requirements exclusively. While teacher guidance is always advisable to obtain the best from the workbook, it has also been designed such that the more ambitious student can progress with the minimum of supervision, whether in a formal class, school or privately, or working at home. Answers and support will be available on the internet – check webpages for information.

The teaching pages are liberally interspersed with exercise pages. More difficult concepts such as time-signatures and tones/semitones (steps) are dealt with diagrammatically. The book has a glossary of Italian terms at the back, along with daily practice pieces. A few easy-play carols along with over 50 well-known and traditional pieces have been included in the appendix. Also included is a variety of manuscript paper with differing pitch sizes which can be copied.

See webpage <u>www.musicworkbook.com</u> *on the internet for more information.*
Answers to exercises, hints and tips on Lulu. See <u>www.theorybook.co.uk</u>.
<u>http://www.lulu.com/content/e-book/music-theory-exercises/7251289</u>

ISBN Claire's Music Workbook 0-9544406-4-1. Available from RPL Ltd., La Romaine, Trinidad.

Just Released! Claire's Traditional Carolbook. 39 tunes. ISBN 0-9544406-1-7.
- ➢ Created and inspired by young people - not just old reprints
- ➢ Modern arrangements to suit the modern piano player
- ➢ Simple progressions- most are two note harmonies
- ➢ No big jumps - octave stretches a rarity!
- ➢ No long stretches - ideal for small hands
- ➢ Harmony is retained while maintaining simplicity
- ➢ Rhythm is maintained
- ➢ Two easy keys - C major and G major
- ➢ No key signatures
- ➢ Easy for guitar players who can recognise basic chords
- ➢ Guide fingering without unnecessary clutter
- ➢ Practice exercises based on carol arrangements included
- ➢ Playable by amateurs and more advanced pianists
- ➢ Two versions of some popular carols (English and American)
- ➢ Every carol has the words edition on the facing page in clear type. this is photocopiable for use in schools, churches, hospitals, youth and other institutions.
    And a new carol, "Little Angels"
This little "music-box" type jingle is very popular with children and is easy to play.

Available from Amazon.com, selected music shops or directly from publisher:
Musicworkbook Ltd., 5 Bryant Avenue, Berkshire, England SL2 1LF, United Kingdom. © MMXII
Tel. +44 (0)7017 000 559   E-MAIL musicworkbook@yahoo.com
ISBN's   Main edition: Claire's MusicWorkBook 0-9544406-4-1.

ISBN 0-9544406-6-8

9 780954 440664